SUPER HOROSCOPE
VIRGO

2008
AUGUST 22 – SEPTEMBER 22

BERKLEY BOOKS, NEW YORK

THE BERKLEY PUBLISHING GROUP
Published by the Penguin Group
Penguin Group (USA) Inc.
375 Hudson Street, New York, New York 10014, USA
Penguin Group (Canada), 90 Eglinton Avenue East, Suite 700, Toronto, Ontario M4P 2Y3, Canada
(a division of Pearson Penguin Canada Inc.)
Penguin Books Ltd., 80 Strand, London WC2R 0RL, England
Penguin Group Ireland, 25 St. Stephen's Green, Dublin 2, Ireland (a division of Penguin Books Ltd.)
Penguin Group (Australia), 250 Camberwell Road, Camberwell, Victoria 3124, Australia
(a division of Pearson Australia Group Pty. Ltd.)
Penguin Books India Pvt. Ltd., 11 Community Centre, Panchsheel Park, New Delhi—110 017, India
Penguin Group (NZ), 67 Apollo Drive, Rosedale, North Shore 0745, Auckland, New Zealand
(a division of Pearson New Zealand Ltd.)
Penguin Books (South Africa) (Pty.) Ltd., 24 Sturdee Avenue, Rosebank, Johannesburg 2196,
South Africa

Penguin Books Ltd., Registered Offices: 80 Strand, London WC2R 0RL, England

2008 SUPER HOROSCOPE VIRGO

The publishers regret that they cannot answer individual letters requesting personal horoscope information.

Copyright © 1974, 1978, 1979, 1980, 1981, 1982 by Grosset & Dunlap, Inc.

Copyright © 1983, 1984 by Charter Communications, Inc.

Copyright © 1985, 1986, 1987, 1988, 1989, 1990, 1991, 1992, 1993, 1994, 1995, 1996, 1997, 1998, 1999, 2000, 2001, 2002, 2003, 2004, 2005, 2006, 2007 by The Berkley Publishing Group.

Cover design by Steven Ferlauto.

All rights reserved.
No part of this book may be reproduced, scanned, or distributed in any printed or electronic form without permission. Please do not participate in or encourage piracy of copyrighted materials in violation of the author's rights. Purchase only authorized editions.
BERKLEY is a registered trademark of Penguin Group (USA) Inc.
The "B" design is a trademark belonging to Penguin Group (USA) Inc.

PRINTING HISTORY
Berkley trade paperback edition / July 2007

Berkley trade paperback ISBN: 978-0-425-21548-7

Library of Congress Cataloging-in-Publication Data

ISSN: 1535-9108

PRINTED IN THE UNITED STATES OF AMERICA

10 9 8 7 6 5 4 3 2 1

CONTENTS

THE CUSP-BORN VIRGO 4
   The Cusps of Virgo 5
THE ASCENDANT: VIRGO RISING 6
   Rising Signs for Virgo 8
THE PLACE OF ASTROLOGY IN TODAY'S WORLD 10
   Astrology and Relationships 10
   The Challenge of Love 11
   Astrology and Science 12
   Know Thyself—Why? 14
WHAT IS A HOROSCOPE? 16
   The Zodiac 16
   The Sun Sign and the Cusp 17
   The Rising Sign and the Zodiacal Houses 17
   The Planets in the Houses 20
   How To Use These Predictions 21
HISTORY OF ASTROLOGY 22
ASTROLOGICAL BRIDGE TO THE 21st CENTURY 28
THE SIGNS OF THE ZODIAC 31
   Dominant Characteristics 31
   Sun Sign Personalities 56
   Key Words 58
   The Elements and Qualities of the Signs 59
THE PLANETS OF THE SOLAR SYSTEM 67
   The Planets and the Signs They Rule 67
   Characteristics of the Planets 68
THE MOON IN EACH SIGN 78
MOON TABLES 85
   Time Conversions 85
   Moon Sign Dates for 2008 86
   Moon Phases for 2008 90
   Fishing Guide for 2008 90
   Planting Guide for 2008 91
   Moon's Influence Over Plants 91
   Moon's Influence Over Health and Daily Affairs 92
VIRGO 93
   Character Analysis 94
   Love and Marriage 100
VIRGO LUCKY NUMBERS FOR 2008 128
VIRGO YEARLY FORECAST FOR 2008 129
VIRGO DAILY FORECAST FOR 2008 133
   November and December Daily Forecasts for 2007 231

THE CUSP-BORN VIRGO

Are you *really* a Virgo? If your birthday falls during the fourth week of August, at the beginning of Virgo, will you still retain the traits of Leo, the sign of the Zodiac before Virgo? And what if you were born late in September—are you more Libra than Virgo? Many people born at the edge, or cusp, of a sign have great difficulty determining exactly what sign they are. If you are one of these people, here's how you can figure it out, once and for all.

Consult the cusp table on the facing page, then locate the year of your birth. The table will tell you the precise days on which the Sun entered and left your sign for the year of your birth. In that way you can determine if you are a true Virgo—or whether you are a Leo or Libra—according to the variations in cusp dates from year to year (see also page 17).

If you were born either at the beginning or the end of Virgo, yours is a lifetime reflecting a process of subtle transformation. Your life on earth will symbolize a significant change in consciousness, for you are either about to enter a whole new way of living or are leaving one behind.

If you were born at the beginning of Virgo, you may want to read the horoscope book for Leo as well as Virgo, for Leo holds the key to much of your complexity of spirit, reflects certain hidden weaknesses and compulsions, and your unspoken wishes. Your tie to Leo symbolizes your romantic dilemma and your unusual—often timid—approach to love. You are afraid of taking a gamble and letting everything ride on your emotions. You may resist giving up the rational, logical, clear-minded approach to life, but you can never really flee from your need for love.

You symbolize the warmth and fullness of a late summer day, a natural ripeness and maturity that is mellow and comfortable to be near.

If you were born sometime after the third week of September, you may want to read the horoscope book for Libra as well as Virgo, for Libra is possibly your greatest asset. Though you are eager to get involved with another person and you crave warmth and companionship, you may hover between stiff mental analyzing and poetic romanticism. You have that Garboesque desire to be secluded, untouched—yet you want to share your life with another. You are a blend of monastic, spartan simplicity with grace, harmony, and gentle beauty. You combine a profound power to sift, purify, and analyze with the sensibilities of recognizing what is right, beautiful, and just. You can be picky and faultfinding, inconsistent and small, needing someone desperately but rejecting the one you love most. Yet you are fundamentally a thoughtful, loving person with the sincere wish to serve and make someone happy.

Developing your capacity to share will aid you in joint financial ventures, bring your values into harmony, and create a balance in your life.

THE CUSPS OF VIRGO

DATES SUN ENTERS VIRGO (LEAVES LEO)

August 23 every year from 1900 to 2010, except for the following:

August 22				August 24	
1960	1980	1992	2001	1903	1919
64	84	93	2004	07	23
68	88	96	2005	11	27
72	89	97	2008	15	
76		2000	2009		

DATES SUN LEAVES VIRGO (ENTERS LIBRA)

September 23 every year from 1900 to 2010, except for the following:

September 22					September 24
1948	1968	1981	1992	2001	1903
52	72	84	93	2004	07
56	76	85	96	2005	
60	77	88	97	2008	
64	80	89	2000	2009	

THE ASCENDANT: VIRGO RISING

Could you be a "double" Virgo? That is, could you have Virgo as your Rising sign as well as your Sun sign? The tables on pages 8–9 will tell you Virgos what your Rising sign happens to be. Just find the hour of your birth, then find the day of your birth, and you will see which sign of the Zodiac is your Ascendant, as the Rising sign is called. The Ascendant is called that because it is the sign rising on the eastern horizon at the time of your birth. For a more detailed discussion of the Rising sign and the twelve houses of the Zodiac, see pages 17–20.

The Ascendant, or Rising sign, is placed on the 1st house in a horoscope, of which there are twelve houses. The first house represents your response to the environment—your unique response. Call it identity, personality, ego, self-image, facade, come-on, body-mind-spirit—whatever term best conveys to you the meaning of the you that acts and reacts in the world. It is a you that is always changing, discovering a new you. Your identity started with birth and early environment, over which you had little conscious control, and continues to experience, to adjust, to express itself. The 1st house also represents how others see you. Has anyone ever guessed your sign to be your Rising sign? People may respond to that personality, that facade, that body type governed by your Rising sign.

Your Ascendant, or Rising sign, modifies your basic Sun sign personality, and it affects the way you act out the daily predictions for your Sun sign. If your Rising sign is indeed Virgo, what follows is a description of its effects on your horoscope. If your Rising sign is not Virgo, but some other sign of the Zodiac, you may wish to read the horoscope book for that sign as well.

With Virgo on the Ascendant, that is, in the 1st house, your ruling planet Mercury is therefore in the 1st house. You are known for your inquiring mind, sharp verbal skills, love of learning. Your very appearance—fastidious, lean, efficient—gives the impression of a great openness to the environment; you seem to pick up clues from the most cursory observations, filing them away for future use. Mercury in the 1st house, however, can make you too self-absorbed with your own interests and thus lacking in sympathy for other people. And your quick wit and loquaciousness, if put into the service of petty gossip, could make you a tattletale who gets in trouble with people.

Your striving for perfection and your liking for details make many of you with Virgo Rising master craftspeople. That talent is not restricted to the arts of fashioning jewelry, fabric, metals, food, and other materials of the earth, though you are an earth sign. Mercury, your ruler, gives you a quicksilver mind, and you excel in the mathematical and scientific arts. Your memory is splendid, too. If you are not actually working in complex systems such as computer science or engineering, your talent for organizing details and structuring information certainly benefits your work life, as well as your social life.

Your love of learning has few boundaries, and no limits if you with Virgo Rising consistently apply yourself. You are equally attracted to medicine, art, science, literature. Your analytical mind, scalpel-sharp, can cut through a mass of confused information, selecting the wheat from the chaff, so to speak. Certainly you can distinguish theory from practice, and you know when and how to use the practice. Many of you, for that reason, and also because you like to help people, find yourselves in health and medical service careers.

Personally you are interested in the perfection of the body and the purity of the mind. Translated into everyday activities, you could be very fussy about your diet, your clothes, your living quarters, your spiritual beliefs, your exercise programs. It is not unlikely that you experiment often in these areas, and sometimes you're accused of being a faddist. If you cannot change where you live frequently, you'll be satisfied to take a few long trips and many short ones during your lifetime.

Basically you are patient, methodical, ambitious sometimes in a secretive way. Your caustic wit, which strips the facade from people, hides your true feelings and melancholy of spirit. As much as you like to quip in bright dialogue with others, you like to be alone. Even your travels can be solitary adventures; you commune with the nature around you. Some of these experiences may motivate an in-depth study of art and literature at some point in your lifetime. And you may well become a writer, merging a myriad of facts with personal data you are loathe to talk about.

For you with Virgo Rising, two key words are self-mastery and service. But while you are perfecting your knowledge and skills in serving others, don't forget your own needs. Develop compassion for yourself.

RISING SIGNS FOR VIRGO

Hour of Birth*	Day of Birth		
	August 22–26	August 27–31	September 1–5
Midnight	Gemini	Gemini	Cancer
1 am	Cancer	Cancer	Cancer
2 am	Cancer	Cancer	Cancer
3 am	Leo	Leo	Leo
4 am	Leo	Leo	Leo
5 am	Leo	Leo; Virgo 8/31	Virgo
6 am	Virgo	Virgo	Virgo
7 am	Virgo	Virgo	Virgo
8 am	Libra	Libra	Libra
9 am	Libra	Libra	Libra
10 am	Libra	Libra; Scorpio 8/29	Scorpio
11 am	Scorpio	Scorpio	Scorpio
Noon	Scorpio	Scorpio	Scorpio
1 pm	Sagittarius	Sagittarius	Sagittarius
2 pm	Sagittarius	Sagittarius	Sagittarius
3 pm	Sagittarius	Capricorn	Capricorn
4 pm	Capricorn	Capricorn	Capricorn
5 pm	Capricorn; Aquarius 8/26	Aquarius	Aquarius
6 pm	Aquarius	Aquarius	Aquarius; Pisces 9/3
7 pm	Pisces	Pisces	Pisces
8 pm	Aries	Aries	Aries
9 pm	Aries; Taurus 8/26	Taurus	Taurus
10 pm	Taurus	Taurus	Taurus; Gemini 9/3
11 pm	Gemini	Gemini	Gemini

*Hour of birth given here is for Standard Time in any time zone. If your hour of birth was recorded in Daylight Saving Time, subtract one hour from it and consult that hour in the table above. For example, if you were born at 7 PM D.S.T., see 6 PM above.

YOUR RISING SIGN / 9

Hour of Birth*	Day of Birth		
	September 6–10	September 11–15	September 16–24
Midnight	Cancer	Cancer	Cancer
1 am	Cancer	Cancer	Cancer; Leo 9/21
2 am	Leo	Leo	Leo
3 am	Leo	Leo	Leo
4 am	Leo	Leo; Virgo 9/14	Virgo
5 am	Virgo	Virgo	Virgo
6 am	Virgo	Virgo	Virgo; Libra 9/21
7 am	Libra	Libra	Libra
8 am	Libra	Libra	Libra
9 am	Libra	Scorpio	Scorpio
10 am	Scorpio	Scorpio	Scorpio
11 am	Scorpio	Scorpio	Scorpio; Sagittarius 9/21
Noon	Sagittarius	Sagittarius	Sagittarius
1 pm	Sagittarius	Sagittarius	Sagittarius
2 pm	Sagittarius	Capricorn	Capricorn
3 pm	Capricorn	Capricorn	Capricorn
4 pm	Capricorn; Aquarius 9/10	Aquarius	Aquarius
5 pm	Aquarius	Aquarius	Pisces
6 pm	Pisces	Pisces	Pisces; Aries 9/21
7 pm	Aries	Aries	Aries
8 pm	Aries; Taurus 9/10	Taurus	Taurus
9 pm	Taurus	Taurus	Gemini
10 pm	Gemini	Gemini	Gemini
11 pm	Gemini	Gemini	Cancer

*See note on facing page.

THE PLACE OF ASTROLOGY IN TODAY'S WORLD

Does astrology have a place in the fast-moving, ultra-scientific world we live in today? Can it be justified in a sophisticated society whose outriders are already preparing to step off the moon into the deep space of the planets themselves? Or is it just a hangover of ancient superstition, a psychological dummy for neurotics and dreamers of every historical age?

These are the kind of questions that any inquiring person can be expected to ask when they approach a subject like astrology which goes beyond, but never excludes, the materialistic side of life.

The simple, single answer is that astrology works. It works for many millions of people in the western world alone. In the United States there are 10 million followers and in Europe, an estimated 25 million. America has more than 4000 practicing astrologers, Europe nearly three times as many. Even down-under Australia has its hundreds of thousands of adherents. In the eastern countries, astrology has enormous followings, again, because it has been proved to work. In India, for example, brides and grooms for centuries have been chosen on the basis of their astrological compatibility.

Astrology today is more vital than ever before, more practicable because all over the world the media devotes much space and time to it, more valid because science itself is confirming the precepts of astrological knowledge with every new exciting step. The ordinary person who daily applies astrology intelligently does not have to wonder whether it is true nor believe in it blindly. He can see it working for himself. And, if he can use it—and this book is designed to help the reader to do just that—he can make living a far richer experience, and become a more developed personality and a better person.

Astrology and Relationships

Astrology is the science of relationships. It is not just a study of planetary influences on man and his environment. It is the study of man himself.

We are at the center of our personal universe, of all our relationships. And our happiness or sadness depends on how we act, how we relate to the people and things that surround us. The emotions that we generate have a distinct effect—for better or worse—on the world around us. Our friends and our enemies will confirm this. Just look in the mirror the next time you are angry. In other words, each of us is a kind of sun or planet or star radiating our feelings on the environment around us. Our influence on our personal universe, whether loving, helpful, or destructive, varies with our changing moods, expressed through our individual character.

Our personal "radiations" are potent in the way they affect our moods and our ability to control them. But we usually are able to throw off our emotion in some sort of action—we have a good cry, walk it off, or tell someone our troubles—before it can build up too far and make us physically ill. Astrology helps us to understand the universal forces working on us, and through this understanding, we can become more properly adjusted to our surroundings so that we find ourselves coping where others may flounder.

The Challenge of Love

The challenge of love lies in recognizing the difference between infatuation, emotion, sex, and, sometimes, the intentional deceit of the other person. Mankind, with its record of broken marriages, despair, and disillusionment, is obviously not very good at making these distinctions.

Can astrology help?

Yes. In the same way that advance knowledge can usually help in any human situation. And there is probably no situation as human, as poignant, as pathetic and universal, as the failure of man's love.

Love, of course, is not just between man and woman. It involves love of children, parents, home, and friends. But the big problems usually involve the choice of partner.

Astrology has established degrees of compatibility that exist between people born under the various signs of the Zodiac. Because people are individuals, there are numerous variations and modifications. So the astrologer, when approached on mate and marriage matters, makes allowances for them. But the fact remains that some groups of people are suited for each other and some are not, and astrology has expressed this in terms of characteristics we all can study and use as a personal guide.

No matter how much enjoyment and pleasure we find in the different aspects of each other's character, if it is not an overall compatibility, the chances of our finding fulfillment or enduring happiness in each other are pretty hopeless. And astrology can help us to find someone compatible.

Astrology and Science

Closely related to our emotions is the "other side" of our personal universe, our physical welfare. Our body, of course, is largely influenced by things around us over which we have very little control. The phone rings, we hear it. The train runs late. We snag our stocking or cut our face shaving. Our body is under a constant bombardment of events that influence our daily lives to varying degrees.

The question that arises from all this is, what makes each of us act so that we have to involve other people and keep the ball of activity and evolution rolling? This is the question that both science and astrology are involved with. The scientists have attacked it from different angles: anthropology, the study of human evolution as body, mind and response to environment; anatomy, the study of bodily structure; psychology, the science of the human mind; and so on. These studies have produced very impressive classifications and valuable information, but because the approach to the problem is fragmented, so is the result. They remain "branches" of science. Science generally studies effects. It keeps turning up wonderful answers but no lasting solutions. Astrology, on the other hand, approaches the question from the broader viewpoint. Astrology began its inquiry with the totality of human experience and saw it as an effect. It then looked to find the cause, or at least the prime movers, and during thousands of years of observation of man and his *universal* environment came up with the extraordinary principle of planetary influence—or astrology, which, from the Greek, means the science of the stars.

Modern science, as we shall see, has confirmed much of astrology's foundations—most of it unintentionally, some of it reluctantly, but still, indisputably.

It is not difficult to imagine that there must be a connection between outer space and Earth. Even today, scientists are not too sure how our Earth was created, but it is generally agreed that it is only a tiny part of the universe. And as a part of the universe, people on Earth see and feel the influence of heavenly bodies in almost every aspect of our existence. There is no doubt that the Sun has the greatest influence on life on this planet. Without it there would be no life, for without it there would be no warmth, no division into day and night, no cycles of time or season at all. This is clear and easy to see. The influence of the Moon, on the other hand, is more subtle, though no less definite.

There are many ways in which the influence of the Moon manifests itself here on Earth, both on human and animal life. It is a well-known fact, for instance, that the large movements of water on our planet—that is the ebb and flow of the tides—are caused by the Moon's gravitational pull. Since this is so, it follows that these water movements do not occur only in the oceans, but that all bodies of water are affected, even down to the tiniest puddle.

The human body, too, which consists of about 70 percent water, falls within the scope of this lunar influence. For example the menstrual cycle of most women corresponds to the 28-day lunar month; the period of pregnancy in humans is 273 days, or equal to nine lunar months. Similarly, many illnesses reach a crisis at the change of the Moon, and statistics in many countries have shown that the crime rate is highest at the time of the Full Moon. Even human sexual desire has been associated with the phases of the Moon. But it is in the movement of the tides that we get the clearest demonstration of planetary influence, which leads to the irresistible correspondence between the so-called metaphysical and the physical.

Tide tables are prepared years in advance by calculating the future positions of the Moon. Science has known for a long time that the Moon is the main cause of tidal action. But only in the last few years has it begun to realize the possible extent of this influence on mankind. To begin with, the ocean tides do not rise and fall as we might imagine from our personal observations of them. The Moon as it orbits around Earth sets up a circular wave of attraction which pulls the oceans of the world after it, broadly in an east to west direction. This influence is like a phantom wave crest, a loop of power stretching from pole to pole which passes over and around the Earth like an invisible shadow. It travels with equal effect across the land masses and, as scientists were recently amazed to observe, caused oysters placed in the dark in the middle of the United States where there is no sea to open their shells to receive the nonexistent tide. If the land-locked oysters react to this invisible signal, what effect does it have on us who not so long ago in evolutionary time came out of the sea and still have its salt in our blood and sweat?

Less well known is the fact that the Moon is also the primary force behind the circulation of blood in human beings and animals, and the movement of sap in trees and plants. Agriculturists have established that the Moon has a distinct influence on crops, which explains why for centuries people have planted according to Moon cycles. The habits of many animals, too, are directed by the movement of the Moon. Migratory birds, for instance, depart only at or near the time of the Full Moon. And certain sea creatures, eels in particular, move only in accordance with certain phases of the Moon.

Know Thyself—Why?

In today's fast-changing world, everyone still longs to know what the future holds. It is the one thing that everyone has in common: rich and poor, famous and infamous, all are deeply concerned about tomorrow.

But the key to the future, as every historian knows, lies in the past. This is as true of individual people as it is of nations. You cannot understand your future without first understanding your past, which is simply another way of saying that you must first of all know yourself.

The motto "know thyself" seems obvious enough nowadays, but it was originally put forward as the foundation of wisdom by the ancient Greek philosophers. It was then adopted by the "mystery religions" of the ancient Middle East, Greece, Rome, and is still used in all genuine schools of mind training or mystical discipline, both in those of the East, based on yoga, and those of the West. So it is universally accepted now, and has been through the ages.

But how do you go about discovering what sort of person you are? The first step is usually classification into some sort of system of types. Astrology did this long before the birth of Christ. Psychology has also done it. So has modern medicine, in its way.

One system classifies people according to the source of the impulses they respond to most readily: the muscles, leading to direct bodily action; the digestive organs, resulting in emotion; or the brain and nerves, giving rise to thinking. Another such system says that character is determined by the endocrine glands, and gives us such labels as "pituitary," "thyroid," and "hyperthyroid" types. These different systems are neither contradictory nor mutually exclusive. In fact, they are very often different ways of saying the same thing.

Very popular, useful classifications were devised by Carl Jung, the eminent disciple of Freud. Jung observed among the different faculties of the mind, four which have a predominant influence on character. These four faculties exist in all of us without exception, but not in perfect balance. So when we say, for instance, that someone is a "thinking type," it means that in any situation he or she tries to be rational. Emotion, which may be the opposite of thinking, will be his or her weakest function. This thinking type can be sensible and reasonable, or calculating and unsympathetic. The emotional type, on the other hand, can often be recognized by exaggerated language—everything is either marvelous or terrible—and in extreme cases they even invent dramas and quarrels out of nothing just to make life more interesting.

The other two faculties are intuition and physical sensation. The sensation type does not only care for food and drink, nice clothes and furniture; he or she is also interested in all forms of physical experience. Many scientists are sensation types as are athletes and nature-lovers. Like sensation, intuition is a form of perception and we all possess it. But it works through that part of the mind which is not under conscious control—consequently it sees meanings and connections which are not obvious to thought or emotion. Inventors and original thinkers are always intuitive, but so, too, are superstitious people who see meanings where none exist.

Thus, sensation tells us what is going on in the world, feeling (that is, emotion) tells us how important it is to ourselves, thinking enables us to interpret it and work out what we should do about it, and intuition tells us what it means to ourselves and others. All four faculties are essential, and all are present in every one of us. But some people are guided chiefly by one, others by another. In addition, Jung also observed a division of the human personality into the extrovert and the introvert, which cuts across these four types.

A disadvantage of all these systems of classification is that one cannot tell very easily where to place oneself. Some people are reluctant to admit that they act to please their emotions. So they deceive themselves for years by trying to belong to whichever type they think is the "best." Of course, there is no best; each has its faults and each has its good points.

The advantage of the signs of the Zodiac is that they simplify classification. Not only that, but your date of birth is personal—

it is unarguably yours. What better way to know yourself than by going back as far as possible to the very moment of your birth? And this is precisely what your horoscope is all about, as we shall see in the next section.

WHAT IS A HOROSCOPE?

If you had been able to take a picture of the skies at the moment of your birth, that photograph would be your horoscope. Lacking such a snapshot, it is still possible to recreate the picture—and this is at the basis of the astrologer's art. In other words, your horoscope is a representation of the skies with the planets in the exact positions they occupied at the time you were born.

The year of birth tells an astrologer the positions of the distant, slow-moving planets Jupiter, Saturn, Uranus, Neptune, and Pluto. The month of birth indicates the Sun sign, or birth sign as it is commonly called, as well as indicating the positions of the rapidly moving planets Venus, Mercury, and Mars. The day and time of birth will locate the position of our Moon. And the moment—the exact hour and minute—of birth determines the houses through what is called the Ascendant, or Rising sign.

With this information the astrologer consults various tables to calculate the specific positions of the Sun, Moon, and other planets relative to your birthplace at the moment you were born. Then he or she locates them by means of the Zodiac.

The Zodiac

The Zodiac is a band of stars (constellations) in the skies, centered on the Sun's apparent path around the Earth, and is divided into twelve equal segments, or signs. What we are actually dividing up is the Earth's path around the Sun. But from our point of view here on Earth, it seems as if the Sun is making a great circle around our planet in the sky, so we say it is the Sun's apparent path. This twelvefold division, the Zodiac, is a reference system for the astrologer. At any given moment the planets—and in astrology both the Sun and Moon are considered to be planets—can all be located at a specific point along this path.

Now where in all this are you, the subject of the horoscope? Your character is largely determined by the sign the Sun is in. So that is where the astrologer looks first in your horoscope, at your Sun sign.

The Sun Sign and the Cusp

There are twelve signs in the Zodiac, and the Sun spends approximately one month in each sign. But because of the motion of the Earth around the Sun—the Sun's apparent motion—the dates when the Sun enters and leaves each sign may change from year to year. Some people born near the cusp, or edge, of a sign have difficulty determining which is their Sun sign. But in this book a Table of Cusps is provided for the years 1900 to 2010 (page 5) so you can find out what your true Sun sign is.

Here are the twelve signs of the Zodiac, their ancient zodiacal symbol, and the dates when the Sun enters and leaves each sign for the year 2008. Remember, these dates may change from year to year.

ARIES	Ram	March 20–April 19
TAURUS	Bull	April 19–May 20
GEMINI	Twins	May 20–June 20
CANCER	Crab	June 20–July 22
LEO	Lion	July 22–August 22
VIRGO	Virgin	August 22–September 22
LIBRA	Scales	September 22–October 22
SCORPIO	Scorpion	October 22–November 21
SAGITTARIUS	Archer	November 21–December 21
CAPRICORN	Sea Goat	December 21–January 20
AQUARIUS	Water Bearer	January 20–February 19
PISCES	Fish	February 19–March 20

It is possible to draw significant conclusions and make meaningful predictions based simply on the Sun sign of a person. There are many people who have been amazed at the accuracy of the description of their own character based only on the Sun sign. But an astrologer needs more information than just your Sun sign to interpret the photograph that is your horoscope.

The Rising Sign and the Zodiacal Houses

An astrologer needs the exact time and place of your birth in order to construct and interpret your horoscope. The illustration on the next page shows the flat chart, or natural wheel, an astrologer uses. Note the inner circle of the wheel labeled 1 through 12. These 12 divisions are known as the houses of the Zodiac.

18 / WHAT IS A HOROSCOPE?

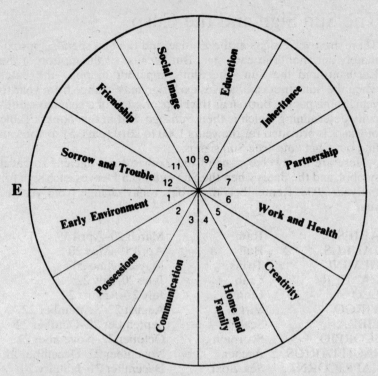

The 1st house always starts from the position marked E, which corresponds to the eastern horizon. The rest of the houses 2 through 12 follow around in a "counterclockwise" direction. The point where each house starts is known as a cusp, or edge.

The cusp, or edge, of the 1st house (point E) is where an astrologer would place your Rising sign, the Ascendant. And, as already noted, the exact time of your birth determines your Rising sign. Let's see how this works.

As the Earth rotates on its axis once every 24 hours, each one of the twelve signs of the Zodiac appears to be "rising" on the horizon, with a new one appearing about every 2 hours. Actually it is the turning of the Earth that exposes each sign to view, but in our astrological work we are discussing apparent motion. This Rising sign marks the Ascendant, and it colors the whole orientation of a horoscope. It indicates the sign governing the 1st house of the chart, and will thus determine which signs will govern all the other houses.

To visualize this idea, imagine two color wheels with twelve divisions superimposed upon each other. For just as the Zodiac is divided into twelve constellations that we identify as the signs, another twelvefold division is used to denote the houses. Now imagine one wheel (the signs) moving slowly while the other wheel (the houses) remains still. This analogy may help you see how the signs keep shifting the "color" of the houses as the Rising sign continues to change every two hours. To simplify things, a Table of Rising Signs has been provided (pages 8–9) for your specific Sun sign.

Once your Rising sign has been placed on the cusp of the 1st house, the signs that govern the rest of the 11 houses can be placed on the chart. In any individual's horoscope the signs do not necessarily correspond with the houses. For example, it could be that a sign covers part of two adjacent houses. It is the interpretation of such variations in an individual's horoscope that marks the professional astrologer.

But to gain a workable understanding of astrology, it is not necessary to go into great detail. In fact, we just need a description of the houses and their meanings, as is shown in the illustration above and in the table below.

THE 12 HOUSES OF THE ZODIAC

1st	Individuality, body appearance, general outlook on life	Personality house
2nd	Finance, possessions, ethical principles, gain or loss	Money house
3rd	Relatives, communication, short journeys, writing, education	Relatives house
4th	Family and home, parental ties, land and property, security	Home house
5th	Pleasure, children, creativity, entertainment, risk	Pleasure house
6th	Health, harvest, hygiene, work and service, employees	Health house
7th	Marriage and divorce, the law, partnerships and alliances	Marriage house
8th	Inheritance, secret deals, sex, death, regeneration	Inheritance house
9th	Travel, sports, study, philosophy Ω house	Travel house
10th	Career, social standing, success and honor	Business house
11th	Friendship, social life, hopes and wishes	Friends house
12th	Troubles, illness, secret enemies, hidden agendas	Trouble house

The Planets in the Houses

An astrologer, knowing the exact time and place of your birth, will use tables of planetary motion in order to locate the planets in your horoscope chart. He or she will determine which planet or planets are in which sign and in which house. It is not uncommon, in an individual's horoscope, for there to be two or more planets in the same sign and in the same house.

The characteristics of the planets modify the influence of the Sun according to their natures and strengths.

Sun: Source of life. Basic temperament according to the Sun sign. The conscious will. Human potential.
Moon: Emotions. Moods. Customs. Habits. Changeable. Adaptive. Nurturing.
Mercury: Communication. Intellect. Reasoning power. Curiosity. Short travels.
Venus: Love. Delight. Charm. Harmony. Balance. Art. Beautiful possessions.
Mars: Energy. Initiative. War. Anger. Adventure. Courage. Daring. Impulse.
Jupiter: Luck. Optimism. Generous. Expansive. Opportunities. Protection.
Saturn: Pessimism. Privation. Obstacles. Delay. Hard work. Research. Lasting rewards after long struggle.
Uranus: Fashion. Electricity. Revolution. Independence. Freedom. Sudden changes. Modern science.
Neptune: Sensationalism. Theater. Dreams. Inspiration. Illusion. Deception.
Pluto: Creation and destruction. Total transformation. Lust for power. Strong obsessions.

Superimpose the characteristics of the planets on the functions of the house in which they appear. Express the result through the character of the Sun sign, and you will get the basic idea.

Of course, many other considerations have been taken into account in producing the carefully worked out predictions in this book: the aspects of the planets to each other; their strength according to position and sign; whether they are in a house of exaltation or decline; whether they are natural enemies or not; whether a planet occupies its own sign; the position of a planet in relation to its own house or sign; whether the sign is male or female; whether the sign is a fire, earth, water, or air sign. These are only a few of the colors on the astrologer's pallet which he or she must mix with the inspiration of the artist and the accuracy of the mathematician.

How To Use These Predictions

A person reading the predictions in this book should understand that they are produced from the daily position of the planets for a group of people and are not, of course, individually specialized. To get the full benefit of them our readers should relate the predictions to their own character and circumstances, coordinate them, and draw their own conclusions from them.

If you are a serious observer of your own life, you should find a definite pattern emerging that will be a helpful and reliable guide.

The point is that we always retain our free will. The stars indicate certain directional tendencies but we are not compelled to follow. We can do or not do, and wisdom must make the choice.

We all have our good and bad days. Sometimes they extend into cycles of weeks. It is therefore advisable to study daily predictions in a span ranging from the day before to several days ahead.

Daily predictions should be taken very generally. The word "difficult" does not necessarily indicate a whole day of obstruction or inconvenience. It is a warning to you to be cautious. Your caution will often see you around the difficulty before you are involved. This is the correct use of astrology.

In another section (pages 78–84), detailed information is given about the influence of the Moon as it passes through each of the twelve signs of the Zodiac. There are instructions on how to use the Moon Tables (pages 85–92), which provide Moon Sign Dates throughout the year as well as the Moon's role in health and daily affairs. This information should be used in conjunction with the daily forecasts to give a fuller picture of the astrological trends.

HISTORY OF ASTROLOGY

The origins of astrology have been lost far back in history, but we do know that reference is made to it as far back as the first written records of the human race. It is not hard to see why. Even in primitive times, people must have looked for an explanation for the various happenings in their lives. They must have wanted to know why people were different from one another. And in their search they turned to the regular movements of the Sun, Moon, and stars to see if they could provide an answer.

It is interesting to note that as soon as man learned to use his tools in any type of design, or his mind in any kind of calculation, he turned his attention to the heavens. Ancient cave dwellings reveal dim crescents and circles representative of the Sun and Moon, rulers of day and night. Mesopotamia and the civilization of Chaldea, in itself the foundation of those of Babylonia and Assyria, show a complete picture of astronomical observation and well-developed astrological interpretation.

Humanity has a natural instinct for order. The study of anthropology reveals that primitive people—even as far back as prehistoric times—were striving to achieve a certain order in their lives. They tried to organize the apparent chaos of the universe. They had the desire to attach meaning to things. This demand for order has persisted throughout the history of man. So that observing the regularity of the heavenly bodies made it logical that primitive peoples should turn heavenward in their search for an understanding of the world in which they found themselves so random and alone.

And they did find a significance in the movements of the stars. Shepherds tending their flocks, for instance, observed that when the cluster of stars now known as the constellation Aries was in sight, it was the time of fertility and they associated it with the Ram. And they noticed that the growth of plants and plant life corresponded with different phases of the Moon, so that certain times were favorable for the planting of crops, and other times were not. In this way, there grew up a tradition of seasons and causes connected with the passage of the Sun through the twelve signs of the Zodiac.

Astrology was valued so highly that the king was kept informed of the daily and monthly changes in the heavenly bodies, and the results of astrological studies regarding events of the future. Head astrologers were clearly men of great rank and position, and the office was said to be a hereditary one.

Omens were taken, not only from eclipses and conjunctions of the Moon or Sun with one of the planets, but also from storms and earthquakes. In the eastern civilizations, particularly, the reverence inspired by astrology appears to have remained unbroken since the very earliest days. In ancient China, astrology, astronomy, and religion went hand in hand. The astrologer, who was also an astronomer, was part of the official government service and had his own corner in the Imperial Palace. The duties of the Imperial astrologer, whose office was one of the most important in the land, were clearly defined, as this extract from early records shows:

> This exalted gentleman must concern himself with the stars in the heavens, keeping a record of the changes and movements of the Planets, the Sun and the Moon, in order to examine the movements of the terrestrial world with the object of prognosticating good and bad fortune. He divides the territories of the nine regions of the empire in accordance with their dependence on particular celestial bodies. All the fiefs and principalities are connected with the stars and from this their prosperity or misfortune should be ascertained. He makes prognostications according to the twelve years of the Jupiter cycle of good and evil of the terrestrial world. From the colors of the five kinds of clouds, he determines the coming of floods or droughts, abundance or famine. From the twelve winds, he draws conclusions about the state of harmony of heaven and earth, and takes note of good and bad signs that result from their accord or disaccord. In general, he concerns himself with five kinds of phenomena so as to warn the Emperor to come to the aid of the government and to allow for variations in the ceremonies according to their circumstances.

The Chinese were also keen observers of the fixed stars, giving them such unusual names as Ghost Vehicle, Sun of Imperial Concubine, Imperial Prince, Pivot of Heaven, Twinkling Brilliance, Weaving Girl. But, great astrologers though they may have been, the Chinese lacked one aspect of mathematics that the Greeks applied to astrology—deductive geometry. Deductive geometry was the basis of much classical astrology in and after the time of the Greeks, and this explains the different methods of prognostication used in the East and West.

Down through the ages the astrologer's art has depended, not so much on the uncovering of new facts, though this is important, as on the interpretation of the facts already known. This is the essence of the astrologer's skill.

But why should the signs of the Zodiac have any effect at all on the formation of human character? It is easy to see why people thought they did, and even now we constantly use astrological expressions in our everyday speech. The thoughts of "lucky star," "ill-fated," "star-crossed," "mooning around," are interwoven into the very structure of our language.

Wherever the concept of the Zodiac is understood and used, it could well appear to have an influence on the human character. Does this mean, then, that the human race, in whose civilization the idea of the twelve signs of the Zodiac has long been embedded, is divided into only twelve types? Can we honestly believe that it is really as simple as that? If so, there must be pretty wide ranges of variation within each type. And if, to explain the variation, we call in heredity and environment, experiences in early childhood, the thyroid and other glands, and also the four functions of the mind together with extroversion and introversion, then one begins to wonder if the original classification was worth making at all. No sensible person believes that his favorite system explains everything. But even so, he will not find the system much use at all if it does not even save him the trouble of bothering with the others.

In the same way, if we were to put every person under only one sign of the Zodiac, the system becomes too rigid and unlike life. Besides, it was never intended to be used like that. It may be convenient to have only twelve types, but we know that in practice there is every possible gradation between aggressiveness and timidity, or between conscientiousness and laziness. How, then, do we account for this?

A person born under any given Sun sign can be mainly influenced by one or two of the other signs that appear in their individual horoscope. For instance, famous persons born under the sign of Gemini include Henry VIII, whom nothing and no one could have induced to abdicate, and Edward VIII, who did just that. Obviously, then, the sign Gemini does not fully explain the complete character of either of them.

Again, under the opposite sign, Sagittarius, were both Stalin, who was totally consumed with the notion of power, and Charles V, who freely gave up an empire because he preferred to go into a monastery. And we find under Scorpio many uncompromising characters such as Luther, de Gaulle, Indira Gandhi, and Montgomery, but also Petain, a successful commander whose name later became synonymous with collaboration.

A single sign is therefore obviously inadequate to explain the differences between people; it can only explain resemblances, such as the combativeness of the Scorpio group, or the far-reaching devotion of Charles V and Stalin to their respective ideals—the Christian heaven and the Communist utopia.

But very few people have only one sign in their horoscope chart.

In addition to the month of birth, the day and, even more, the hour to the nearest minute if possible, ought to be considered. Without this, it is impossible to have an actual horoscope, for the word horoscope literally means "a consideration of the hour."

The month of birth tells you only which sign of the Zodiac was occupied by the Sun. The day and hour tell you what sign was occupied by the Moon. And the minute tells you which sign was rising on the eastern horizon. This is called the Ascendant, and, as some astrologers believe, it is supposed to be the most important thing in the whole horoscope.

The Sun is said to signify one's heart, that is to say, one's deepest desires and inmost nature. This is quite different from the Moon, which signifies one's superficial way of behaving. When the ancient Romans referred to the Emperor Augustus as a Capricorn, they meant that he had the Moon in Capricorn. Or, to take another example, a modern astrologer would call Disraeli a Scorpion because he had Scorpio Rising, but most people would call him Sagittarius because he had the Sun there. The Romans would have called him Leo because his Moon was in Leo.

So if one does not seem to fit one's birth month, it is always worthwhile reading the other signs, for one may have been born at a time when any of them were rising or occupied by the Moon. It also seems to be the case that the influence of the Sun develops as life goes on, so that the month of birth is easier to guess in people over the age of forty. The young are supposed to be influenced mainly by their Ascendant, the Rising sign, which characterizes the body and physical personality as a whole.

It is nonsense to assume that all people born at a certain time will exhibit the same characteristics, or that they will even behave in the same manner. It is quite obvious that, from the very moment of its birth, a child is subject to the effects of its environment, and that this in turn will influence its character and heritage to a decisive extent. Also to be taken into account are education and economic conditions, which play a very important part in the formation of one's character as well.

People have, in general, certain character traits and qualities which, according to their environment, develop in either a positive or a negative manner. Therefore, selfishness (inherent selfishness, that is) might emerge as unselfishness; kindness and consideration as cruelty and lack of consideration toward others. In the same way, a naturally constructive person may, through frustration, become destructive, and so on. The latent characteristics with which people are born can, therefore, through environment and good or bad training, become something that would appear to be its opposite, and so give the lie to the astrologer's description of their character.

But this is not the case. The true character is still there, but it is buried deep beneath these external superficialities.

Careful study of the character traits of various signs of the Zodiac are of immeasurable help, and can render beneficial service to the intelligent person. Undoubtedly, the reader will already have discovered that, while he is able to get on very well with some people, he just "cannot stand" others. The causes sometimes seem inexplicable. At times there is intense dislike, at other times immediate sympathy. And there is, too, the phenomenon of love at first sight, which is also apparently inexplicable. People appear to be either sympathetic or unsympathetic toward each other for no apparent reason.

Now if we look at this in the light of the Zodiac, we find that people born under different signs are either compatible or incompatible with each other. In other words, there are good and bad interrelating factors among the various signs. This does not, of course, mean that humanity can be divided into groups of hostile camps. It would be quite wrong to be hostile or indifferent toward people who happen to be born under an incompatible sign. There is no reason why everybody should not, or cannot, learn to control and adjust their feelings and actions, especially after they are aware of the positive qualities of other people by studying their character analyses, among other things.

Every person born under a certain sign has both positive and negative qualities, which are developed more or less according to our free will. Nobody is entirely good or entirely bad, and it is up to each of us to learn to control ourselves on the one hand and at the same time to endeavor to learn about ourselves and others.

It cannot be emphasized often enough that it is free will that determines whether we will make really good use of our talents and abilities. Using our free will, we can either overcome our failings or allow them to rule us. Our free will enables us to exert sufficient willpower to control our failings so that they do not harm ourselves or others.

Astrology can reveal our inclinations and tendencies. Astrology can tell us about ourselves so that we are able to use our free will to overcome our shortcomings. In this way astrology helps us do our best to become needed and valuable members of society as well as helpmates to our family and our friends. Astrology also can save us a great deal of unhappiness and remorse.

Yet it may seem absurd that an ancient philosophy could be a prop to modern men and women. But below the materialistic surface of modern life, there are hidden streams of feeling and thought. Symbology is reappearing as a study worthy of the scholar; the psychosomatic factor in illness has passed from the writings of the crank to those of the specialist; spiritual healing in all its forms is no longer a pious hope but an accepted phenomenon. And it is into this context that we consider astrology, in the sense that it is an analysis of human types.

Astrology and medicine had a long journey together, and only parted company a couple of centuries ago. There still remain in medical language such astrological terms as "saturnine," "choleric," and "mercurial," used in the diagnosis of physical tendencies. The herbalist, for long the handyman of the medical profession, has been dominated by astrology since the days of the Greeks. Certain herbs traditionally respond to certain planetary influences, and diseases must therefore be treated to ensure harmony between the medicine and the disease.

But the stars are expected to foretell and not only to diagnose.

Astrological forecasting has been remarkably accurate, but often it is wide of the mark. The brave person who cares to predict world events takes dangerous chances. Individual forecasting is less clear cut; it can be a help or a disillusionment. Then we come to the nagging question: if it is possible to foreknow, is it right to foretell? This is a point of ethics on which it is hard to pronounce judgment. The doctor faces the same dilemma if he finds that symptoms of a mortal disease are present in his patient and that he can only prognosticate a steady decline. How much to tell an individual in a crisis is a problem that has perplexed many distinguished scholars. Honest and conscientious astrologers in this modern world, where so many people are seeking guidance, face the same problem.

Five hundred years ago it was customary to call in a learned man who was an astrologer who was probably also a doctor and a philosopher. By his knowledge of astrology, his study of planetary influences, he felt himself qualified to guide those in distress. The world has moved forward at a fantastic rate since then, and yet people are still uncertain of themselves. At first sight it seems fantastic in the light of modern thinking that they turn to the most ancient of all studies, and get someone to calculate a horoscope for them. But is it really so fantastic if you take a second look? For astrology is concerned with tomorrow, with survival. And in a world such as ours, tomorrow and survival are the keywords for the twenty-first century.

ASTROLOGICAL BRIDGE TO THE 21st CENTURY

Themes connecting past, present, and future are in play as the first decade reveals hidden paths and personal hints for achieving your potential. Make the most of the messages from the planets.

With the dawning of the twenty-first century look first to Jupiter, the planet of good fortune. Each new yearly Jupiter cycle follows the natural progression of the Zodiac. First is Jupiter in Aries and in Taurus through spring 2000, next Jupiter is in Gemini to summer 2001, then in Cancer to midsummer 2002, in Leo to late summer 2003, in Virgo to early autumn 2004, in Libra to midautumn 2005, and so on through Jupiter in Pisces through June 2010. The beneficent planet Jupiter promotes your professional and educational goals while urging informed choice and deliberation, providing a rich medium for creativity. Planet Jupiter's influence is protective, the generous helper that comes to the rescue just in the nick of time. And while safeguarding good luck, Jupiter can turn unusual risks into achievable aims.

In order to take advantage of luck and opportunity, to gain wisdom from experience, to persevere against adversity, look to beautiful planet Saturn. Saturn, planet of reason and responsibility, began a new cycle in earthy Taurus at the turn of the century. Saturn in Taurus until spring 2001 inspires industry and affection, blends practicality and imagination, all the while inviting caution and care. Saturn in Taurus lends beauty, order, and structure to your life. Then Saturn is in Gemini, the sign of mind and communication, until June 2003. Saturn in Gemini gives a lively intellectual capacity, so the limits of creativity can be stretched and boundaries broken. Saturn in Gemini holds the promise of fruitful endeavor through sustained study, learning, and application. Saturn in Cancer from early June 2003 to mid-July 2005 poses issues of long-term security versus immediate gratification. Rely on deliberation and choice to make sense out of diversity and change. Saturn in Cancer can be a revealing cycle, leading to the desired outcomes of growth and maturity. Saturn in Leo from mid-July 2005 to early September 2007 can be a test of boldness versus caution. Here every challenge must be met with benevolent authority, matched by a caring and generous outlook. Saturn in Virgo early September 2007 into October 2009 sharpens and deepens the mind, conferring precise writing and teaching skills. Saturn in Virgo presents chances to excel, to accomplish a great deal, and to gain prominence through good words and good works.

Uranus, planet of innovation and surprise, started an important new cycle in January of 1996. At that time Uranus entered its natural home in airy Aquarius. Uranus in Aquarius into the year 2003 has a profound effect on your personality and the lens through which you see the world. A basic change in the way you project yourself is just one impact of Uranus in Aquarius. More significantly, a whole new consciousness is evolving. Winds of change blowing your way emphasize movement and freedom. Uranus in Aquarius poses involvement in the larger community beyond self, family, friends, lovers, associates. Radical ideas and progressive thought signal a journey of liberation. As the new century begins, follow Uranus on the path of humanitarianism. A new Uranus cycle begins March 2003 when Uranus visits Pisces, briefly revisits Aquarius, then returns late in 2003 to Pisces where it will stay into May 2010. Uranus in Pisces, a strongly intuitive force, urges work and service for the good of humankind to make the world a better place for all people.

Neptune, planet of vision and mystery, is enjoying a long cycle that excites creativity and imaginative thinking. Neptune is in airy Aquarius from November 1998 to February of 2012. Neptune in Aquarius, the sign of the Water Bearer, represents two sides of the coin of wisdom: inspiration and reason. Here Neptune stirs powerful currents bearing a rich and varied harvest, the fertile breeding ground for idealistic aims and practical considerations. Neptune's fine intuition tunes in to your dreams, your imagination, your spirituality. You can never turn your back on the mysteries of life. Uranus and Neptune, the planets of enlightenment and idealism, give you glimpses into the future, letting you peek through secret doorways into the twenty-first century.

Pluto, dwarf planet of beginnings and endings, started a new cycle of transformative power in the year 2008. Pluto entered the earthy sign of Capricorn and journeys there for sixteen years until 2024. Pluto in Capricorn over the course of this extensive journey has the capacity to change the landscape as well as the humanscape. The transforming energy of Pluto combines with the persevering power of Capricorn to give depth and character to potential change. Pluto in Capricorn can bring focus and cohesion to disparate, diverse creativities. As new forms arise and take root, Pluto in Capricorn organizes the rebuilding process. Freedom versus limitation, freedom versus authority is part of the picture. Reasonableness struggles with recklessness to solve divisive issues. Pluto in Capricorn can teach important lessons about adversity, and the lessons will be learned.

THE SIGNS OF THE ZODIAC

Dominant Characteristics

Aries: March 21–April 20

The Positive Side of Aries

The Aries has many positive points to his character. People born under this first sign of the Zodiac are often quite strong and enthusiastic. On the whole, they are forward-looking people who are not easily discouraged by temporary setbacks. They know what they want out of life and they go out after it. Their personalities are strong. Others are usually quite impressed by the Ram's way of doing things. Quite often they are sources of inspiration for others traveling the same route. Aries men and women have a special zest for life that can be contagious; for others, they are a fine example of how life should be lived.

The Aries person usually has a quick and active mind. He is imaginative and inventive. He enjoys keeping busy and active. He generally gets along well with all kinds of people. He is interested in mankind, as a whole. He likes to be challenged. Some would say he thrives on opposition, for it is when he is set against that he often does his best. Getting over or around obstacles is a challenge he generally enjoys. All in all, Aries is quite positive and young-thinking. He likes to keep abreast of new things that are happening in the world. Aries are often fond of speed. They like things to be done quickly, and this sometimes aggravates their slower colleagues and associates.

The Aries man or woman always seems to remain young. Their whole approach to life is youthful and optimistic. They never say die, no matter what the odds. They may have an occasional setback, but it is not long before they are back on their feet again.

The Negative Side of Aries

Everybody has his less positive qualities—and Aries is no exception. Sometimes the Aries man or woman is not very tactful in communicating with others; in his hurry to get things done he is apt to be a little callous or inconsiderate. Sensitive people are likely to find him somewhat sharp-tongued in some situations. Often in his eagerness to get the show on the road, he misses the mark altogether and cannot achieve his aims.

At times Aries can be too impulsive. He can occasionally be stubborn and refuse to listen to reason. If things do not move quickly enough to suit the Aries man or woman, he or she is apt to become rather nervous or irritable. The uncultivated Aries is not unfamiliar with moments of doubt and fear. He is capable of being destructive if he does not get his way. He can overcome some of his emotional problems by steadily trying to express himself as he really is, but this requires effort.

Taurus: April 21–May 20

The Positive Side of Taurus

The Taurus person is known for his ability to concentrate and for his tenacity. These are perhaps his strongest qualities. The Taurus man or woman generally has very little trouble in getting along with others; it's his nature to be helpful toward people in need. He can always be depended on by his friends, especially those in trouble.

Taurus generally achieves what he wants through his ability to persevere. He never leaves anything unfinished but works on something until it has been completed. People can usually take him at his word; he is honest and forthright in most of his dealings. The Taurus person has a good chance to make a success of his life because of his many positive qualities. The Taurus who aims high seldom falls short of his mark. He learns well by experience. He is thorough and does not believe in shortcuts of any kind. The Bull's thoroughness pays off in the end, for through his deliberateness he learns how to rely on himself and what he has learned. The Taurus person tries to get along with others, as a rule. He is not overly critical and likes people to be themselves. He is a tolerant person and enjoys peace and harmony—especially in his home life.

Taurus is usually cautious in all that he does. He is not a person

who believes in taking unnecessary risks. Before adopting any one line of action, he will weigh all of the pros and cons. The Taurus person is steadfast. Once his mind is made up it seldom changes. The person born under this sign usually is a good family person—reliable and loving.

The Negative Side of Taurus

Sometimes the Taurus man or woman is a bit too stubborn. He won't listen to other points of view if his mind is set on something. To others, this can be quite annoying. Taurus also does not like to be told what to do. He becomes rather angry if others think him not too bright. He does not like to be told he is wrong, even when he is. He dislikes being contradicted.

Some people who are born under this sign are very suspicious of others—even of those persons close to them. They find it difficult to trust people fully. They are often afraid of being deceived or taken advantage of. The Bull often finds it difficult to forget or forgive. His love of material things sometimes makes him rather avaricious and petty.

Gemini: May 21–June 20

The Positive Side of Gemini

The person born under this sign of the Heavenly Twins is usually quite bright and quick-witted. Some of them are capable of doing many different things. The Gemini person very often has many different interests. He keeps an open mind and is always anxious to learn new things.

Gemini is often an analytical person. He is a person who enjoys making use of his intellect. He is governed more by his mind than by his emotions. He is a person who is not confined to one view; he can often understand both sides to a problem or question. He knows how to reason, how to make rapid decisions if need be.

He is an adaptable person and can make himself at home almost anywhere. There are all kinds of situations he can adapt to. He is a person who seldom doubts himself; he is sure of his talents and his ability to think and reason. Gemini is generally most satisfied when he is in a situation where he can make use of his intellect. Never

short of imagination, he often has strong talents for invention. He is rather a modern person when it comes to life; Gemini almost always moves along with the times—perhaps that is why he remains so youthful throughout most of his life.

Literature and art appeal to the person born under this sign. Creativity in almost any form will interest and intrigue the Gemini man or woman.

The Gemini is often quite charming. A good talker, he often is the center of attraction at any gathering. People find it easy to like a person born under this sign because he can appear easygoing and usually has a good sense of humor.

The Negative Side of Gemini

Sometimes the Gemini person tries to do too many things at one time—and as a result, winds up finishing nothing. Some Twins are easily distracted and find it rather difficult to concentrate on one thing for too long a time. Sometimes they give in to trifling fancies and find it rather boring to become too serious about any one thing. Some of them are never dependable, no matter what they promise.

Although the Gemini man or woman often appears to be well-versed on many subjects, this is sometimes just a veneer. His knowledge may be only superficial, but because he speaks so well he gives people the impression of erudition. Some Geminis are sharp-tongued and inconsiderate; they think only of themselves and their own pleasure.

Cancer: June 21–July 20

The Positive Side of Cancer

The Moon Child's most positive point is his understanding nature. On the whole, he is a loving and sympathetic person. He would never go out of his way to hurt anyone. The Cancer man or woman is often very kind and tender; they give what they can to others. They hate to see others suffering and will do what they can to help someone in less fortunate circumstances than themselves. They are often very concerned about the world. Their interest in people generally goes beyond that of just their own families and close friends; they have a deep sense of community and respect humanitarian values. The Moon Child means what he says, as a rule; he is honest about his feelings.

The Cancer man or woman is a person who knows the art of patience. When something seems difficult, he is willing to wait until the situation becomes manageable again. He is a person who knows how to bide his time. Cancer knows how to concentrate on one thing at a time. When he has made his mind up he generally sticks with what he does, seeing it through to the end.

Cancer is a person who loves his home. He enjoys being surrounded by familiar things and the people he loves. Of all the signs, Cancer is the most maternal. Even the men born under this sign often have a motherly or protective quality about them. They like to take care of people in their family—to see that they are well loved and well provided for. They are usually loyal and faithful. Family ties mean a lot to the Cancer man or woman. Parents and in-laws are respected and loved. Young Cancer responds very well to adults who show faith in him. The Moon Child has a strong sense of tradition. He is very sensitive to the moods of others.

The Negative Side of Cancer

Sometimes Cancer finds it rather hard to face life. It becomes too much for him. He can be a little timid and retiring, when things don't go too well. When unfortunate things happen, he is apt to just shrug and say, "Whatever will be will be." He can be fatalistic to a fault. The uncultivated Cancer is a bit lazy. He doesn't have very much ambition. Anything that seems a bit difficult he'll gladly leave to others. He may be lacking in initiative. Too sensitive, when he feels he's been injured, he'll crawl back into his shell and nurse his imaginary wounds. The immature Moon Child often is given to crying when the smallest thing goes wrong.

Some Cancers find it difficult to enjoy themselves in environments outside their homes. They make heavy demands on others, and need to be constantly reassured that they are loved. Lacking such reassurance, they may resort to sulking in silence.

Leo: July 21–August 21

The Positive Side of Leo

Often Leos make good leaders. They seem to be good organizers and administrators. Usually they are quite popular with others. Whatever group it is that they belong to, the Leo man or woman is almost sure to be or become the leader. Loyalty, one of the Lion's noblest traits, enables him or her to maintain this leadership position.

Leo is generous most of the time. It is his best characteristic. He or she likes to give gifts and presents. In making others happy, the Leo person becomes happy himself. He likes to splurge when spending money on others. In some instances it may seem that the Lion's generosity knows no boundaries. A hospitable person, the Leo man or woman is very fond of welcoming people to his house and entertaining them. He is never short of company.

Leo has plenty of energy and drive. He enjoys working toward some specific goal. When he applies himself correctly, he gets what he wants most often. The Leo person is almost never unsure of himself. He has plenty of confidence and aplomb. He is a person who is direct in almost everything he does. He has a quick mind and can make a decision in a very short time.

He usually sets a good example for others because of his ambitious manner and positive ways. He knows how to stick to something once he's started. Although Leo may be good at making a joke, he is not superficial or glib. He is a loving person, kind and thoughtful.

There is generally nothing small or petty about the Leo man or woman. He does what he can for those who are deserving. He is a person others can rely upon at all times. He means what he says. An honest person, generally speaking, he is a friend who is valued and sought out.

The Negative Side of Leo

Leo, however, does have his faults. At times, he can be just a bit too arrogant. He thinks that no one deserves a leadership position except him. Only he is capable of doing things well. His opinion of himself is often much too high. Because of his conceit, he is

sometimes rather unpopular with a good many people. Some Leos are too materialistic; they can only think in terms of money and profit.

Some Leos enjoy lording it over others—at home or at their place of business. What is more, they feel they have the right to. Egocentric to an impossible degree, this sort of Leo cares little about how others think or feel. He can be rude and cutting.

Virgo: August 22–September 22

The Positive Side of Virgo

The person born under the sign of Virgo is generally a busy person. He knows how to arrange and organize things. He is a good planner. Above all, he is practical and is not afraid of hard work.

Often called the sign of the Harvester, Virgo knows how to attain what he desires. He sticks with something until it is finished. He never shirks his duties, and can always be depended upon. The Virgo person can be thoroughly trusted at all times.

The man or woman born under this sign tries to do everything to perfection. He doesn't believe in doing anything halfway. He always aims for the top. He is the sort of a person who is always learning and constantly striving to better himself—not because he wants more money or glory, but because it gives him a feeling of accomplishment.

The Virgo man or woman is a very observant person. He is sensitive to how others feel, and can see things below the surface of a situation. He usually puts this talent to constructive use.

It is not difficult for the Virgo to be open and earnest. He believes in putting his cards on the table. He is never secretive or underhanded. He's as good as his word. The Virgo person is generally plainspoken and down to earth. He has no trouble in expressing himself.

The Virgo person likes to keep up to date on new developments in his particular field. Well-informed, generally, he sometimes has a keen interest in the arts or literature. What he knows, he knows well. His ability to use his critical faculties is well-developed and sometimes startles others because of its accuracy.

Virgos adhere to a moderate way of life; they avoid excesses. Virgo is a responsible person and enjoys being of service.

The Negative Side of Virgo

Sometimes a Virgo person is too critical. He thinks that only he can do something the way it should be done. Whatever anyone else does is inferior. He can be rather annoying in the way he quibbles over insignificant details. In telling others how things should be done, he can be rather tactless and mean.

Some Virgos seem rather emotionless and cool. They feel emotional involvement is beneath them. They are sometimes too tidy, too neat. With money they can be rather miserly. Some Virgos try to force their opinions and ideas on others.

Libra: September 23–October 22

The Positive Side of Libra

Libras love harmony. It is one of their most outstanding character traits. They are interested in achieving balance; they admire beauty and grace in things as well as in people. Generally speaking, they are kind and considerate people. Libras are usually very sympathetic. They go out of their way not to hurt another person's feelings. They are outgoing and do what they can to help those in need.

People born under the sign of Libra almost always make good friends. They are loyal and amiable. They enjoy the company of others. Many of them are rather moderate in their views; they believe in keeping an open mind, however, and weighing both sides of an issue fairly before making a decision.

Alert and intelligent, Libra, often known as the Lawgiver, is always fair-minded and tries to put himself in the position of the other person. They are against injustice; quite often they take up for the underdog. In most of their social dealings, they try to be tactful and kind. They dislike discord and bickering, and most Libras strive for peace and harmony in all their relationships.

The Libra man or woman has a keen sense of beauty. They appreciate handsome furnishings and clothes. Many of them are artistically inclined. Their taste is usually impeccable. They know how to use color. Their homes are almost always attractively arranged and inviting. They enjoy entertaining people and see to it that their guests always feel at home and welcome.

Libra gets along with almost everyone. He is well-liked and socially much in demand.

The Negative Side of Libra

Some people born under this sign tend to be rather insincere. So eager are they to achieve harmony in all relationships that they will even go so far as to lie. Many of them are escapists. They find facing the truth an ordeal and prefer living in a world of make-believe.

In a serious argument, some Libras give in rather easily even when they know they are right. Arguing, even about something they believe in, is too unsettling for some of them.

Libras sometimes care too much for material things. They enjoy possessions and luxuries. Some are vain and tend to be jealous.

Scorpio: October 23–November 22

The Positive Side of Scorpio

The Scorpio man or woman generally knows what he or she wants out of life. He is a determined person. He sees something through to the end. Scorpio is quite sincere, and seldom says anything he doesn't mean. When he sets a goal for himself he tries to go about achieving it in a very direct way.

The Scorpion is brave and courageous. They are not afraid of hard work. Obstacles do not frighten them. They forge ahead until they achieve what they set out for. The Scorpio man or woman has a strong will.

Although Scorpio may seem rather fixed and determined, inside he is often quite tender and loving. He can care very much for others. He believes in sincerity in all relationships. His feelings about someone tend to last; they are profound and not superficial.

The Scorpio person is someone who adheres to his principles no matter what happens. He will not be deterred from a path he believes to be right.

Because of his many positive strengths, the Scorpion can often achieve happiness for himself and for those that he loves.

He is a constructive person by nature. He often has a deep understanding of people and of life, in general. He is perceptive and unafraid. Obstacles often seem to spur him on. He is a positive person who enjoys winning. He has many strengths and resources; challenge of any sort often brings out the best in him.

The Negative Side of Scorpio

The Scorpio person is sometimes hypersensitive. Often he imagines injury when there is none. He feels that others do not bother to recognize him for his true worth. Sometimes he is given to excessive boasting in order to compensate for what he feels is neglect.

Scorpio can be proud, arrogant, and competitive. They can be sly when they put their minds to it and they enjoy outwitting persons or institutions noted for their cleverness.

Their tactics for getting what they want are sometimes devious and ruthless. They don't care too much about what others may think. If they feel others have done them an injustice, they will do their best to seek revenge. The Scorpion often has a sudden, violent temper; and this person's interest in sex is sometimes quite unbalanced or excessive.

Sagittarius: November 23–December 20

The Positive Side of Sagittarius

People born under this sign are honest and forthright. Their approach to life is earnest and open. Sagittarius is often quite adult in his way of seeing things. They are broad-minded and tolerant people. When dealing with others the person born under the sign of the Archer is almost always open and forthright. He doesn't believe in deceit or pretension. His standards are high. People who associate with Sagittarius generally admire and respect his tolerant viewpoint.

The Archer trusts others easily and expects them to trust him. He is never suspicious or envious and almost always thinks well of others. People always enjoy his company because he is so friendly and easygoing. The Sagittarius man or woman is often good-humored. He can always be depended upon by his friends, family, and co-workers.

The person born under this sign of the Zodiac likes a good joke every now and then. Sagittarius is eager for fun and laughs, which makes him very popular with others.

A lively person, he enjoys sports and outdoor life. The Archer is fond of animals. Intelligent and interesting, he can begin an ani-

mated conversation with ease. He likes exchanging ideas and discussing various views.

He is not selfish or proud. If someone proposes an idea or plan that is better than his, he will immediately adopt it. Imaginative yet practical, he knows how to put ideas into practice.

The Archer enjoys sport and games, and it doesn't matter if he wins or loses. He is a forgiving person, and never sulks over something that has not worked out in his favor.

He is seldom critical, and is almost always generous.

The Negative Side of Sagittarius

Some Sagittarius are restless. They take foolish risks and seldom learn from the mistakes they make. They don't have heads for money and are often mismanaging their finances. Some of them devote much of their time to gambling.

Some are too outspoken and tactless, always putting their feet in their mouths. They hurt others carelessly by being honest at the wrong time. Sometimes they make promises which they don't keep. They don't stick close enough to their plans and go from one failure to another. They are undisciplined and waste a lot of energy.

Capricorn: December 21–January 19

The Positive Side of Capricorn

The person born under the sign of Capricorn, known variously as the Mountain Goat or Sea Goat, is usually very stable and patient. He sticks to whatever tasks he has and sees them through. He can always be relied upon and he is not averse to work.

An honest person, Capricorn is generally serious about whatever he does. He does not take his duties lightly. He is a practical person and believes in keeping his feet on the ground.

Quite often the person born under this sign is ambitious and knows how to get what he wants out of life. The Goat forges ahead and never gives up his goal. When he is determined about something, he almost always wins. He is a good worker—a hard worker. Although things may not come easy to him, he will not complain, but continue working until his chores are finished.

He is usually good at business matters and knows the value of money. He is not a spendthrift and knows how to put something away for a rainy day; he dislikes waste and unnecessary loss.

Capricorn knows how to make use of his self-control. He can apply himself to almost anything once he puts his mind to it. His ability to concentrate sometimes astounds others. He is diligent and does well when involved in detail work.

The Capricorn man or woman is charitable, generally speaking, and will do what is possible to help others less fortunate. As a friend, he is loyal and trustworthy. He never shirks his duties or responsibilities. He is self-reliant and never expects too much of the other fellow. He does what he can on his own. If someone does him a good turn, then he will do his best to return the favor.

The Negative Side of Capricorn

Like everyone, Capricorn, too, has faults. At times, the Goat can be overcritical of others. He expects others to live up to his own high standards. He thinks highly of himself and tends to look down on others.

His interest in material things may be exaggerated. The Capricorn man or woman thinks too much about getting on in the world and having something to show for it. He may even be a little greedy.

He sometimes thinks he knows what's best for everyone. He is too bossy. He is always trying to organize and correct others. He may be a little narrow in his thinking.

Aquarius: January 20–February 18

The Positive Side of Aquarius

The Aquarius man or woman is usually very honest and forthright. These are his two greatest qualities. His standards for himself are generally very high. He can always be relied upon by others. His word is his bond.

Aquarius is perhaps the most tolerant of all the Zodiac personalities. He respects other people's beliefs and feels that everyone is entitled to his own approach to life.

He would never do anything to injure another's feelings. He is never unkind or cruel. Always considerate of others, the Water

Bearer is always willing to help a person in need. He feels a very strong tie between himself and all the other members of mankind.

The person born under this sign, called the Water Bearer, is almost always an individualist. He does not believe in teaming up with the masses, but prefers going his own way. His ideas about life and mankind are often quite advanced. There is a saying to the effect that the average Aquarius is fifty years ahead of his time.

Aquarius is community-minded. The problems of the world concern him greatly. He is interested in helping others no matter what part of the globe they live in. He is truly a humanitarian sort. He likes to be of service to others.

Giving, considerate, and without prejudice, Aquarius have no trouble getting along with others.

The Negative Side of Aquarius

Aquarius may be too much of a dreamer. He makes plans but seldom carries them out. He is rather unrealistic. His imagination has a tendency to run away with him. Because many of his plans are impractical, he is always in some sort of a dither.

Others may not approve of him at all times because of his unconventional behavior. He may be a bit eccentric. Sometimes he is so busy with his own thoughts that he loses touch with the realities of existence.

Some Aquarius feel they are more clever and intelligent than others. They seldom admit to their own faults, even when they are quite apparent. Some become rather fanatic in their views. Their criticism of others is sometimes destructive and negative.

Pisces: February 19–March 20

The Positive Side of Pisces

Known as the sign of the Fishes, Pisces has a sympathetic nature. Kindly, he is often dedicated in the way he goes about helping others. The sick and the troubled often turn to him for advice and assistance. Possessing keen intuition, Pisces can easily understand people's deepest problems.

He is very broad-minded and does not criticize others for their faults. He knows how to accept people for what they are. On the whole, he is a trustworthy and earnest person. He is loyal to his friends and will do what he can to help them in time of need. Generous and good-natured, he is a lover of peace; he is often willing to help others solve their differences. People who have taken a wrong turn in life often interest him and he will do what he can to persuade them to rehabilitate themselves.

He has a strong intuitive sense and most of the time he knows how to make it work for him. Pisces is unusually perceptive and often knows what is bothering someone before that person, himself, is aware of it. The Pisces man or woman is an idealistic person, basically, and is interested in making the world a better place in which to live. Pisces believes that everyone should help each other. He is willing to do more than his share in order to achieve cooperation with others.

The person born under this sign often is talented in music or art. He is a receptive person; he is able to take the ups and downs of life with philosophic calm.

The Negative Side of Pisces

Some Pisces are often depressed; their outlook on life is rather glum. They may feel that they have been given a bad deal in life and that others are always taking unfair advantage of them. Pisces sometimes feel that the world is a cold and cruel place. The Fishes can be easily discouraged. The Pisces man or woman may even withdraw from the harshness of reality into a secret shell of his own where he dreams and idles away a good deal of his time.

Pisces can be lazy. He lets things happen without giving the least bit of resistance. He drifts along, whether on the high road or on the low. He can be lacking in willpower.

Some Pisces people seek escape through drugs or alcohol. When temptation comes along they find it hard to resist. In matters of sex, they can be rather permissive.

Sun Sign Personalities

ARIES: Hans Christian Andersen, Pearl Bailey, Marlon Brando, Wernher Von Braun, Charlie Chaplin, Joan Crawford, Da Vinci, Bette Davis, Doris Day, W.C. Fields, Alec Guinness, Adolf Hitler, William Holden, Thomas Jefferson, Nikita Khrushchev, Elton John, Arturo Toscanini, J.P. Morgan, Paul Robeson, Gloria Steinem, Sarah Vaughn, Vincent van Gogh, Tennessee Williams

TAURUS: Fred Astaire, Charlotte Brontë, Carol Burnett, Irving Berlin, Bing Crosby, Salvador Dali, Tchaikovsky, Queen Elizabeth II, Duke Ellington, Ella Fitzgerald, Henry Fonda, Sigmund Freud, Orson Welles, Joe Louis, Lenin, Karl Marx, Golda Meir, Eva Peron, Bertrand Russell, Shakespeare, Kate Smith, Benjamin Spock, Barbra Streisand, Shirley Temple, Harry Truman

GEMINI: Ruth Benedict, Josephine Baker, Rachel Carson, Carlos Chavez, Walt Whitman, Bob Dylan, Ralph Waldo Emerson, Judy Garland, Paul Gauguin, Allen Ginsberg, Benny Goodman, Bob Hope, Burl Ives, John F. Kennedy, Peggy Lee, Marilyn Monroe, Joe Namath, Cole Porter, Laurence Olivier, Harriet Beecher Stowe, Queen Victoria, John Wayne, Frank Lloyd Wright

CANCER: "Dear Abby," Lizzie Borden, David Brinkley, Yul Brynner, Pearl Buck, Marc Chagall, Princess Diana, Babe Didrikson, Mary Baker Eddy, Henry VIII, John Glenn, Ernest Hemingway, Lena Horne, Oscar Hammerstein, Helen Keller, Ann Landers, George Orwell, Nancy Reagan, Rembrandt, Richard Rodgers, Ginger Rogers, Rubens, Jean-Paul Sartre, O.J. Simpson

LEO: Neil Armstrong, James Baldwin, Lucille Ball, Emily Brontë, Wilt Chamberlain, Julia Child, William J. Clinton, Cecil B. De Mille, Ogden Nash, Amelia Earhart, Edna Ferber, Arthur Goldberg, Alfred Hitchcock, Mick Jagger, George Meany, Annie Oakley, George Bernard Shaw, Napoleon, Jacqueline Onassis, Henry Ford, Francis Scott Key, Andy Warhol, Mae West, Orville Wright

VIRGO: Ingrid Bergman, Warren Burger, Maurice Chevalier, Agatha Christie, Sean Connery, Lafayette, Peter Falk, Greta Garbo, Althea Gibson, Arthur Godfrey, Goethe, Buddy Hackett, Michael Jackson, Lyndon Johnson, D.H. Lawrence, Sophia Loren, Grandma Moses, Arnold Palmer, Queen Elizabeth I, Walter Reuther, Peter Sellers, Lily Tomlin, George Wallace

LIBRA: Brigitte Bardot, Art Buchwald, Truman Capote, Dwight D. Eisenhower, William Faulkner, F. Scott Fitzgerald, Gandhi, George Gershwin, Micky Mantle, Helen Hayes, Vladimir Horowitz, Doris Lessing, Martina Navratalova, Eugene O'Neill, Luciano Pavarotti, Emily Post, Eleanor Roosevelt, Bruce Springsteen, Margaret Thatcher, Gore Vidal, Barbara Walters, Oscar Wilde

SCORPIO: Vivien Leigh, Richard Burton, Art Carney, Johnny Carson, Billy Graham, Grace Kelly, Walter Cronkite, Marie Curie, Charles de Gaulle, Linda Evans, Indira Gandhi, Theodore Roosevelt, Rock Hudson, Katherine Hepburn, Robert F. Kennedy, Billie Jean King, Martin Luther, Georgia O'Keeffe, Pablo Picasso, Jonas Salk, Alan Shepard, Robert Louis Stevenson

SAGITTARIUS: Jane Austen, Louisa May Alcott, Woody Allen, Beethoven, Willy Brandt, Mary Martin, William F. Buckley, Maria Callas, Winston Churchill, Noel Coward, Emily Dickinson, Walt Disney, Benjamin Disraeli, James Doolittle, Kirk Douglas, Chet Huntley, Jane Fonda, Chris Evert Lloyd, Margaret Mead, Charles Schulz, John Milton, Frank Sinatra, Steven Spielberg

CAPRICORN: Muhammad Ali, Isaac Asimov, Pablo Casals, Dizzy Dean, Marlene Dietrich, James Farmer, Ava Gardner, Barry Goldwater, Cary Grant, J. Edgar Hoover, Howard Hughes, Joan of Arc, Gypsy Rose Lee, Martin Luther King, Jr., Rudyard Kipling, Mao Tse-tung, Richard Nixon, Gamal Nasser, Louis Pasteur, Albert Schweitzer, Stalin, Benjamin Franklin, Elvis Presley

AQUARIUS: Marian Anderson, Susan B. Anthony, Jack Benny, John Barrymore, Mikhail Baryshnikov, Charles Darwin, Charles Dickens, Thomas Edison, Clark Gable, Jascha Heifetz, Abraham Lincoln, Yehudi Menuhin, Mozart, Jack Nicklaus, Ronald Reagan, Jackie Robinson, Norman Rockwell, Franklin D. Roosevelt, Gertrude Stein, Charles Lindbergh, Margaret Truman

PISCES: Edward Albee, Harry Belafonte, Alexander Graham Bell, Chopin, Adelle Davis, Albert Einstein, Golda Meir, Jackie Gleason, Winslow Homer, Edward M. Kennedy, Victor Hugo, Mike Mansfield, Michelangelo, Edna St. Vincent Millay, Liza Minelli, John Steinbeck, Linus Pauling, Ravel, Renoir, Diana Ross, William Shirer, Elizabeth Taylor, George Washington

The Signs and Their Key Words

		POSITIVE	NEGATIVE
ARIES	self	courage, initiative, pioneer instinct	brash rudeness, selfish impetuosity
TAURUS	money	endurance, loyalty, wealth	obstinacy, gluttony
GEMINI	mind	versatility	capriciousness, unreliability
CANCER	family	sympathy, homing instinct	clannishness, childishness
LEO	children	love, authority, integrity	egotism, force
VIRGO	work	purity, industry, analysis	faultfinding, cynicism
LIBRA	marriage	harmony, justice	vacillation, superficiality
SCORPIO	sex	survival, regeneration	vengeance, discord
SAGITTARIUS	travel	optimism, higher learning	lawlessness
CAPRICORN	career	depth	narrowness, gloom
AQUARIUS	friends	human fellowship, genius	perverse unpredictability
PISCES	confinement	spiritual love, universality	diffusion, escapism

The Elements and Qualities of The Signs

Every sign has both an *element* and a *quality* associated with it. The element indicates the basic makeup of the sign, and the quality describes the kind of activity associated with each.

Element	Sign	Quality	Sign
FIRE	ARIES LEO SAGITTARIUS	CARDINAL	ARIES LIBRA CANCER CAPRICORN
EARTH	TAURUS VIRGO CAPRICORN	FIXED	TAURUS LEO SCORPIO AQUARIUS
AIR	GEMINI LIBRA AQUARIUS	MUTABLE	GEMINI VIRGO SAGITTARIUS PISCES
WATER	CANCER SCORPIO PISCES		

Signs can be grouped together according to their element and quality. Signs of the same element share many basic traits in common. They tend to form stable configurations and ultimately harmonious relationships. Signs of the same quality are often less harmonious, but they share many dynamic potentials for growth as well as profound fulfillment.

Further discussion of each of these sign groupings is provided on the following pages.

The Fire Signs

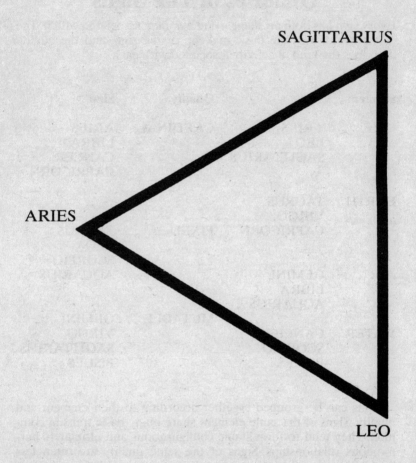

This is the fire group. On the whole these are emotional, volatile types, quick to anger, quick to forgive. They are adventurous, powerful people and act as a source of inspiration for everyone. They spark into action with immediate exuberant impulses. They are intelligent, self-involved, creative, and idealistic. They all share a certain vibrancy and glow that outwardly reflects an inner flame and passion for living.

The Earth Signs

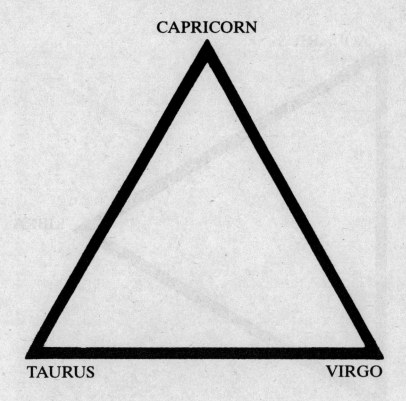

This is the earth group. They are in constant touch with the material world and tend to be conservative. Although they are all capable of spartan self-discipline, they are earthy, sensual people who are stimulated by the tangible, elegant, and luxurious. The thread of their lives is always practical, but they do fantasize and are often attracted to dark, mysterious, emotional people. They are like great cliffs overhanging the sea, forever married to the ocean but always resisting erosion from the dark, emotional forces that thunder at their feet.

The Air Signs

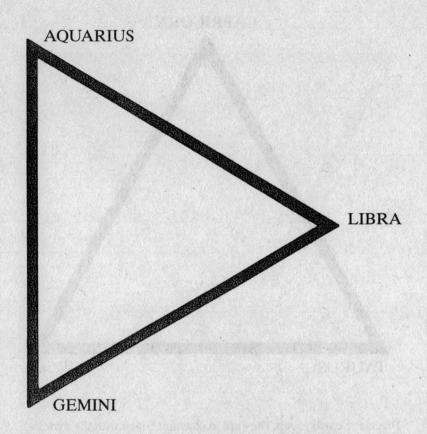

This is the air group. They are light, mental creatures desirous of contact, communication, and relationship. They are involved with people and the forming of ties on many levels. Original thinkers, they are the bearers of human news. Their language is their sense of word, color, style, and beauty. They provide an atmosphere suitable and pleasant for living. They add change and versatility to the scene, and it is through them that we can explore new territory of human intelligence and experience.

The Water Signs

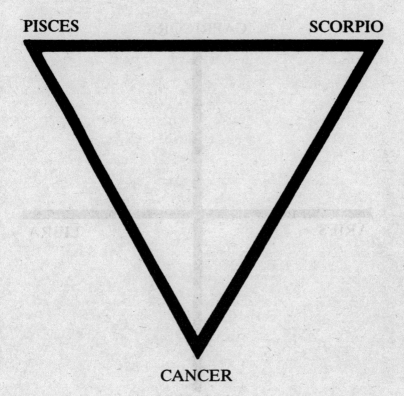

This is the water group. Through the water people, we are all joined together on emotional, nonverbal levels. They are silent, mysterious types whose magic hypnotizes even the most determined realist. They have uncanny perceptions about people and are as rich as the oceans when it comes to feeling, emotion, or imagination. They are sensitive, mystical creatures with memories that go back beyond time. Through water, life is sustained. These people have the potential for the depths of darkness or the heights of mysticism and art.

The Cardinal Signs

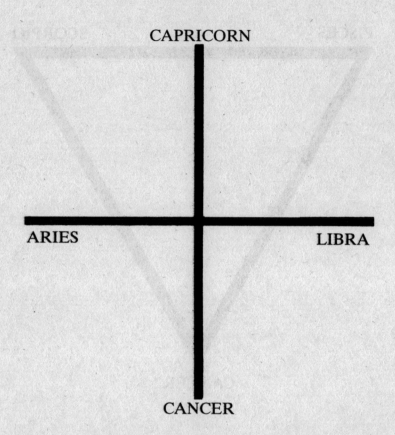

Put together, this is a clear-cut picture of dynamism, activity, tremendous stress, and remarkable achievement. These people know the meaning of great change since their lives are often characterized by significant crises and major successes. This combination is like a simultaneous storm of summer, fall, winter, and spring. The danger is chaotic diffusion of energy; the potential is irrepressible growth and victory.

The Fixed Signs

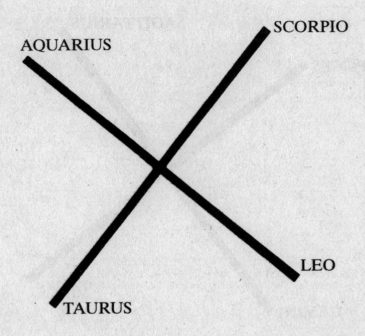

Fixed signs are always establishing themselves in a given place or area of experience. Like explorers who arrive and plant a flag, these people claim a position from which they do not enjoy being deposed. They are staunch, stalwart, upright, trusty, honorable people, although their obstinacy is well-known. Their contribution is fixity, and they are the angels who support our visible world.

The Mutable Signs

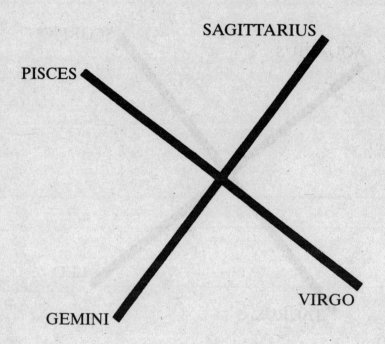

Mutable people are versatile, sensitive, intelligent, nervous, and deeply curious about life. They are the translators of all energy. They often carry out or complete tasks initiated by others. Combinations of these signs have highly developed minds; they are imaginative and jumpy and think and talk a lot. At worst their lives are a Tower of Babel. At best they are adaptable and ready creatures who can assimilate one kind of experience and enjoy it while anticipating coming changes.

THE PLANETS OF THE SOLAR SYSTEM

This section describes the planets of the solar system. In astrology, both the Sun and the Moon are considered to be planets. Because of the Moon's influence in our day-to-day lives, the Moon is described in a separate section following this one.

The Planets and the Signs They Rule

The signs of the Zodiac are linked to the planets in the following way. Each sign is governed or ruled by one or more planets. No matter where the planets are located in the sky at any given moment, they still rule their respective signs, and when they travel through the signs they rule, they have special dignity and their effects are stronger.

Following is a list of the planets and the signs they rule. After looking at the list, read the definitions of the planets and see if you can determine how the planet ruling *your* Sun sign has affected your life.

SIGNS	RULING PLANETS
Aries	Mars, Pluto
Taurus	Venus
Gemini	Mercury
Cancer	Moon
Leo	Sun
Virgo	Mercury
Libra	Venus
Scorpio	Mars, Pluto
Sagittarius	Jupiter
Capricorn	Saturn
Aquarius	Saturn, Uranus
Pisces	Jupiter, Neptune

Characteristics of the Planets

The following pages give the meaning and characteristics of the planets of the solar system. They all travel around the Sun at different speeds and different distances. Taken with the Sun, they all distribute individual intelligence and ability throughout the entire chart.

The planets modify the influence of the Sun in a chart according to their own particular natures, strengths, and positions. Their positions must be calculated for each year and day, and their function and expression in a horoscope will change as they move from one area of the Zodiac to another.

We start with a description of the sun.

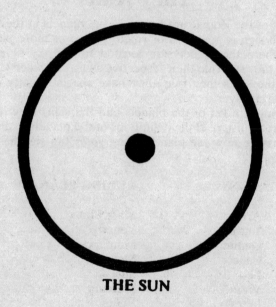

THE SUN

SUN

This is the center of existence. Around this flaming sphere all the planets revolve in endless orbits. Our star is constantly sending out its beams of light and energy without which no life on Earth would be possible. In astrology it symbolizes everything we are trying to become, the center around which all of our activity in life will always revolve. It is the symbol of our basic nature and describes the natural and constant thread that runs through everything that we do from birth to death on this planet.

To early astrologers, the Sun seemed to be another planet because it crossed the heavens every day, just like the rest of the bodies in the sky.

It is the only star near enough to be seen well—it is, in fact, a dwarf star. Approximately 860,000 miles in diameter, it is about ten times as wide as the giant planet Jupiter. The next nearest star is nearly 300,000 times as far away, and if the Sun were located as far away as most of the bright stars, it would be too faint to be seen without a telescope.

Everything in the horoscope ultimately revolves around this singular body. Although other forces may be prominent in the charts of some individuals, still the Sun is the total nucleus of being and symbolizes the complete potential of every human being alive. It is vitality and the life force. Your whole essence comes from the position of the Sun.

You are always trying to express the Sun according to its position by house and sign. Possibility for all development is found in the Sun, and it marks the fundamental character of your personal radiations all around you.

It is the symbol of strength, vigor, wisdom, dignity, ardor, and generosity, and the ability for a person to function as a mature individual. It is also a creative force in society. It is consciousness of the gift of life.

The underdeveloped solar nature is arrogant, pushy, undependable, and proud, and is constantly using force.

MERCURY

Mercury is the planet closest to the Sun. It races around our star, gathering information and translating it to the rest of the system. Mercury represents your capacity to understand the desires of your own will and to translate those desires into action.

In other words it is the planet of mind and the power of communication. Through Mercury we develop an ability to think, write, speak, and observe—to become aware of the world around us. It colors our attitudes and vision of the world, as well as our capacity to communicate our inner responses to the outside world. Some people who have serious disabilities in their power of verbal communication have often wrongly been described as people lacking intelligence.

Although this planet (and its position in the horoscope) indicates your power to communicate your thoughts and perceptions to the world, intelligence is something deeper. Intelligence is distributed throughout all the planets. It is the relationship of the planets to each other that truly describes what we call intelligence. Mercury rules speaking, language, mathematics, draft and design, students, messengers, young people, offices, teachers, and any pursuits where the mind of man has wings.

VENUS

Venus is beauty. It symbolizes the harmony and radiance of a rare and elusive quality: beauty itself. It is refinement and delicacy, softness and charm. In astrology it indicates grace, balance, and the aesthetic sense. Where Venus is we see beauty, a gentle drawing in of energy and the need for satisfaction and completion. It is a special touch that finishes off rough edges. It is sensitivity, and affection, and it is always the place for that other elusive phenomenon: love. Venus describes our sense of what is beautiful and loving. Poorly developed, it is vulgar, tasteless, and self-indulgent. But its ideal is the flame of spiritual love—Aphrodite, goddess of love, and the sweetness and power of personal beauty.

MARS

Mars is raw, crude energy. The planet next to Earth but outward from the Sun is a fiery red sphere that charges through the horoscope with force and fury. It represents the way you reach out for new adventure and new experience. It is energy and drive, initiative, courage, and daring. It is the power to start something and see it through. It can be thoughtless, cruel and wild, angry and hostile, causing cuts, burns, scalds, and wounds. It can stab its way through a chart, or it can be the symbol of healthy spirited adventure, well-channeled constructive power to begin and keep up the drive. If you have trouble starting things, if you lack the get-up-and-go to start the ball rolling, if you lack aggressiveness and self-confidence, chances are there's another planet influencing your Mars. Mars rules soldiers, butchers, surgeons, salesmen—any field that requires daring, bold skill, operational technique, or self-promotion.

JUPITER

This is the largest planet of the solar system. Scientists have recently learned that Jupiter reflects more light than it receives from the Sun. In a sense it is like a star itself. In astrology it rules good luck and good cheer, health, wealth, optimism, happiness, success, and joy. It is the symbol of opportunity and always opens the way for new possibilities in your life. It rules exuberance, enthusiasm, wisdom, knowledge, generosity, and all forms of expansion in general. It rules actors, statesmen, clerics, professional people, religion, publishing, and the distribution of many people over large areas.

Sometimes Jupiter makes you think you deserve everything, and you become sloppy, wasteful, careless and rude, prodigal and lawless, in the illusion that nothing can ever go wrong. Then there is the danger of overconfidence, exaggeration, undependability, and overindulgence.

Jupiter is the minimization of limitation and the emphasis on spirituality and potential. It is the thirst for knowledge and higher learning.

SATURN

Saturn circles our system in dark splendor with its mysterious rings, forcing us to be awakened to whatever we have neglected in the past. It will present real puzzles and problems to be solved, causing delays, obstacles, and hindrances. By doing so, Saturn stirs our own sensitivity to those areas where we are laziest.

Here we must patiently develop *method*, and only through painstaking effort can our ends be achieved. It brings order to a horoscope and imposes reason just where we are feeling least reasonable. By creating limitations and boundary, Saturn shows the consequences of being human and demands that we accept the changing cycles inevitable in human life. Saturn rules time, old age, and sobriety. It can bring depression, gloom, jealousy, and greed, or serious acceptance of responsibilities out of which success will develop. With Saturn there is nothing to do but face facts. It rules laborers, stones, granite, rocks, and crystals of all kinds.

THE OUTER PLANETS: URANUS, NEPTUNE, PLUTO

Uranus, Neptune, Pluto are the outer planets. They liberate human beings from cultural conditioning, and in that sense are the lawbreakers. In early times it was thought that Saturn was the last planet of the system—the outer limit beyond which we could never go. The discovery of the next three planets ushered in new phases of human history, revolution, and technology.

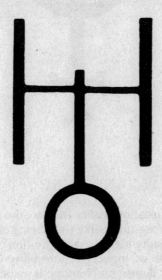

URANUS

Uranus rules unexpected change, upheaval, revolution. It is the symbol of total independence and asserts the freedom of an individual from all restriction and restraint. It is a breakthrough planet and indicates talent, originality, and genius in a horoscope. It usually causes last-minute reversals and changes of plan, unwanted separations, accidents, catastrophes, and eccentric behavior. It can add irrational rebelliousness and perverse bohemianism to a personality or a streak of unaffected brilliance in science and art. It rules technology, aviation, and all forms of electrical and electronic advancement. It governs great leaps forward and topsy-turvy situations, and *always* turns things around at the last minute. Its effects are difficult to predict, since it rules sudden last-minute decisions and events that come like lightning out of the blue.

NEPTUNE

Neptune dissolves existing reality the way the sea erodes the cliffs beside it. Its effects are subtle like the ringing of a buoy's bell in the fog. It suggests a reality higher than definition can usually describe. It awakens a sense of higher responsibility often causing guilt, worry, anxieties, or delusions. Neptune is associated with all forms of escape and can make things seem a certain way so convincingly that you are absolutely sure of something that eventually turns out to be quite different.

It is the planet of illusion and therefore governs the invisible realms that lie beyond our ordinary minds, beyond our simple factual ability to prove what is "real." Treachery, deceit, disillusionment, and disappointment are linked to Neptune. It describes a vague reality that promises eternity and the divine, yet in a manner so complex that we cannot really fathom it at all. At its worst Neptune is a cheap intoxicant; at its best it is the poetry, music, and inspiration of the higher planes of spiritual love. It has dominion over movies, photographs, and much of the arts.

PLUTO

Pluto lies at the outpost of our system and therefore rules finality in a horoscope—the final closing of chapters in your life, the passing of major milestones and points of development from which there is no return. It is a final wipeout, a closeout, an evacuation. It is a distant, subtle but powerful catalyst in all transformations that occur. It creates, destroys, then recreates. Sometimes Pluto starts its influence with a minor event or insignificant incident that might even go unnoticed. Slowly but surely, little by little, everything changes, until at last there has been a total transformation in the area of your life where Pluto has been operating. It rules mass thinking and the trends that society first rejects, then adopts, and finally outgrows.

Pluto rules the dead and the underworld—all the powerful forces of creation and destruction that go on all the time beneath, around, and above us. It can bring a lust for power with strong obsessions.

It is the planet that rules the metamorphosis of the caterpillar into a butterfly, for it symbolizes the capacity to change totally and forever a person's lifestyle, way of thought, and behavior.

THE MOON IN EACH SIGN

The Moon is the nearest planet to the Earth. It exerts more observable influence on us from day to day than any other planet. The effect is very personal, very intimate, and if we are not aware of how it works it can make us quite unstable in our ideas. And the annoying thing is that at these times we often see our own instability but can do nothing about it. A knowledge of what can be expected may help considerably. We can then be prepared to stand strong against the Moon's negative influences and use its positive ones to help us to get ahead. Who has not heard of going with the tide?

The Moon reflects, has no light of its own. It reflects the Sun—the life giver—in the form of vital movement. The Moon controls the tides, the blood rhythm, the movement of sap in trees and plants. Its nature is inconstancy and change so it signifies our moods, our superficial behavior—walking, talking, and especially thinking. Being a true reflector of other forces, the Moon is cold, watery like the surface of a still lake, brilliant and scintillating at times, but easily ruffled and disturbed by the winds of change.

The Moon takes about 27⅓ days to make a complete transit of the Zodiac. It spends just over 2¼ days in each sign. During that time it reflects the qualities, energies, and characteristics of the sign and, to a degree, the planet which rules the sign. When the Moon in its transit occupies a sign incompatible with our own birth sign, we can expect to feel a vague uneasiness, perhaps a touch of irritableness. We should not be discouraged nor let the feeling get us down, or, worse still, allow ourselves to take the discomfort out on others. Try to remember that the Moon has to change signs within 55 hours and, provided you are not physically ill, your mood will probably change with it. It is amazing how frequently depression lifts with the shift in the Moon's position. And, of course, when the Moon is transiting a sign compatible or sympathetic to yours, you will probably feel some sort of stimulation or just be plain happy to be alive.

THE MOON IN EACH SIGN / 79

In the horoscope, the Moon is such a powerful indicator that competent astrologers often use the sign it occupied at birth as the birth sign of the person. This is done particularly when the Sun is on the cusp, or edge, of two signs. Most experienced astrologers, however, coordinate both Sun and Moon signs by reading and confirming from one to the other and secure a far more accurate and personalized analysis.

For these reasons, the Moon tables which follow this section (see pages 86–92) are of great importance to the individual. They show the days and the exact times the Moon will enter each sign of the Zodiac for the year. Remember, you have to adjust the indicated times to local time. The corrections, already calculated for most of the main cities, are at the beginning of the tables. What follows now is a guide to the influences that will be reflected to the Earth by the Moon while it transits each of the twelve signs. The influence is at its peak about 26 hours after the Moon enters a sign. As you read the daily forecast, check the Moon sign for any given day and glance back at this guide.

MOON IN ARIES
This is a time for action, for reaching out beyond the usual self-imposed limitations and faint-hearted cautions. If you have plans in your head or on your desk, put them into practice. New ventures, applications, new jobs, new starts of any kind—all have a good chance of success. This is the period when original and dynamic impulses are being reflected onto Earth. Such energies are extremely vital and favor the pursuit of pleasure and adventure in practically every form. Sick people should feel an improvement. Those who are well will probably find themselves exuding confidence and optimism. People fond of physical exercise should find their bodies growing with tone and well-being. Boldness, strength, determination should characterize most of your activities with a readiness to face up to old challenges. Yesterday's problems may seem petty and exaggerated—so deal with them. Strike out alone. Self-reliance will attract others to you. This is a good time for making friends. Business and marriage partners are more likely to be impressed with the man and woman of action. Opposition will be overcome or thrown aside with much less effort than usual. CAUTION: Be dominant but not domineering.

MOON IN TAURUS
The spontaneous, action-packed person of yesterday gives way to the cautious, diligent, hardworking "thinker." In this period ideas will probably be concentrated on ways of improving finances. A great deal of time may be spent figuring out and going over

schemes and plans. It is the right time to be careful with detail. People will find themselves working longer than usual at their desks. Or devoting more time to serious thought about the future. A strong desire to put order into business and financial arrangements may cause extra work. Loved ones may complain of being neglected and may fail to appreciate that your efforts are for their ultimate benefit. Your desire for system may extend to criticism of arrangements in the home and lead to minor upsets. Health may be affected through overwork. Try to secure a reasonable amount of rest and relaxation, although the tendency will be to "keep going" despite good advice. Work done conscientiously in this period should result in a solid contribution to your future security. CAUTION: Try not to be as serious with people as the work you are engaged in.

MOON IN GEMINI

The humdrum of routine and too much work should suddenly end. You are likely to find yourself in an expansive, quicksilver world of change and self-expression. Urges to write, to paint, to experience the freedom of some sort of artistic outpouring, may be very strong. Take full advantage of them. You may find yourself finishing something you began and put aside long ago. Or embarking on something new which could easily be prompted by a chance meeting, a new acquaintance, or even an advertisement. There may be a yearning for a change of scenery, the feeling to visit another country (not too far away), or at least to get away for a few days. This may result in short, quick journeys. Or, if you are planning a single visit, there may be some unexpected changes or detours on the way. Familiar activities will seem to give little satisfaction unless they contain a fresh element of excitement or expectation. The inclination will be toward untried pursuits, particularly those that allow you to express your inner nature. The accent is on new faces, new places. CAUTION: Do not be too quick to commit yourself emotionally.

MOON IN CANCER

Feelings of uncertainty and vague insecurity are likely to cause problems while the Moon is in Cancer. Thoughts may turn frequently to the warmth of the home and the comfort of loved ones. Nostalgic impulses could cause you to bring out old photographs and letters and reflect on the days when your life seemed to be much more rewarding and less demanding. The love and understanding of parents and family may be important, and, if it is not forthcoming, you may have to fight against bouts of self-pity. The cordiality of friends and the thought of good times with them that are sure to be repeated will help to restore you to a happier frame of mind. The desire to be alone may follow minor setbacks or rebuffs at this time, but solitude is unlikely to help. Better to get on the telephone or visit someone. This period often causes peculiar dreams and upsurges of imaginative thinking which can be helpful to authors of occult and mystical works. Preoccupation with the personal world of simple human needs can overshadow any material strivings. CAUTION: Do not spend too much time thinking—seek the company of loved ones or close friends.

MOON IN LEO
New horizons of exciting and rather extravagant activity open up. This is the time for exhilarating entertainment, glamorous and lavish parties, and expensive shopping sprees. Any merrymaking that relies upon your generosity as a host has every chance of being a spectacular success. You should find yourself right in the center of the fun, either as the life of the party or simply as a person whom happy people like to be with. Romance thrives in this heady atmosphere and friendships are likely to explode unexpectedly into serious attachments. Children and younger people should be attracted to you and you may find yourself organizing a picnic or a visit to a fun-fair, the movies, or the beach. The sunny company and vitality of youthful companions should help you to find some unsuspected energy. In career, you could find an opening for promotion or advancement. This should be the time to make a direct approach. The period favors those engaged in original research. CAUTION: Bask in popularity, not in flattery.

MOON IN VIRGO
Off comes the party cap and out steps the busy, practical worker. He wants to get his personal affairs straight, to rearrange them, if necessary, for more efficiency, so he will have more time for more work. He clears up his correspondence, pays outstanding bills, makes numerous phone calls. He is likely to make inquiries, or sign up for some new insurance and put money into gilt-edged investment. Thoughts probably revolve around the need for future security—to tie up loose ends and clear the decks. There may be a tendency to be "finicky," to interfere in the routine of others, particularly friends and family members. The motive may be a genuine desire to help with suggestions for updating or streamlining their affairs, but these will probably not be welcomed. Sympathy may be felt for less fortunate sections of the community and a flurry of some sort of voluntary service is likely. This may be accompanied by strong feelings of responsibility on several fronts and health may suffer from extra efforts made. CAUTION: Everyone may not want your help or advice.

MOON IN LIBRA

These are days of harmony and agreement and you should find yourself at peace with most others. Relationships tend to be smooth and sweet-flowing. Friends may become closer and bonds deepen in mutual understanding. Hopes will be shared. Progress by cooperation could be the secret of success in every sphere. In business, established partnerships may flourish and new ones get off to a good start. Acquaintances could discover similar interests that lead to congenial discussions and rewarding exchanges of some sort. Love, as a unifying force, reaches its optimum. Marriage partners should find accord. Those who wed at this time face the prospect of a happy union. Cooperation and tolerance are felt to be stronger than dissension and impatience. The argumentative are not quite so loud in their bellowings, nor as inflexible in their attitudes. In the home, there should be a greater recognition of the other point of view and a readiness to put the wishes of the group before selfish insistence. This is a favorable time to join an art group. CAUTION: Do not be too independent—let others help you if they want to.

MOON IN SCORPIO

Driving impulses to make money and to economize are likely to cause upsets all around. No area of expenditure is likely to be spared the ax, including the household budget. This is a time when the desire to cut down on extravagance can become near fanatical. Care must be exercised to try to keep the aim in reasonable perspective. Others may not feel the same urgent need to save and may retaliate. There is a danger that possessions of sentimental value will be sold to realize cash for investment. Buying and selling of stock for quick profit is also likely. The attention turns to organizing, reorganizing, tidying up at home and at work. Neglected jobs could suddenly be done with great bursts of energy. The desire for solitude may intervene. Self-searching thoughts could disturb. The sense of invisible and mysterious energies in play could cause some excitability. The reassurance of loves ones may help. CAUTION: Be kind to the people you love.

MOON IN SAGITTARIUS

These are days when you are likely to be stirred and elevated by discussions and reflections of a religious and philosophical nature. Ideas of faraway places may cause unusual response and excitement. A decision may be made to visit someone overseas, perhaps a person whose influence was important to your earlier character development. There could be a strong resolution to get away from present intellectual patterns, to learn new subjects, and to meet more interesting people. The superficial may be rejected in all its forms. An impatience with old ideas and unimaginative contacts could lead to a change of companions and interests. There may be an upsurge of religious feeling and metaphysical inquiry. Even a new insight into the significance of astrology and other occult studies is likely under the curious stimulus of the Moon in Sagittarius. Physically, you may express this need for fundamental change by spending more time outdoors: sports, gardening, long walks appeal. CAUTION: Try to channel any restlessness into worthwhile study.

MOON IN CAPRICORN

Life in these hours may seem to pivot around the importance of gaining prestige and honor in the career, as well as maintaining a spotless reputation. Ambitious urges may be excessive and could be accompanied by quite acquisitive drives for money. Effort should be directed along strictly ethical lines where there is no possibility of reproach or scandal. All endeavors are likely to be characterized by great earnestness, and an air of authority and purpose which should impress those who are looking for leadership or reliability. The desire to conform to accepted standards may extend to sharp criticism of family members. Frivolity and unconventional actions are unlikely to amuse while the Moon is in Capricorn. Moderation and seriousness are the orders of the day. Achievement and recognition in this period could come through community work or organizing for the benefit of some amateur group. CAUTION: Dignity and esteem are not always self-awarded.

MOON IN AQUARIUS

Moon in Aquarius is in the second last sign of the Zodiac where ideas can become disturbingly fine and subtle. The result is often a mental "no-man's land" where imagination cannot be trusted with the same certitude as other times. The dangers for the individual are the extremes of optimism and pessimism. Unless the imagination is held in check, situations are likely to be misread, and rosy conclusions drawn where they do not exist. Consequences for the unwary can be costly in career and business. Best to think twice and not speak or act until you think again. Pessimism can be a cruel self-inflicted penalty for delusion at this time. Between the two extremes are strange areas of self-deception which, for example, can make the selfish person think he is actually being generous. Eerie dreams which resemble the reality and even seem to continue into the waking state are also possible. CAUTION: Look for the fact and not just for the image in your mind.

MOON IN PISCES

Everything seems to come to the surface now. Memory may be crystal clear, throwing up long-forgotten information which could be valuable in the career or business. Flashes of clairvoyance and intuition are possible along with sudden realizations of one's own nature, which may be used for self-improvement. A talent, never before suspected, may be discovered. Qualities not evident before in friends and marriage partners are likely to be noticed. As this is a period in which the truth seems to emerge, the discovery of false characteristics is likely to lead to disenchantment or a shift in attachments. However, when qualities are accepted, it should lead to happiness and deeper feeling. Surprise solutions could bob up for old problems. There may be a public announcement of the solving of a crime or mystery. People with secrets may find someone has "guessed" correctly. The secrets of the soul or the inner self also tend to reveal themselves. Religious and philosophical groups may make some interesting discoveries. CAUTION: Not a time for activities that depend on secrecy.

NOTE: When you read your daily forecasts, use the Moon Sign Dates that are provided in the following section of Moon Tables. Then you may want to glance back here for the Moon's influence in a given sign.

MOON TABLES

CORRECTION FOR NEW YORK TIME, FIVE HOURS WEST OF GREENWICH

Atlanta, Boston, Detroit, Miami, Washington, Montreal,
  Ottawa, Quebec, Bogota, Havana, Lima, Santiago ... Same time
Chicago, New Orleans, Houston, Winnipeg, Churchill,
  Mexico City .... Deduct 1 hour
Albuquerque, Denver, Phoenix, El Paso, Edmonton,
  Helena .... Deduct 2 hours
Los Angeles, San Francisco, Reno, Portland,
  Seattle, Vancouver .... Deduct 3 hours
Honolulu, Anchorage, Fairbanks, Kodiak .... Deduct 5 hours
Nome, Samoa, Tonga, Midway .... Deduct 6 hours
Halifax, Bermuda, San Juan, Caracas, La Paz,
  Barbados .... Add 1 hour
St. John's, Brasilia, Rio de Janeiro, Sao Paulo,
  Buenos Aires, Montevideo .... Add 2 hours
Azores, Cape Verde Islands .... Add 3 hours
Canary Islands, Madeira, Reykjavik .... Add 4 hours
London, Paris, Amsterdam, Madrid, Lisbon,
  Gibraltar, Belfast, Raba .... Add 5 hours
Frankfurt, Rome, Oslo, Stockholm, Prague,
  Belgrade .... Add 6 hours
Bucharest, Beirut, Tel Aviv, Athens, Istanbul, Cairo,
  Alexandria, Cape Town, Johannesburg .... Add 7 hours
Moscow, Leningrad, Baghdad, Dhahran,
  Addis Ababa, Nairobi, Teheran, Zanzibar ...... Add 8 hours
Bombay, Calcutta, Sri Lanka .... Add $10^{1/2}$
Hong Kong, Shanghai, Manila, Peking, Perth ..... Add 13 hours
Tokyo, Okinawa, Darwin, Pusan .... Add 14 hours
Sydney, Melbourne, Port Moresby, Guam .... Add 15 hours
Auckland, Wellington, Suva, Wake .... Add 17 hours

2008 MOON SIGN DATES—
NEW YORK TIME

JANUARY		FEBRUARY		MARCH	
Day Moon Enters		Day Moon Enters		Day Moon Enters	
1. Scorp.	8:33 pm	1. Sagitt.		1. Capric.	1:34 pm
2. Scorp.		2. Sagitt.		2. Capric.	
3. Scorp.		3. Capric.	4:53 am	3. Aquar.	11:26 pm
4. Sagitt.	9:14 am	4. Capric.		4. Aquar.	
5. Sagitt.		5. Aquar.	2:11 pm	5. Aquar.	
6. Capric.	8:44 pm	6. Aquar.		6. Pisces	5:54 am
7. Capric.		7. Pisces	8:47 pm	7. Pisces	
8. Capric.		8. Pisces		8. Aries	9:24 am
9. Aquar.	6:14 am	9. Pisces		9. Aries	
10. Aquar.		10. Aries	1:18 am	10. Taurus	11:15 am
11. Pisces	1:45 pm	11. Aries		11. Taurus	
12. Pisces		12. Taurus	4:35 am	12. Gemini	12:55 pm
13. Aries	7:24 pm	13. Taurus		13. Gemini	
14. Aries		14. Gemini	7:20 am	14. Cancer	3:39 pm
15. Taurus	11:14 pm	15. Gemini		15. Cancer	
16. Taurus		16. Cancer	10:13 am	16. Leo	8:05 pm
17. Taurus		17. Cancer		17. Leo	
18. Gemini	1:31 am	18. Leo	1:52 pm	18. Leo	
19. Gemini		19. Leo		19. Virgo	5:26 am
20. Cancer	3:06 am	20. Virgo	7:07 pm	20. Virgo	
21. Cancer		21. Virgo		21. Libra	10:46 am
22. Leo	5:21 am	22. Virgo		22. Libra	
23. Leo		23. Libra	2:46 am	23. Scorp.	9:07 pm
24. Virgo	9:49 am	24. Libra		24. Scorp.	
25. Virgo		25. Scorp.	1:07 pm	25. Scorp.	
26. Libra	5:36 pm	26. Scorp.		26. Sagitt.	9:12 am
27. Libra		27. Scorp.		27. Sagitt.	
28. Libra		28. Sagitt.	1:23 am	28. Capric.	9:44 pm
29. Scorp.	4:36 am	29. Sagitt.		29. Capric.	
30. Scorp.				30. Capric.	
31. Sagitt.	5:09 pm			31. Aquar.	8:35 am

Daylight saving time to be considered where applicable.

2008 MOON SIGN DATES— NEW YORK TIME

APRIL
Day Moon Enters
1. Aquar.
2. Pisces   3:56 pm
3. Pisces
4. Aries   7:28 pm
5. Aries
6. Taurus   8:21 pm
7. Taurus
8. Gemini   8:28 pm
9. Gemini
10. Cancer   9:44 pm
11. Cancer
12. Cancer
13. Leo   1:30 am
14. Leo
15. Virgo   8:08 am
16. Virgo
17. Libra   5:11 pm
18. Libra
19. Libra
20. Scorp.   4:01 am
21. Scorp.
22. Sagitt.   4:08 pm
23. Sagitt.
24. Sagitt.
25. Capric.   4:48 am
26. Capric.
27. Aquar.   4:28 pm
28. Aquar.
29. Aquar.
30. Pisces   1:12 am

MAY
Day Moon Enters
1. Pisces
2. Aries   5:52 am
3. Aries
4. Taurus   6:59 am
5. Taurus
6. Gemini   6:18 am
7. Gemini
8. Cancer   6:03 am
9. Cancer
10. Leo   8:11 am
11. Leo
12. Virgo   1:49 pm
13. Virgo
14. Libra   10:47 pm
15. Libra
16. Libra
17. Scorp.   10:00 am
18. Scorp.
19. Sagitt.   10:20 pm
20. Sagitt.
21. Sagitt.
22. Capric.   10:56 am
23. Capric.
24. Aquar.   10:53 pm
25. Aquar.
26. Aquar.
27. Pisces   8:39 am
28. Pisces
29. Aries   2:54 pm
30. Aries
31. Taurus   5:20 pm

JUNE
Day Moon Enters
1. Taurus
2. Gemini   5:07 pm
3. Gemini
4. Cancer   4:17 pm
5. Cancer
6. Leo   5:01 pm
7. Leo
8. Virgo   9:02 pm
9. Virgo
10. Virgo
11. Libra   4:56 am
12. Libra
13. Scorp.   3:54 pm
14. Scorp.
15. Scorp.
16. Sagitt.   4:21 am
17. Sagitt.
18. Capric.   4:53 pm
19. Capric.
20. Capric.
21. Aquar.   4:35 am
22. Aquar.
23. Pisces   3:33 pm
24. Pisces
25. Aries   9:50 pm
26. Aries
27. Aries
28. Taurus   1:51 am
29. Taurus
30. Gemini   3:04 am

Daylight saving time to be considered where applicable.

2008 MOON SIGN DATES— NEW YORK TIME

JULY
Day Moon Enters
1. Gemini
2. Cancer 2:54 am
3. Cancer
4. Leo 3:16 am
5. Leo
6. Virgo 5:05 am
7. Virgo
8. Libra 12:32 pm
9. Libra
10. Scorp. 10:36 pm
11. Scorp.
12. Scorp.
13. Sagitt. 10:51 am
14. Sagitt.
15. Capric. 11:21 pm
16. Capric.
17. Capric.
18. Aquar. 10:41 am
19. Aquar.
20. Pisces 8:09 pm
21. Pisces
22. Pisces
23. Aries 1:23 am
24. Aries
25. Taurus 8:15 am
26. Taurus
27. Gemini 10:56 am
28. Gemini
29. Cancer 12:13 pm
30. Cancer
31. Leo 1:23 pm

AUGUST
Day Moon Enters
1. Leo
2. Virgo 4:00 pm
3. Virgo
4. Libra 9:29 pm
5. Libra
6. Libra
7. Scorp. 6:27 am
8. Scorp.
9. Sagitt. 6:11 pm
10. Sagitt.
11. Sagitt.
12. Capric. 6:43 am
13. Capric.
14. Aquar. 5:57 pm
15. Aquar.
16. Aquar.
17. Pisces 2:47 am
18. Pisces
19. Aries 9:11 am
20. Aries
21. Taurus 1:39 pm
22. Taurus
23. Gemini 4:49 pm
24. Gemini
25. Cancer 7:20 pm
26. Cancer
27. Leo 9:52 pm
28. Leo
29. Leo
30. Virgo 1:19 am
31. Virgo

SEPTEMBER
Day Moon Enters
1. Libra 6:46 am
2. Libra
3. Scorp. 3:03 pm
4. Scorp.
5. Scorp.
6. Sagitt. 2:12 am
7. Sagitt.
8. Capric. 2:46 pm
9. Capric.
10. Capric.
11. Aquar. 2:21 am
12. Aquar.
13. Pisces 11:06 am
14. Pisces
15. Aries 4:40 pm
16. Aries
17. Taurus 7:58 pm
18. Taurus
19. Gemini 10:18 pm
20. Gemini
21. Gemini
22. Cancer 12:50 am
23. Cancer
24. Leo 4:15 am
25. Leo
26. Virgo 8:53 am
27. Virgo
28. Libra 3:07 pm
29. Libra
30. Scorp. 11:27 pm

Daylight saving time to be considered where applicable.

2008 MOON SIGN DATES—
NEW YORK TIME

OCTOBER		NOVEMBER		DECEMBER	
Day Moon Enters		**Day Moon Enters**		**Day Moon Enters**	
1. Scorp.		1. Sagitt.		1. Capric.	
2. Scorp.		2. Capric.	6:14 am	2. Aquar.	1:46 am
3. Sagitt.	10:15 am	3. Capric.		3. Aquar.	
4. Sagitt.		4. Aquar.	7:03 pm	4. Pisces	1:24 pm
5. Capric.	10:50 pm	5. Aquar.		5. Pisces	
6. Capric.		6. Aquar.		6. Aries	9:45 pm
7. Capric.		7. Pisces	5:44 am	7. Aries	
8. Aquar.	11:04 am	8. Pisces		8. Aries	
9. Aquar.		9. Aries	12:47 pm	9. Taurus	1:53 am
10. Pisces	8:32 pm	10. Aries		10. Taurus	
11. Pisces		11. Taurus	3:06 pm	11. Gemini	2:34 am
12. Pisces		12. Taurus		12. Gemini	
13. Aries	2:08 am	13. Gemini	3:12 pm	13. Cancer	1:41 am
14. Aries		14. Gemini		14. Cancer	
15. Taurus	4:32 am	15. Cancer	2:53 pm	15. Leo	1:24 am
16. Taurus		16. Cancer		16. Leo	
17. Gemini	5:26 am	17. Leo	4:09 pm	17. Virgo	3:37 am
18. Gemini		18. Leo		18. Virgo	
19. Cancer	6:41 am	19. Virgo	8:14 pm	19. Libra	9:24 am
20. Cancer		20. Virgo		20. Libra	
21. Leo	9:36 am	21. Virgo		21. Scorp.	6:38 pm
22. Leo		22. Libra	3:21 am	22. Scorp.	
23. Virgo	2:41 pm	23. Libra		23. Scorp.	
24. Virgo		24. Scorp.	12:55 pm	24. Sagitt.	6:14 am
25. Libra	9:49 pm	25. Scorp.		25. Sagitt.	
26. Libra		26. Scorp.		26. Capric.	6:57 pm
27. Libra		27. Sagitt.	12:15 am	27. Capric.	
28. Scorp.	6:48 am	28. Sagitt.		28. Capric.	
29. Scorp.		29. Capric.	12:49 pm	29. Aquar.	7:44 am
30. Sagitt.	5:42 pm	30. Capric.		30. Aquar.	
31. Sagitt.				31. Pisces	7:28 pm

Daylight saving time to be considered where applicable.

2008 PHASES OF THE MOON—
NEW YORK TIME

New Moon	First Quarter	Full Moon	Last Quarter
Jan. 8	Jan. 15	Jan. 22	Jan. 30
Feb. 6	Feb. 13	Feb. 20	Feb. 28
March 7	March 14	March 21	March 29
April 5	April 12	April 20	April 28
May 5	May 11	May 19	May 27
June 3	June 10	June 18	June 26
July 2	July 9	July 18	July 25
August 1	August 8	August 16	August 23
August 30	Sept. 7	Sept. 15	Sept. 22
Sept. 29	Oct. 7	Oct. 14	Oct. 21
Oct. 28	Nov. 5	Nov. 13	Nov. 19
Nov. 27	Dec. 5	Dec. 12	Dec. 19
Dec. 27	Jan. 4 ('09)	Jan. 10 ('09)	Jan. 17 ('09)

Each phase of the Moon lasts approximately seven to eight days, during which the Moon's shape gradually changes as it comes out of one phase and goes into the next.

There will be a solar eclipse during the New Moon phase on February 6 and August 1.

There will be a lunar eclipse during the Full Moon phase on February 20 and August 16.

2008 FISHING GUIDE

	Good	Best
January	15-22-23-24-25	8-20-21-30
February	6-12-18-19-20-21-22-28	17-23
March	14-19-20	7-21-22-23-24-25-29
April	6-18-23-24-28	12-19-20-21-22
May	12-19-20-21	5-16-17-18-23-28
June	3-11-16-17-18-21-22-26	15-19
July	14-15-19-20	3-10-16-17-18-21-25
August	1-15-16-17-19-20-23	8-13-18
September	7-11-12-16-17	14-15-18-23-29
October	13-14-17-21	7-11-12-16-29
November	5-10-11-13-14-15-20-27	12-16
December	11-12-15-19	6-9-10-13-14-27

2008 PLANTING GUIDE

	Aboveground Crops	Root Crops
January	12-16-17-20-21	2-3-27-28-29-30-31
February	8-9-12-13-16-17	3-4-23-24-25-26-27
March	11-15-16	2-3-22-23-24-25-29-30
April	7-8-11-12-18-19	3-4-20-21-25-26
May	9-15-16-17-18	1-23-24-28
June	5-6-11-12-13-14-15	1-19-24-25-28-29
July	3-9-10-11-12-16	2-3-21-22-25-26-30
August	5-6-7-8-12-13	18-22-26-27
September	1-2-3-4-5-9-14-29-30	18-19-22-23
October	1-2-6-7-11-12-29	16-20-26-27
November	2-3-4-8-12-30	16-17-23-24-25-26
December	1-5-6-9-10-27-28	13-14-20-21-22-23

	Pruning	Weeds and Pests
January	2-3-29-30	4-5-23-24-25
February	26-27	1-2-6-21-22-28-29
March	24-25	4-26-27
April	3-4-20-21	1-5-23-24-28-29
May	1-28	3-20-21-26-30
June	24-25	22-26-27-30
July	2-21-22-30	1-19-20-23-24-28
August	18-26-27	20-24-25-28-29-30
September	22-23	16-17-20-21-25-26-27
October	20	17-18-22-23-24
November	16-17-25-26	14-18-19-20-21
December	13-14-22-23	15-16-17-18-25-26

MOON'S INFLUENCE OVER PLANTS

Centuries ago it was established that seeds planted when the Moon is in signs and phases called Fruitful will produce more growth than seeds planted when the Moon is in a Barren sign.
Fruitful Signs: Taurus, Cancer, Libra, Scorpio, Capricorn, Pisces
Barren Signs: Aries, Gemini, Leo, Virgo, Sagittarius, Aquarius
Dry Signs: Aries, Gemini, Sagittarius, Aquarius

Activity	Moon In
Mow lawn, trim plants	**Fruitful sign:** 1st & 2nd quarter
Plant flowers	**Fruitful sign:** 2nd quarter; best in Cancer and Libra
Prune	**Fruitful sign:** 3rd & 4th quarter
Destroy pests; spray	**Barren sign:** 4th quarter
Harvest potatoes, root crops	**Dry sign:** 3rd & 4th quarter; Taurus, Leo, and Aquarius

MOON'S INFLUENCE OVER YOUR HEALTH

ARIES	Head, brain, face, upper jaw
TAURUS	Throat, neck, lower jaw
GEMINI	Hands, arms, lungs, shoulders, nervous system
CANCER	Esophagus, stomach, breasts, womb, liver
LEO	Heart, spine
VIRGO	Intestines, liver
LIBRA	Kidneys, lower back
SCORPIO	Sex and eliminative organs
SAGITTARIUS	Hips, thighs, liver
CAPRICORN	Skin, bones, teeth, knees
AQUARIUS	Circulatory system, lower legs
PISCES	Feet, tone of being

Try to avoid work being done on that part of the body when the Moon is in the sign governing that part.

MOON'S INFLUENCE OVER DAILY AFFAIRS

The Moon makes a complete transit of the Zodiac every 27 days 7 hours and 43 minutes. In making this transit the Moon forms different aspects with the planets and consequently has favorable or unfavorable bearings on affairs and events for persons according to the sign of the Zodiac under which they were born.

When the Moon is in conjunction with the Sun it is called a New Moon; when the Moon and Sun are in opposition it is called a Full Moon. From New Moon to Full Moon, first and second quarter—which takes about two weeks—the Moon is increasing or waxing. From Full Moon to New Moon, third and fourth quarter, the Moon is decreasing or waning.

Activity	Moon In
Business: buying and selling new, requiring public support	Sagittarius, Aries, Gemini, Virgo 1st and 2nd quarter
meant to be kept quiet	3rd and 4th quarter
Investigation	3rd and 4th quarter
Signing documents	1st & 2nd quarter, Cancer, Scorpio, Pisces
Advertising	2nd quarter, Sagittarius
Journeys and trips	1st & 2nd quarter, Gemini, Virgo
Renting offices, etc.	Taurus, Leo, Scorpio, Aquarius
Painting of house/apartment	3rd & 4th quarter, Taurus, Scorpio, Aquarius
Decorating	Gemini, Libra, Aquarius
Buying clothes and accessories	Taurus, Virgo
Beauty salon or barber shop visit	1st & 2nd quarter, Taurus, Leo, Libra, Scorpio, Aquarius
Weddings	1st & 2nd quarter

Virgo

VIRGO

Character Analysis

People born under the sign of Virgo are generally practical. They believe in doing things thoroughly; there is nothing slipshod or haphazard about the way they do things. They are precise and methodical. The man or woman born under this sixth sign of the Zodiac respects common sense and tries to be rational in his or her approach to tasks or problems.

Virgo is the sign of work and service. It is the symbol of the farmer at harvest time, and so the man or woman born under this sign is sometimes called the Harvester. These people's tireless efforts to bring the fruits of the Earth to the table of humanity create great joy and beneficence. Celebration through work and harvest is the characteristic of the sign of Virgo.

Sincerity, zeal, and devotion mark the working methods of the Virgo man and woman. They have excellent critical abilities; they know how to analyze a problem and come up with a solution. Virgo is seldom fooled by superficialities, and can go straight to the heart of the matter.

Virgo knows how to break things down to the minutest detail; he or she prefers to work on things piece by piece. Inwardly, he is afraid of being overwhelmed by things that seem larger than life. For this reason, one often finds the Virgo occupied with details. His powers of concentration are greatest when he can concentrate on small, manageable things.

The Virgo person believes in doing things correctly; he's thorough and precise. He's seldom carried away by fantasy; he believes in keeping his feet firmly on the ground. People who seem a bit flighty or impractical sometimes irritate him.

Virgo knows how to criticize other people. It is very easy for him to point out another's weaknesses or faults; he is seldom wrong. However, Virgo is sometimes a bit sharp in making criticisms and often offends a good friend or acquaintance. The cultivated Virgo, however, knows how to apply criticism tactfully. He or she is considerate of another's feelings.

The Virgo person believes in applying himself in a positive manner to whatever task is set before him. He is a person full of purpose and goodwill. He is diligent and methodical. He is seldom given to impulse, but works along steadily and constructively.

Anything that is scientific, technological, and practical arouses Virgo's interest. The technical and craft aspects of the arts impress these people, and many Virgos become expert designers, graphic artists, and handicrafters. The precision so important to these disciplines is a quality Virgo possesses in abundance. Combined with imagination and flair, the attention to detail often makes Virgos first-rate artists.

Whether or not individual Virgos are talented in artistic areas, most of these people are usually very interested in anything of an artistic nature. Virgos also are great readers. They have a deep appreciation for the way the intricacies of life weave together, then unravel, and finally are rewoven into a new fabric or design.

Virgos also possess an innate verbal ability that is especially suited to the study of a language, whether the language is a machine language such as in computers or a tongue spoken by other people. Virgo has no trouble applying his or her native intelligence and skill either in a learning or teaching capacity. Virgos enjoy school. They often study a wide range of subjects, but not in great depth, in order to have a well-rounded education. Virgos like friends and colleagues to be as well-informed as they are if not more so. Virgo has a deep respect for culture, education, and intellect.

Usually, Virgo takes in stride whatever comes into his or her life. Basically, he is an uncomplicated person, who views things clearly and sharply. He has a way of getting right down to the meat of the matter. Generally a serious-minded person, he believes in being reliable. He is not one who will take great risks in life as he has no interest in playing the hero or the idealist. Virgo believes in doing what he can, but without flourishes.

Quite often he is a quiet, modest person. He believes that appearance is important and thus does his best to look well-groomed. He feels that being neat is important and dislikes untidiness in anything.

The Virgo man or woman likes to deal with life on a practical level and they usually look for the uncomplicated answer or solution to any problem or dilemma. Even if Virgos are urged to look into the mystical side of existence, they may dismiss it as being either unfounded or irrelevant.

On the whole, the Virgo person is even-tempered. He or she does not allow himself to become angry easily. He knows how to take the bitter with the sweet. But if someone does him a wrong turn, he is not likely to forget it. His good nature is not to be abused.

Health

Many persons born under this sign are amazingly healthy. They frequently live to see a ripe old age. This longevity is generally due to the fact that people born under this sign take all things in moderation. Virgo is not the type of person who burns the candle at both ends. They acknowledge their limits and avoid excess.

Frequently Virgos are small and neat-featured. Virgo women are sometimes quite attractive in a sort of dry way. Both men and women of this sign have a youthful appearance throughout life. When young, Virgos are generally very active. However, as they reach middle age and beyond they have a tendency to put on a bit of weight.

The Virgo person usually enjoys good health, although some have a tendency to be overly concerned about it. They imagine ailments they do not really have. Still, they do manage to stay fit. Other Virgos see themselves as being rather strong and resourceful, even when they are ill. For that reason they seldom feel moved to feel sorry for another ailing Virgo. Actually, serious illnesses frighten Virgos. They will do all they can to remain in good health.

The medicine cabinet of someone born under this sign is often filled with all sorts of pills, tablets, and ointments. Most of them will never be used.

As a rule, Virgo watches his diet. He stays away from foods that won't agree with him. He keeps a balanced diet and is moderate in his drinking habits. Virgos need plenty of exercise to keep the body fit. Most Virgos do not have a particular liking for strenuous sport. But the wise Virgo always will get some kind of energetic exercise, preferably a brisk and long walk, or a daily workout. Another thing that Virgos need is rest. They should get at least eight hours sleep per day.

On the whole, Virgo is a sensitive person. His nerves may be easily affected if he finds himself in a disagreeable situation. The stomach is another area of concern. When a Virgo becomes sick, this area is usually affected. Digestion complaints are not rare among persons born under this sign. Regular meals are important for the Virgo. Quick snacks and fast food may play havoc with his digestive system. In spite of this particular weakness, Virgos manage to lead normal, healthy lives. They should try to avoid becoming too concerned with ups and downs. Many of their illnesses may turn out to be imaginary.

Occupation

Virgos delight in keeping busy. They are not afraid of hard work. By nature, they are ambitious people and are happiest when they are putting their talents and abilities to good use. They can best be described as goal-directed; they never lose sight of their objective once committed. They are very thorough in whatever they undertake. Even routine work is something that they can do without finding fault. In fact, work that is scheduled—or that follows a definite pattern—is well suited to their steady natures. Virgos will put aside other things, if necessary, in order to attain a goal. They prefer to work under peaceful conditions, and will seldom do anything to irritate their superiors.

They learn well and are not afraid to undertake any kind of work—even the most menial—if it is necessary. Sometimes, however, they neglect their own conditions because they are so involved in their work. For this reason, Virgos occasionally fall ill or become a bit nervous. Any kind of work that allows them to make use of their talent for criticism will please them.

Virgo men and women usually shine as bookkeepers, accountants, teachers, and pharmacists. The cultivated Virgo person often turns to the world of science where they are likely to do well. Some great writers and poets have been born under this sixth sign of the Zodiac.

It is very important that Virgo has the kind of work that is suited to his personality. It may take a while before he actually finds his niche in life, and he may have to struggle at times in order to make ends meet. But because he is not afraid of work, he manages to come out on top.

Virgo is a perfectionist. He or she is always looking for ways to improve the work scheme or technique. He is never satisfied until things are working smoothly. He will even do more than his share in order to secure regularity and precision in a job he is doing. It is not unusual for the average Virgo to have various ideas about how to better the job they are doing, how to streamline things. They are extremely resourceful people as far as energy is concerned. In most cases, they can work longer than others, without letting it show. Because Virgo is so concerned with detail, they may seem obsessive or compulsive to co-workers.

The enterprising Virgo can go far in business if a partner is somewhat adventurous and enthusiastic, qualities which tend to balance those of the Virgo person. At times, Virgo can be quite a worrier. Battling problems large and small may prevent him from making the headway he feels is necessary in his work. A partner who knows how to cut the work and worries in half by taking advantage of shortcuts is someone the average Virgo businessperson could learn to value. People enjoying working with Virgo men and women, because they are so reliable and honest. They usually set a good example for others on the job.

If not careful, the ambitious Virgo can become the type of person who thinks about nothing else but the job. They are not afraid of taking on more than the average worker. But they can make the mistake of expecting the same of others. This attitude can lead to conflict and unpleasantness. Generally, Virgo does achieve what he sets out for, because he knows how to apply himself. He is seldom the envy of others because he is not the type of person who is easily noticed or recognized.

Virgo is a quiet person. He or she enjoys working in peaceful and harmonious surroundings. Conflict at work is bound to upset him and affect his nerves. He works well under people. He is not against taking orders from those who prove themselves his superiors. On the whole, the man or woman born under this sign does not like to be delegated with the full responsibility of a task or project. He or she would rather have a supporting or a subordinate role.

Virgo men and women frequently excel in a trade. They often make good metalsmiths and carpenters, jewelers and wood carvers. They can work in miniature, creating a variety of pleasing items.

The Virgo person is one who is very concerned about security. Now and again he may have cause to worry about his financial position. On the whole, he is conscious of the value of money. He or she is a person who will never risk security by going out on a limb. He knows how to put money away for a rainy day. Many times he will scout about for new ways of increasing his savings. Bettering his financial situation is something that constantly concerns him. When he does invest, it usually turns out to his advantage. He generally makes sure that the investment he makes is a sure thing. He does not believe in gambling or taking big risks.

Sometimes the Virgo, because of his keen interest in money and profit, is the victim of a fraud. Dishonest people may try to take advantage of his interest in monetary gain. The well-off Virgo is extremely generous and enjoys looking after the needs of others. He sees to it that those he cares for live in comfort.

Not all Virgos are fortunate enough to become extremely wealthy, but all of them work hard for what they achieve.

Home and Family

People born under this sign are generally homebodies. They like to spend as much time as possible surrounded by the things and the people they enjoy. They make excellent hosts and enjoy entertaining guests and visitors. It is important to Virgos that the people around them be happy and content. Virgo is most at ease when companions behave correctly, that is, if they are respectful of individuals' needs and property. Virgos do not like people to take advantage of their hospitality or to abuse what they consider a privilege. But on the whole Virgos are easygoing. The demands they may make of guests and family are reasonable.

A harmonious atmosphere at home is important to the person

born under this sign. As long as this can be guaranteed, Virgo remains in good humor. They are likely to have a number of insurance policies on the home, family, and possessions. They believe that you can never be safe enough.

In spite of their love of home, Virgo is likely to have an avid interest in travel. If they cannot make many changes in their environment, they are bound to make them in their home. The Virgo homemaker never tires of rearranging things. Generally, Virgos have a good sense of beauty and harmony. They know how to make a room inviting and comfortable. Change is always of interest to the person born under this sign. They like to read of faraway places, even if they never get a chance to visit them. A new job or a new home address from time to time can brighten Virgo's spirits immeasurably.

The Virgo woman is as neat as a pin. Usually she is an excellent cook, and takes care that her kitchen never gets out of order or becomes untidy even while she is working in it. She believes that everything has its proper place and should be kept there. Because she is so careful with her possessions, they often appear brand new.

Others may feel that the Virgo man or woman, because of his or her cool, calm ways, is not especially cut out to be a good parent. But the opposite is true. Virgo people know how to bring up their youngsters correctly. They generally pass on their positive qualities to their children without any trouble. They teach them that honesty and diligence are important. They instill them with an appreciation for common sense in all matters.

Although the Virgo father or mother may deeply love their children, they have a tendency to be rather strict. They are always concerned that their children turn out well. Sometimes they expect too much of them. Some of them can be old-fashioned and believe that a child belongs in a child's place. They expect this not only of their own youngsters but also of other people's children.

Social Relationships

The Virgo man or woman is particular about the friends he makes. He is fond of people who have a particular direction in life. He is inclined to avoid drifters or irresolute people. Those who have made their mark win his admiration. Virgo likes intelligent people, those who are somewhat cultured in their interests.

As a good friend, Virgo is invaluable; there is nothing he or she would not do to help someone in need. Virgo stands by friends even in their most difficult moments. The only demand he makes is that his interest in another's affairs be valued. He does not like to feel that his help is not appreciated. It is important that Virgo be thanked for even the slightest favor.

Quite often people born under this sign are rather timid or at least retiring; they have to be drawn out by others. After Virgos get to know someone well, however, they bloom. In spite of their initial shyness, they do not enjoy being alone. They like company; they like to be reassured by people. They prefer intelligent, informed people as companions. Virgo can overlook negative qualities in someone if they feel that person is basically sincere toward others. The Virgo person needs friends. In solitude, the average Virgo is apt to feel stranded or deserted. They enjoy having someone around who will make a fuss over them, no matter how small.

Virgo is a perfectionist. Sometimes they criticize others too strongly for their faults, and as a result, they may not have as many friends as they would like.

Virgo can be cliquey, enjoying a fairly closed circle of friends and acquaintances. Gossip and intrigue might be a mainstay of such a clique. The smaller the circle, the more comfortable Virgo will feel and the more chances there will be for Virgo to orchestrate the social and recreational activities. In an intimate group setting Virgo's shyness disappears, giving way to the delicious wit and clever turn of phrase basic to this verbal, mental sign.

Gala parties with lots of hangers-on and freeloaders are not Virgo's style. A typical noisy blast can be a turn-off to one who is finicky and fastidious. The mere sight of overindulgence and overfamiliarity can make Virgo long for the glamour of posh surroundings accompanied only by a lover or close friend.

Frequent home entertaining also can be a problem. The fussy Virgo will fret about all the details that must be arranged to host a successful social. Then the neat, tidy Virgo will worry about the mess created in the house after a perfect get-together. On the whole, Virgo men and women prefer socializing in a few select places known for gracious service and fine food.

Of all the signs in the Zodiac, Virgo is most drawn to human welfare issues, a fact that leads these men and women into groups whose goal is to improve people's lot in life. The Virgo dedication to a cause is remarkable. Their example is an inspiration for everyone to follow. Doing someone a good turn comes naturally to Virgo. Their qualities of service and kindness are genuine, as friends who admire and respect them will testify.

Love and Marriage

In love and romance, the person born under the sign of Virgo is not inclined to be overly romantic. To a partner, they may seem reserved and inhibited. Their practical nature prevails even in affairs of the heart. They are least likely to be swept off their feet when in love. Chances are they may flirt a bit in the beginning of a relationship, but soon thereafter they settle down to the serious side of love. Virgo standards are very high, and it may be some time before they find someone who can measure up to them. As a consequence, Virgo frequently marries rather late in life.

It is important for the Virgo man or woman to find the right person because they are easily influenced by someone they love. On the other hand, Virgo has a protective side to their nature. When in love they will try to shield the object of their affection from the unpleasant things in life.

The person born under the sign of Virgo may be disappointed in love more than once. People whom they set great store in may prove to be unsuitable. Sometimes it is Virgo's own fault. They may be too critical of small weaknesses that a partner or lover has.

Some Virgos seem prim and proper when it comes to romance. They would prefer to think that it is not absolutely necessary and that intellect is everything. It may take some doing to get such a Virgo to change this attitude. At any rate, they are not fond of being demonstrative as far as affection goes. They do not like to make a show of love in front of others.

If their lover is too demanding or forceful in the relationship, they may feel inclined to break off the affair. Virgo appreciates gentleness and consideration in love life. On the whole, they are not easy to approach. The person who finds him or her interesting will have to be very tactful and patient when trying to convince Virgo of their love.

In married life, Virgo is apt to be very practical. They are interested in preserving the happiness they have found and will do everything in their power to keep the relationship alive. It is quite important that the Virgo man or woman marry someone with a similar outlook. Someone quite opposite may misinterpret Virgo's calm and cool manner as being unfeeling. Virgo makes a faithful mate. He or she can always be depended upon. They know how to keep things in the home running smoothly. They will do what they can to preserve harmony because they dislike discord and unpleasantness. A cooperative person, Virgo is willing to make concessions if they seem necessary. In short, the Virgo man or woman can make a success of marriage if they have had the good fortune to choose the right person.

Romance and the Virgo Woman

The Virgo woman is often a serious person. She knows what she wants out of life and what to expect from people. She is discriminating in her choice of men. It may take considerable time before she will admit to herself that she is in love. She is not afraid to wait in matters of romance; it is important to her that she select the right person. She may be more easily attracted to an intelligent man than to a handsome one. She values intellect more than physical attributes.

It is important for the Virgo woman to trust someone before she falls in love with him. She will allow a relationship to develop into a love affair only after she has gotten to know the man well on strictly a companionship basis at first.

The Virgo woman is reputed to be prim and proper about sex. But this description does not tell the whole story, or even the right story. In fact, Virgo can exhibit extremes in sexual attitudes and behavior. It is an age-old dilemma, contrast, contradiction—call it what you will—between the madonna and the hooker. There is Virgo the Virgin, whose purity is renowned and whose frigidity is assumed. Then there is Virgo the Harvester, whose promiscuity is whispered and whose fruitfulness is celebrated.

Indeed, the difference between an old-fashioned Virgo and a liberated Virgo are remarkable but very hard to discern in the beginning of an affair. One thing is sure, though. Cheat on your Virgo woman, and you can kiss the relationship good-bye. That is, unless you have discussed the possibility of having an open relationship— on both sides and managed in good taste. Remember, no matter what her sexual proclivities are, the Virgo woman cannot stand vulgarity in any form.

The Virgo woman generally makes a good wife. She knows how to keep the household shipshape. She likes looking after people she loves. She is efficient and industrious. There is almost nothing she will not do for the man she loves. She is capable of deep affection and love, but must be allowed to express herself in her own way.

As a mother, she is ideal. She teaches all her youngsters to be polite and well-mannered, and constantly worries about their health and welfare. Fearing all manner of mishaps, injuries, illnesses, and minor ailments, the Virgo mother may tend to restrict the kids' freedom at play and in school. However, she always has the children's best interests at heart.

Romance and the Virgo Man

The Virgo man, practical and analytical as he is in most matters, is rather cautious when it comes to love and romance. He is not what one would call romantic. He may be shy and hesitant. It may be up to the female to begin the relationship. He may prefer not to start an affair until he has dated for a while.

Virgo is particular. If his love partner makes one false move, he is likely to dissolve the relationship. An understanding and patient woman can help him to be a little more realistic and open in his approach to love. But first she must know what kind of man she is dealing with.

The witty, talkative Virgo man enjoys flirting. But he will never press his luck nor take advantage of a compromising situation. He won't accuse you of stringing him along. It may seem as if he is waiting for you to make the next move. And you probably have to be the aggressor if the dating relationship is to get beyond the holding-hands stage and into serious lovemaking. Make sure, though, you don't go overboard with physical demonstrations of affection—especially in public places. Virgo is easily embarrassed by touching and kissing in front of other people. Any degree of sexual intimacy is strictly reserved for the bedroom.

The strong, silent Virgo type usually appeals to women who like the challenge of overcoming his apparent resistance to her feminine charms. Little does she know that he might be scared silly of making a fool of himself or of being criticized. Virgo projects his own personality traits onto people who get close to him. So he naturally believes that a woman who approaches is just as critical and faultfinding as he is. Fortunately, though, he doesn't project the egotism and chauvinism that could turn many a woman off. So if you want to play the seduction game, you will thrill to the ultimate conquest of winning this hard-to-get, nearly perfect guy.

The Virgo man enjoys family life and does everything he can to keep his wife and children happy and secure. He may want to have a hand in running the household because he feels he is more efficient than his mate. He is a calm, steady, and faithful person.

As a father he could be a bit of a fussbudget. He may not know how to communicate with his children effectively in some matters. However, he is loving and responsible. He does what he can to see that they have a proper upbringing.

Woman—Man

VIRGO WOMAN
ARIES MAN

Although it's possible that you could find happiness with a man born under the sign of the Ram, it's uncertain as to how long that happiness would last.

An Aries who has made his mark in the world and is somewhat steadfast in his outlooks and attitudes could be quite a catch for you. On the other hand, men under this sign are often swift-footed and quick-minded. Their industrious mannerisms may fail to impress you, especially if you feel that much of their get-up-and-go often leads nowhere.

When it comes to a fine romance, you want someone with a nice, broad shoulder to lean on. You are likely to find a relationship with someone who doesn't stay put for too long somewhat upsetting.

Aries may have a little trouble in understanding you, too, at least in the beginning of the relationship. He may find you a bit too shy and moody. An Aries tends to speak his mind; he's likely to criticize you at the drop of a hat.

You may find a man born under this sign too demanding. He may give you the impression that he expects you to be at his constant beck and call. You have a lot of patience at your disposal, and he may try every last bit of it. He may not be as thorough as you in everything he does. In order to achieve success or a goal quickly, he may overlook small but important details, then regret the oversight when it is far too late.

Being married to an Aries does not mean that you'll have a secure and safe life as far as finances are concerned. Not all Aries are rash with cash, but they lack the sound head you perhaps have for putting away something for that inevitable rainy day. He'll do his best, however, to see that you're adequately provided for, even though his efforts may leave something to be desired as far as you're concerned.

With an Aries man for a mate, you'll find yourself constantly among people. An Aries generally has many friends—and you may not heartily approve of them all. People born under the sign of the Ram are often more interested in interesting people than they are in influential ones. Although there may be a family squabble from time to time, you are stable enough to take it in your stride.

Aries men love children. They make wonderful fathers. Kids take to them like ducks to water. The Ram's quick mind and behavior appeal to the young. Aries ability to jump from one activity to another will suit and delight a child's attention span.

VIRGO WOMAN
TAURUS MAN

Some Taurus men are strong and silent. They do all they can to protect and provide for the women they love. In general, the Taurus man will never let you down. He's steady, sturdy, and reliable. He's pretty honest and practical, too. He says what he means and means what he says. He never indulges in deceit and will always put his cards on the table.

The Taurus man is very affectionate. Being loved, appreciated, and understood is very important for his well-being. Like you, he is also looking for peace and security in his life. If you both work toward these goals together, you'll find that they are easily attained.

If you should marry a Taurus man, you can be sure that the wolf will never darken your door. He is a notoriously good provider and will do everything he can to make his family comfortable and happy.

He'll appreciate the way you have of making a home warm and inviting. A comfortable couch and the evening papers are essential ingredients in making your Taurus husband happy at the end of the workday. Although he may be a big lug of a guy, you'll find that he's fond of gentleness and soft things. If you puff up his pillow and tuck him in at night, he won't complain.

You probably will like his friends. Taurus tends to seek out individuals who are successful or prominent. You also admire people who work hard and achieve their goals.

The Taurus man doesn't care too much for change. He's a stay-at-home of the first order. Chances are that the house you move into after you're married will be the house you'll live in for the rest of your life.

You'll find that the man born under the sign of the Bull is easy to get along with. It's unlikely that you'll have many quarrels or arguments.

Although he'll be gentle and tender with you, your Taurus man is far from being a sensitive type. He's a man's man. More than likely, he loves such sports as fishing and football. He can be earthy as well as down to earth.

The Taurus father loves the children, but he will do everything he can not to spoil them. He believes that children should stay in their place and, in adult company, should be seen but not heard. The Taurus father is an excellent disciplinarian. Your youngsters will be polite and respectful.

VIRGO WOMAN
GEMINI MAN

The Gemini man is a good catch. Many a woman has set her cap for him and failed to bag him. Generally, Gemini men are intelligent, witty, and outgoing. Many of them tend to be versatile.

On the other hand, some of them seem to lack that sort of common sense that you set so much store in. Their tendency to start a half-dozen projects, then toss them up in the air out of boredom may do nothing more than exasperate you.

One thing that causes a Twin's mind and affection to wander is a bore. But it is unlikely that an active woman like you would ever allow herself to be accused of being one. The Gemini man who has caught your heart will admire you for your ideas and intellect, perhaps even more than for your homemaking talents and good looks.

A strong-willed woman could easily fill the role of rudder for her Gemini's ship-without-a-sail. The intelligent Gemini is often aware of his shortcomings and doesn't mind if someone with better bearings gives him a shove in the right direction—when it's needed. The average Gemini doesn't have serious ego hang-ups and will even gracefully accept a well-deserved chewing out from his mate or lover or girl friend.

A successful and serious-minded Gemini could make you a very happy woman, perhaps, if you gave him half a chance. Although he may create the impression that he has a hole in his head, the Gemini man generally has a good head on his shoulders. Some Geminis, who have learned the art of being steadfast, have risen to great heights in their professions.

Once you convince yourself that not all people born under the sign of the Twins are witless grasshoppers, you won't mind dating a few to test your newborn conviction. If you do wind up walking down the aisle with one, accept the fact that married life with him will mean your taking the bitter with the sweet.

Life with a Gemini man can be more fun than a barrel of clowns. You'll never be allowed to experience a dull moment. Don't leave money matters to him, or you'll both wind up behind the eight ball.

Gemini men are always attractive to the opposite sex. You'll perhaps have to allow him a chance to flirt harmlessly. The occasion will seldom amount to more than that if you're his ideal mate.

The Gemini father is a pushover for children. See that you keep the young ones in line, otherwise they'll be running the house. He loves them so much, he generally lets them do what they want. Gemini's sense of humor is infectious, so the children will naturally come to see the fun and funny sides of life.

**VIRGO WOMAN
CANCER MAN**
The man born under the sign of Cancer may very well be the man after your own heart. Generally, Cancers are steady people. They are interested in security and practicality. Despite their seemingly grouchy exterior at times, men born under the sign of the Crab are sensitive and kind individuals.

Cancers are almost always hard workers and are very interested in making successes of themselves economically as well as socially. You'll find that their conservative outlook on many things often agrees with yours. They will be men on whom you can depend come rain or come shine. They will never shirk their responsibilities as providers. They will always see that their family never wants.

Your patience will come in handy if you decide it's a Cancer you want for a mate. He isn't the type that rushes headlong into romance. He wants to be sure about love as you do. If, after the first couple of months of dating, he suggests that you take a walk with him down lovers' lane, don't jump to the conclusion that he's about to make his great play. Chances are he'll only hold your hand and seriously observe the stars.

Don't let his coolness fool you, though. Beneath his starched reserve lies a very warm heart. He's just not interested in showing off as far as affection is concerned. Don't think his interest is wandering if he doesn't kiss you goodnight at the front door; that just isn't his style. For him, affection should only be displayed for two sets of eyes—yours and his. He's passionate only in private, which is something Virgo can understand and appreciate.

He will never step out of line. He's too much of a gentleman for that. When you're alone with him and there's no chance of being disturbed or spied upon, he'll pull out an engagement ring (the one that belonged to his grandmother) and slip it on your trembling finger.

Speaking of relatives, you'll have to get used to the fact that Cancer is overly fond of his mother. When he says his mother's the most wonderful woman in the world, you'd better agree with him, that is, if you want to become his wife.

He'll always be a faithful husband. A Cancer never pussyfoots around after he has taken that marriage vow. He doesn't take marriage responsibilities lightly. He'll see that everything in the house runs smoothly and that bills are paid promptly. He'll take out all kinds of insurance policies on his family and property. He'll arrange it so that when retirement time rolls around, you'll both be very well off.

Cancers make proud, patient, and protective fathers. But they can be a little too protective. Their sheltering instincts can interfere with a youngster's natural inclination toward independence. Still, the Cancer father doesn't want to see his kids learning about life the hard way from the streets.

VIRGO WOMAN
LEO MAN

To know a man born under the sign of the Lion is not necessarily to love him, even though the temptation may be great. When he fixes most girls with his leonine double-whammy, it causes their hearts to pitter-patter and their minds to cloud over.

You are a little too sensible to allow yourself to be bowled over by a regal strut and a roar. Still, there's no denying that Leo has a way with women, even sensible women like yourself. Once he's swept a girl off her feet, it may be hard for her to scramble upright again. Still, you are no pushover for romantic charm, especially if you feel it's all show.

He'll wine you and dine you in the fanciest places. He'll croon to you under the moon and shower you with diamonds if he can get ahold of them. Still, it would be wise to find out just how long that shower is going to last before consenting to be his wife.

Lions in love are hard to ignore, let alone brush off. Your resistance will have a way of nudging him on until he feels he has you completely under his spell. Once mesmerized by this romantic powerhouse, you will probably find yourself doing things of which you never dreamed. Leos can be vain pussycats when involved romantically. They like to be babied and pampered. This may not be your cup of tea exactly. Still when you're romantically dealing with a man born under the sign of Leo, you'll think up ways to make him purr.

Although he may be magnificent and magnanimous while trying to win you, he'll yowl or mew if he thinks he's not quite getting the tender love and care he feels is his due. If you keep him well supplied with affection, you can be sure his eyes will never gaze on someone else and his heart will never wander.

A Leo man often tends to be authoritarian. He can be depended upon to lord it over others in one way or another. If he is the top honcho at his firm, he'll most likely do everything he can to stay on top. If he's not number one, he's probably working on it and will be sitting on the throne before long.

You'll have more security than you can use if he is in a position to support you in the manner to which he feels you should be accustomed. He is inclined to be too lavish, though, at least by your standards.

You'll always have plenty of friends when you have a Leo for a mate. He's a natural-born wheeler-dealer and entertainer. He loves to let his hair down at parties.

As fathers, Leos tend to spoil their children. But they can also be strict when they think that the rules of the royal kingdom are being broken. You'll have to do your best to smooth over the children's roughed-up feelings.

VIRGO WOMAN
VIRGO MAN

The Virgo man is all business or so he may seem to you. He is usually very cool, calm, and collected. He's perhaps too much of a fussbudget to arouse deep romantic interests in a woman like you. Torrid romancing to him is just so much sentimental mush. He can do without it and can make that quite evident in short order. He's keen on chastity and, if necessary, he can lead a sedentary, sexless life without caring very much about the fun others think he's missing. In short, you may find him a first-class dud.

The Virgo man doesn't have much of an imagination; flights of fancy don't interest him. He is always correct and likes to be handled properly. Almost everything about him is orderly. There's a place for everything and everything in its place is an adage he'll fall upon quite regularly.

He does have an honest-to-goodness heart, believe it or not. The woman who finds herself strangely attracted to his cool, feet-flat-on-the-ground ways will discover that his is a constant heart, not one that goes in for flings or sordid affairs. A practical man, even in matters of the heart, he wants to know just what kind of person you are before he takes a chance on you.

The impulsive woman had better not make the mistake of kissing her Virgo friend on the street, even if it's only a peck on the cheek. He's not at all demonstrative and hates public displays of affection. Love, according to him, should be kept within the confines of one's home with the curtains drawn. Once he believes that you are on the level with him as far as your love is concerned, you'll see how fast he can lose his cool. Virgos are considerate, gentle lovers. He'll spend a long time, though, getting to know you. He'll like you before he loves you.

A romance with a Virgo man can be a sometime or, rather, a one-time thing. If the bottom ever falls out, don't bother reaching for the adhesive tape. Nine times out of ten he won't care about patching up. He's a once-burnt-twice-shy guy. When he crosses your telephone number out of his address book, he's crossing you out of his life for good.

Neat as a pin, he's thumbs-down on what he considers sloppy housekeeping. An ashtray with just one stubbed out cigarette in it can annoy him even if it's only two seconds old. Glassware should always sparkle and shine if you want to keep him happy. If you marry him, keep your sunny side up.

If you marry a Virgo man, instill a sense of order in the kids, or at least have them behaving by the time he gets home. The Virgo father wants his children to be kind and courteous and always helpful to the neighbors. The children should be kept as spotless as your house. Kids with dirty faces and hands displease him.

VIRGO WOMAN
LIBRA MAN
Men born under the sign of Libra are frequently too wrapped up in their own private dreams to be really interesting as far as love and

romance are concerned. Many times, the Libra man is a difficult person to bring back down to earth. It is hard for him to face reality. Although he may be very cautious about weighing both sides of an argument, he may never really come to a reasonable decision about anything. Decision making is something that often makes the Libra man uncomfortable. He'd rather leave that job to someone else. Don't ask him why, he probably doesn't know himself.

Qualities such as permanence and constancy are important to you in a love relationship. The Libra man may be an enigma to you. One moment he comes on hard and strong with declarations of his love; the next moment you find he's left you like yesterday's mashed potatoes. It does no good to wonder what went wrong. Chances are it was nothing on which you can put your finger. It's just one of Libra's strange ways.

He is not exactly what you would term an ambitious person. You are perhaps looking for a mate or friend with more drive and fidelity. You are the type of person who is interested in making some headway in the areas that interest you. Libra is often content just to drift along. He does have drive, however, but it's not the long-range kind.

It's not that Libra is shiftless or lazy. He's interested in material things and he appreciates luxuries, but he may not be willing to work hard enough to obtain them. Beauty and harmony interest him. He'll dedicate a lot of time to arranging things so that they are aesthetically pleasing. It would be difficult to call the Libra man practical; nine times out of ten, he isn't.

If you do begin a relationship with a man born under this sign, you will have to coax him now and again to face various situations in a realistic manner. You'll have your hands full, that's for sure. But if you love him, you'll undoubtedly do your best to understand him, no matter how difficult this may be.

If you become involved with a Libra man, either temporarily or permanently, you'd better take over the task of managing his money. Often he has little understanding of financial matters. He tends to spend without thinking, following his whims.

The Libra father is gentle and patient. He can be firm without exercising undue strictness or discipline. Although he can be a harsh judge at times, with the kids he will radiate sweetness and light in the hope that will grow up imitating his gracious manner.

VIRGO WOMAN
SCORPIO MAN
Some people have a hard time understanding the man born under the sign of Scorpio. Few, however, are able to resist his fiery charm.

When angered, he can act like the scorpion he is, ready to strike out and defend himself. His sting can leave an almost permanent mark. If you find yourself interested in the Scorpio man, you'd better learn how to keep on his good side.

The Scorpio man can be rather blunt when he chooses. At times, he may seem hard-hearted. He can be touchy every now and then, and this sensitiveness may get on your nerves after a while. When you feel as though you can't take it anymore, you'd better tiptoe away from the scene rather than chance an explosive confrontation. He's capable of giving you a sounding-out that will make you pack your bags and go back to Mother—for good.

If he finds fault with you, he'll let you know. He might misinterpret your patience and think it a sign of indifference. But you are the type of woman who can adapt to almost any sort of relationship or circumstance if you put your heart and mind to it.

Scorpio men are very perceptive and intelligent. In some respects, they know how to use their brains more effectively than most. They believe in winning, in whatever they do. Second place holds no interest for them. In business, they usually achieve the position they want through a combination of drive and intellect.

Your interest in home life probably won't be shared by him. No matter how comfortable you've managed to make the house, it will have very little influence on him with regard to making him aware of his family responsibilities. He does not like to be tied down, generally, and would rather be out on the battlefield of life, belting away at what he feels to be a just and worthy cause. Don't try to keep the home fires burning too brightly while you wait for him to come home from work; you might run out of firewood.

The Scorpio man is passionate in all things, including love. Most women are easily attracted to him and you are perhaps no exception. Those who allow themselves to be swept off their feet by a Scorpio man soon find that they're dealing with a carton of romantic fireworks. The Scorpio man is passionate with a capital P, make no mistake about that.

Scorpio men are straight to the point. They can be as sharp as a razor blade and just as cutting to anyone who crosses them.

Scorpio fathers like large families, generally. In spite of the extremes in his personality, the Scorpio man is able to transform conflicting characteristics when he becomes a father. He is adept with difficult youngsters because he knows how to tap the best in a child. He believes in preparing his children for the hard knocks life sometimes delivers.

VIRGO WOMAN
SAGITTARIUS MAN

The woman who has set her cap for a man born under the sign of Sagittarius may have to use a great deal of strategy before she can get him to drop down on bended knee. Although some Sagittarius may be marriage-shy, they're not ones to skitter away from romance. A high-spirited woman may find a relationship with a Sagittarius, whether a fling or the real thing, a very enjoyable experience.

As a rule, Sagittarius people are bright, happy, and healthy people. They have a strong sense of fair play. Often they're a source of inspiration to others. They're full of ideas and drive.

You'll be taken by the Archer's infectious grin and his light-hearted friendly nature. If you do wind up being the woman in his life, you'll find that he will treat you more like a buddy than the love of his life. It's his way.

You'll admire his broad-mindedness in most matters, including that of the heart. If, while dating you, he claims that he still wants to play the field, he'll expect you to enjoy the same liberty. Once he's promised to love, honor, and obey, however, he does just that.

A woman who has a keen imagination and a great love of freedom will not be disappointed if she does marry an Archer. The Sagittarius man likes to share his many interests, and he has a genuine belief in equality.

If he does insist on a night out with the boys once a week, he won't scowl if you decide to let him shift for himself in the kitchen while you pursue some of your own interests. He believes in fairness, and he is no male chauvinist.

The Sagittarius is not much of a homebody. Many times he's occupied with faraway places either in his dreams or in reality. He enjoys—just as you do—being on the go. A humdrum existence, especially at home, bores him. At the drop of a hat, he may ask you to take off with him into the wild blue yonder—his idea of a break from routine.

Sagittarius likes surprising people. He'll take great pride in showing you off to his friends. He'll always be a considerate mate; he will never embarrass or disappoint you intentionally. He's very tolerant when it comes to friends; you'll probably spend a lot of time entertaining people.

The Sagittarius father will dote on any son or daughter, but he may be bewildered by the newborn. The Archer usually becomes comfortable with youngsters once they have passed through the baby stage. As soon as the children are old enough to walk and talk, the Sagittarius dad encourages each and every visible sign of talent and skill.

VIRGO WOMAN
CAPRICORN MAN

The Capricorn man is frequently not the romantic lover that attracts most women. Still, with his reserve and calm, he is capable of giving his heart completely once he has found the right woman. The Capricorn man is thorough and deliberate in all that he does. His slow, steady approach is sure to win the one he loves.

He doesn't believe in flirting and would never lead a heart on a merry chase just for the game of it. If you win his trust, he'll give you his heart on a platter. Many times, it is the woman who has to take the lead when romance is in the air. As long as he knows you're making the advances in earnest, he won't mind—in fact, he'll probably be grateful.

But don't start thinking he's a cold fish; he isn't. Although some Capricorns are indeed very capable of expressing passion, others often have difficulty in trying to display affection. He should have no trouble in this area, however, once he has found a patient and understanding lover.

The Capricorn man is very interested in getting ahead. He's quite ambitious and usually knows how to apply himself well to whatever task he undertakes. He certainly isn't a spendthrift. Like you, he knows how to handle money with extreme care. You, with your knack for putting away pennies for that rainy day, should have no difficulty understanding his way with money.

The Capricorn man thinks in terms of future security. He wants to make sure that he and his wife have something to fall back on when they reach retirement age. There's nothing wrong with that; in fact, it's a plus quality.

The Capricorn man will want you to handle household matters efficiently. The fastidious Virgo woman will have no trouble doing so. If he should check up on you from time to time, don't let it irritate you. Once you assure him that you can handle everything to his liking, he'll leave you alone.

Although he's a hard man to catch when it comes to marriage, once he's made that serious step, he's inclined to become possessive. The Capricorn man needs to know that he has the support of his wife in whatever he does, every step of the way.

The Capricorn man wants to be liked. He may seem dull to some, but underneath his reserve there is sometimes an adventurous streak that has never had a chance to express itself. He may be a real daredevil in his heart of hearts. The right woman, the affectionate, adoring woman can bring out that hidden zest in his nature.

Capricorn makes a loving, dutiful father, even though he may not understand his children completely. The Goat believes that there are goals to be achieved, and that there is the right way to achieve them. The Capricorn father can be quite a scold when it comes to disciplining the youngsters. You'll have to step in and bend the rules sometimes.

VIRGO WOMAN
AQUARIUS MAN

You might find the Aquarius man the most broad-minded man you have ever met. On the other hand, you might find him the most impractical. Many times, he's more of a dreamer than a doer. If you don't mind putting up with a man whose heart and mind are as wide as the sky and whose head is almost always in the clouds, then start dating that Aquarius who has somehow captured your fancy. Maybe you, with your good sense, can bring him back down to earth when he gets too starry-eyed.

He's no dumbbell, make no mistake about that. He can be busy making some very complicated and idealistic plans when he's got that out-to-lunch look in his eyes. But more than likely, he'll never execute them. After he's shared one or two of his progressive ideas with you, you may think he's a nut. But don't go jumping to conclusions. There's a saying that Aquarius is a half-century ahead of everybody else in the thinking department.

If you decide to marry him, you'll find out how right his zany whims are on or about your 50th anniversary. Maybe the waiting will be worth it. Could be that you have an Einstein on your hands and heart.

Life with an Aquarius won't be one of total despair if you can learn to temper his airiness with your down-to-earth Virgo practicality. He won't gripe if you do. Aquarius always maintains an open mind. He'll entertain the ideas and opinions of everybody. But he may not agree with all of them.

Don't go tearing your hair out when you find that it's almost impossible to hold a normal conversation with your Aquarius friend at times. Usually chasing the big idea, he can overlook the vital details. Always try to keep in mind that he means well.

His broad-mindedness doesn't stop when it comes to you and your personal freedom. You won't have to give up any of your hobbies or projects after you're married. He will encourage you to continue them and to be as independent as he is.

He'll be a kind and generous husband. He'll never quibble over petty things. Keep track of the money you both spend. He can't. Money burns a hole in his pocket.

At times, you may feel like calling it quits. Chances are, though, that you'll always give him another chance.

The Aquarius is a good family man. He can be a shining example for the children because he sees them as individuals in their own right, not as extensions of himself. Kids love him and vice versa. He'll be tolerant with them as he is with adults.

VIRGO WOMAN
PISCES MAN

The man born under Pisces is quite a dreamer. Sometimes he's so wrapped up in his dreams that he's difficult to reach. To the average, active woman, he may seem a little passive.

He's easygoing most of the time. He seems to take things in his stride. He'll entertain all kinds of views and opinions from just about everyone, nodding or smiling vaguely, giving the impression that he's with them one hundred percent while that may not be the case at all. His attitude may be why bother when he's confronted with someone who is wrong but thinks he's right. The Pisces man will seldom speak his mind if he thinks he'll be rigidly opposed.

The Pisces man is oversensitive at times. He's afraid of getting his feelings hurt. He'll sometimes imagine a personal affront when none's been made. More than likely, you'll find this complex of his maddening. At times you may feel like giving him a swift kick where it hurts the most. It won't do any good, though.

One thing you'll admire about this man is his concern for people who are sickly or troubled. He'll make his shoulder available to anyone in the mood for a good cry. He can listen to one hard-luck story after another without seeming to tire. When his advice is asked, he can be depended upon to offer some wise counsel. He often knows what is upsetting someone before that person is aware of it himself.

Still, at the end of the day, the Pisces man will want some peace and quiet. If you've got a problem when he comes home, don't unload it in his lap. If you do, you might find him short-tempered. He's a good listener, but he can only take so much turmoil.

Pisces are not aimless although they may seem so at times. The positive sort of Pisces man is often successful in his profession and is likely to become rich and influential. Material gain, however, is never a direct goal for a man born under the sign of the Fishes.

The weaker Pisces is usually content to stay on the level where he finds himself.

Because of their seemingly laissez-faire manner, people under the sign of Pisces are immensely popular with children. For tots, the Pisces father plays the double role of confidant and playmate. It will never enter his mind to discipline a child, no matter how spoiled or incorrigible that child becomes.

Man—Woman

**VIRGO MAN
ARIES WOMAN**

The Aries woman may be a little too bossy and busy for you. Generally, Aries is an ambitious creature. She can become a little impatient with a Virgo who by nature is more thorough and deliberate than she is, especially if she feels you're taking too much time.

The Aries woman is a fast worker. Sometimes she's so fast she forgets to look where she's going. When she stumbles or falls, it would be nice if you were there to catch her. But Aries is a proud woman. She doesn't like to be criticized when she errs. The Virgo tongue lashings can turn her into a block of ice.

Don't begin to think that the Aries woman frequently gets tripped up in her plans. Many times she is capable of taking aim and hitting the bull's-eye. You'll be flabbergasted by her accuracy as well as by her ambition. On the other hand, you're apt to spot a flaw in her plans before she does.

You are perhaps somewhat slower than Aries in attaining your goals. Still, you are not inclined to make mistakes along the way. You're almost always well prepared.

The Aries woman can be sensitive at times. She likes to be handled with gentleness and respect. Let her know that you love her for her brains as well as for her good looks. Never give her cause to become jealous. When your Aries date sees green, you'd better forget about sharing a rosy future together. Handle her with tender love and care and she's yours.

The Aries woman can be giving if she feels her partner is deserving. She is no iceberg; she responds to the proper masculine flame. She needs a man she can admire and of whom she can feel proud. She can cause you plenty of heartache if you've made up your mind about her but she hasn't made up hers about you. The Aries woman is very demanding at times. Some tend to be high-strung. They can be difficult if they feel their independence is being hampered.

The cultivated Aries woman makes a wonderful homemaker and hostess. You'll find she's very clever in decorating and using color. Your house will be tastefully furnished; she'll make sure that it radiates harmony. The Aries wife knows how to make guests feel at home.

Although the Aries woman may not be keen on burdensome responsibilities, she is fond of children and the joy they bring. She is skilled at juggling both career and motherhood, so her kids will never feel that she is an absentee parent. In fact, as the youngsters grow older, they might want a little more of the liberation that is so important to her.

VIRGO MAN
TAURUS WOMAN

A Taurus woman could perhaps understand you better than most women. She is very considerate and loving. She is thorough and methodical in whatever she does. She is anxious to avoid mistakes.

Home is very important to the Taurus woman. She is an excellent homemaker. Although your home may not be a palace, it will become, under her care, a comfortable and happy abode. She'll love it when friends drop by for the evening. She is a good cook and enjoys feeding people well.

The Taurus woman is serious about love and affection. When she has taken a tumble for someone, she'll stay by him forever, if possible. She will try to be practical in romance, to some extent. When she decides she wants a certain man, she keeps after him until he's won her. Generally, the Taurus woman is a passionate lover, even though she may appear staid at first glance. She is on the lookout for someone who can return her affection fully. Taurus women are sometimes given to fits of jealousy and possessiveness. They expect fair play in the area of marriage. When it doesn't come about, they can be bitingly sarcastic and mean.

The Taurus woman is usually an easygoing person intent on keeping the peace. She won't argue unless she must. She'll do her best to keep your love relationship on an even keel.

Marriage is generally a one-time thing for Taurus. Once they've taken the serious step, they seldom try to back out of it. Taurus women need love and warmth. With the right man, they become ideal wives.

The Taurus woman will respect you for your steady ways. She'll have confidence in your common sense. She'll share with you all the joys and burdens of parenthood.

Taurus women seldom put up with nonsense from their children. It is not that they are strict, but rather that they are concerned. They like their children to be well behaved and dutiful. Nothing pleases a Taurus mother more than a compliment from a neighbor or teacher about her child's behavior.

Although some children may inwardly resent the iron hand of a Taurus mother, in later life they are often thankful that they were brought up in such an orderly and conscientious way.

VIRGO MAN
GEMINI WOMAN

You may find a romance with a woman born under the sign of the Twins a many-splendored thing. She will provide the intellectual companionship you often look for in a friend or mate. A Gemini partner can appreciate your aims and desires because she travels pretty much the same road as you do intellectually, that is, at least part of the way. She may share your interests but she will lack your tenacity.

She suffers from itchy feet. She can be here, there, all over the place. Her eagerness to be on the move may make you dizzy. Still, you'll enjoy and appreciate her liveliness and mental agility.

The Gemini woman often has a sparkling personality. You'll be attracted to her warmth and grace. While she's on your arm you'll probably notice that many male eyes are drawn to her. She may even return a gaze or two, but don't let that worry you. All women born under this sign have nothing against a harmless flirtation once in a while. But if she feels she is already spoken for, she will never let it get out of hand.

Although she may not be as handy as you'd like in the kitchen, you'll never go without a tasty meal. The Gemini woman is always in a rush. She won't feel she's cheating by breaking out the instant mashed potatoes or the frozen peas. She may not be a good cook but she is clever. With a dash of this and a suggestion of that, she can make an uninteresting TV dinner taste like a gourmet meal. Then, again, maybe you've struck it rich and have a Gemini lover who finds complicated recipes a challenge to her intellect. If so, you'll find every meal a tantalizing and mouth-watering surprise.

When you're beating your brains out over the Sunday crossword puzzle and find yourself stuck, just ask your Gemini woman. She'll give you all the right answers without batting an eyelash.

Just like you, she loves all kinds of people. You may even find that you're a bit more discriminating than she. Often all that a Gemini requires is that her friends be interesting and stay interesting. But one thing she's not able to abide is a dullard.

Leave the party organizing to your Gemini sweetheart or mate, and you'll never have a chance to know what a dull moment is. She'll bring out the swinger in you if you give her half the chance.

A Gemini mother enjoys her children, which can be the truest form of love. Like them, she's often restless, adventurous, and easily bored. She will never complain about their fleeting interests because she understands the changes they will go through as they mature.

VIRGO MAN
CANCER WOMAN
The Cancer woman needs to be protected from the cold, cruel world. She'll love you for your masculine yet gentle manner; you make her feel safe and secure. You don't have to pull any he-man or heroic stunts to win her heart; that's not what interests her.

She's more likely to be impressed by your sure, steady ways—

that way you have of putting your arm around her and making her feel she's the only girl in the world. When she's feeling glum and tears begin to well up in her eyes, you have that knack of saying just the right thing. You know how to calm her fears, no matter how silly some of them may seem.

The woman born under the sign ruled by the Moon is inclined to have her ups and downs. You have that talent for smoothing out the ruffles in her sea of life. She'll probably worship the ground you walk on or put you on a very high pedestal. Don't disappoint her if you can help it. She'll never disappoint you.

The Cancer woman will take great pleasure in devoting the rest of her natural life to you. She'll darn your socks, mend your overalls, scrub floors, wash windows, shop, cook, and do just about anything in order to please you and let you know that she loves you. Sounds like that legendary good old-fashioned girl, doesn't it? Contrary to popular belief, there are still some around, and many of them are Cancers.

Of all the signs of the Zodiac, the Cancer-born are the most maternal. In caring for and bringing up children, Cancer women know just how to combine the right amount of tenderness with the proper dash of discipline. A child couldn't ask for a better mother. Cancer women are sympathetic, affectionate, and patient with their children.

While we're on the subject of motherhood, there's one thing you should be warned about: never be unkind to your mother-in-law. It will be the only golden rule your Cancer wife will probably expect you to follow. No mother-in-law jokes in the presence of your mate, please. They'll go over like a lead balloon. Mother is something pretty special for her. She may be the crankiest, nosiest old bat. But she's your wife's mother. You'd better treat her like she's one of the landed gentry. Sometimes this may be difficult to swallow. But if you want to keep your home together and your wife happy, learn to grin and bear it.

Treat your Cancer wife like a queen, and she'll treat you royally.

VIRGO MAN
LEO WOMAN

The Leo woman can make most men roar like lions. If any woman in the Zodiac has that indefinable something that can make men lose their heads and find their hearts, it's the Leo woman.

She's got more than a fair share of charm and glamour. She knows how to make the most of her assets, especially when she's in the company of the opposite sex. Jealous men are apt to lose their cool or their sanity when trying to woo a woman born under the sign of the Lion. The Lioness likes to kick up her heels quite often and doesn't care who knows it. She frequently makes heads turn and tongues wag. You don't necessarily have to believe any of what you hear—it's probably jealous gossip or wishful thinking. Still, other women in her vicinity turn green with envy and will try anything to put her out of the running.

Although this vamp makes the blood rush to your head and makes you momentarily forget all the things you thought were important and necessary in your life, you may feel differently when you come back down to earth and the stars are out of your eyes. You may feel that she isn't the type of girl you planned to bring home to Mother. Not that your mother might disapprove of your choice, but you might after the shoes and rice are a thing of the past. Although the Leo woman may do her best to be a good wife for you, chances are she'll fall short of your idea of what a good wife should be like.

If you're planning on not going as far as the altar with the Leo woman, you'd better be financially equipped for some very expensive dating. Be prepared to shower her with expensive gifts and to take her dining and dancing to the smartest spots in town. Promise her the moon if you're in a position to go that far. Luxury and glamour are two things that are bound to lower a Leo's resistance. She's got expensive tastes, and you'll have to cater to them if you expect to get to first base with her.

If you've got an important business deal to clinch and you have doubts as to whether you can swing it or not, bring your Leo woman along to the business luncheon. More than likely, with her on your arm, you'll be able to win any business battle with both hands tied. She won't have to say or do anything, just be there at your side. The grouchiest oil magnate can be transformed into a gushing, obedient schoolboy if there's a charming Leo woman in the room.

Leo mothers are sometimes blind to the faults of their children. On the other hand, the Leo mother can be strict when she wants them to learn something. She expects her youngsters to follow the rules, and she is a patient teacher. Being easygoing and friendly, she loves to pal around with the kids while proudly showing them off on every occasion.

VIRGO MAN
VIRGO WOMAN

The Virgo woman may be even too difficult for the Virgo man to understand at first. Her waters run deep. Even when you think you know her, don't take any bets on it. She's capable of keeping things hidden in the deep recesses of her womanly soul—things she'll only release when she's sure that you're the man she wants. But it may take her some time to come around to this decision. Virgos are finicky about almost everything. Many of them have the idea that the only people who can do things correctly are Virgos.

Nothing offends a Virgo woman more than slovenly dress, sloppy character, or a careless display of affection. Make sure your tie is not crooked and your shoes sport a bright shine before you go calling on this lady. Keep your off-color jokes for the locker room; she'll have none of that.

Take her arm when crossing the street, but don't rush the romance. Trying to corner her in the back of a cab may be one way of striking out. Never criticize the way she looks. In fact, the best policy is to agree with her as much as possible.

Still, there's just so much a man can take. All those dos and don'ts you have to observe if you want to get to first base with a Virgo may be just a little too much to ask of you. After a few dates, you may decide that she just isn't worth all that trouble. However, the Virgo woman is usually mysterious enough to keep her men running back for more. Chances are you'll be intrigued by her airs and graces.

If lovemaking means a great deal to you, you'll be disappointed at first in the cool ways of your Virgo woman. However, under her glacial facade there lies a hot cauldron of seething excitement. If you're patient and artful in your romantic approach, you'll find that all the caution was well worth the trouble. When Virgos love, it's all or nothing as far as they're concerned.

One thing a Virgo woman can't stand in love is hypocrisy. She doesn't care what the neighbors say. If her heart tells her to go ahead, she does. She is very concerned with human truths. If her heart stumbles upon another fancy, she will be true to that new heartthrob and leave you standing in the rain.

She's honest to her heart and will be as true to you as you are with her. Do her wrong once, however, and it's farewell.

The Virgo mother has high expectations for her children, and she will strive to bring out the very best in them. She is more tender than strict, though, and will nag rather than discipline. But youngsters sense her unconditional love for them, and usually turn out just as she hoped they would.

VIRGO MAN
LIBRA WOMAN
Libra invented the notion that it's a woman's prerogative to change her mind. Her changeability, in spite of its undeniable charm, could actually drive even a man of your patience up the wall. She's capable of smothering you with love and kisses one day, and on the next avoid you like the plague.

If you think you're a man of steel nerves then perhaps you can tolerate these sudden changes without suffering too much. However, if you admit that you're only a mere mortal who can take so much, then you'd better fasten your attention on a partner who's somewhat more constant.

But don't get the wrong idea. A love affair with a Libra can have a lot of pluses to it. The Libra woman is soft, very feminine, and warm. She doesn't have to vamp all over the place in order to gain a man's attention. Her delicate presence is enough to warm the cockles of any man's heart. One smile, and you're a piece of putty in the palm of her hand.

She can be fluffy and affectionate, which you will like. On the other hand, her indecision about which dress to wear, what to cook for dinner, or whether to redecorate could make you tear your hair out. What will perhaps be more exasperating is her flat denial of the accusation that she cannot make even the simplest decision. The trouble is that she wants to be fair or just in all matters. She'll spend hours weighing pros and cons. Don't make her rush into a decision; that will only irritate her.

The Libra woman likes to be surrounded by beautiful things. Money is no object when beauty is concerned. There will always be plenty of flowers in the house. She'll know how to arrange them tastefully, too. Women under this sign are fond of beautiful clothes and furnishings. They will run up bills without batting an eyelash, if given the chance.

Once she's involved with you, the Libra woman will do everything in her power to make you happy. She'll wait on you hand and foot when you're sick and bring you breakfast in bed Sundays. She'll be very thoughtful and devoted. If anyone dares suggest you're not the grandest man in the world, your Libra wife will give that person a good sounding-out.

The Libra mother works wonders with children. Gentle persuasion and affection are all she uses in bringing them up. It works. She is sensitive and sensible, with an intuitive understanding of what a child needs. Her youngsters will never lack for anything that could make their lives easier and richer. Still, you will always come before the children.

VIRGO MAN
SCORPIO WOMAN
When the Scorpio woman chooses to be sweet, she's apt to give the impression that butter wouldn't melt in her mouth but, of course, it would. When her temper flies, so will everything else that isn't bolted down. She can be as hot as a tamale or as cool as a cucumber when she wants. Whatever mood she's in, you can be

sure it's for real. She doesn't believe in poses or hypocrisy.

The Scorpio woman is often seductive and sultry. Her femme fatale charm can pierce through the hardest of hearts. The Scorpio woman can be a whirlwind of passion. But life with her will not be all smiles and smooth sailing. If you think you can handle a woman who is quick to retaliate and hold a grudge, then try your luck. Your stable and steady nature will probably have a calming effect on her. You're the kind of man she can trust and rely on. But never cross her, even on the smallest thing, or she'll make you pay for it.

Generally, the Scorpio woman will keep family battles within the walls of your home. When company visits, she can be depended upon to give the impression that married life with you is one big joyride. It's just her way of expressing her loyalty to you, at least in front of others. The Scorpio woman will certainly see that others have a high opinion of you both. She'll support you in whatever it is you want to do.

Although she's an individualist, after she has married, she'll put her own interests aside for those of the man she loves. With a woman like this behind you, you can't help but go far. She'll never try to take over your role as boss of the family and she'll give you all the support you need in order to fulfill that role. She won't complain if the going gets rough, for she is a courageous woman. She's as anxious as you to find that place in the sun for you both. She is as determined a person as you are.

Although the Scorpio mother loves her children, she will not put them on a pedestal. She is devoted to developing her youngsters' talents. The Scorpio mother is protective yet encouraging. The opposites within her nature mirror the contradictions within life itself. Under her skillful guidance, the children will learn how to cope with extremes and will grow up to become well-rounded individuals. She will teach her young ones to be courageous and steadfast.

VIRGO MAN
SAGITTARIUS WOMAN

You'll most likely never meet a more good-natured woman than the one under the sign of Sagittarius. Generally, she is full of bounce and good cheer. Her sunny disposition seems almost permanent and can be relied upon even on the rainiest of days.

The woman born under the sign of the Archer is rarely malicious. But she is often a little short on tact and says literally anything that comes into her head, regardless of the occasion. Sometimes the words that tumble out of her mouth are downright cutting and cruel. But no matter what she says, she means well. Unfortunately, the Sagittarius woman is capable of losing some of her friends—

and perhaps even some of yours—through such carelessness.

On the other hand, you will appreciate her honesty and good intentions. To you, these qualities play an important part in life. With a little patience and practice, you can probably help cure your Sagittarius of her loose tongue. In most cases, she'll give in to your better judgment and try to follow your advice.

Chances are, she'll be the outdoors type and sportswoman. Long hikes, fishing trips, and white-water canoeing will probably appeal to her. She's a busy person, one who sets great store in mobility. She won't sit still for one minute if it's not necessary.

She is very friendly and likes lots of company. When your buddies drop by for poker and beer, she won't have any trouble fitting in.

On the whole, she is a very kind and sympathetic woman. If she feels she's made a mistake, she'll be the first to call your attention to it. She's not afraid to own up to her own faults and shortcomings.

You might lose your patience with her once or twice. After she's seen how upset her shortsightedness and careless comments have made you, she'll do her best to please you.

The Sagittarius woman is not the kind who will pry into your business affairs. But she'll always be there, ready to offer advice if you need it.

The Sagittarius woman is seldom suspicious. Your word will almost always be good enough for her.

The Sagittarius mother is a wonderful and loving friend to her children. She is not afraid if a youngster learns some street smarts along the way. To bolster such knowledge, or to counteract it, she may preach a bit too much for the kids. Then you can switch the focus to the practical. But you will appreciate how she encourages the children to study in order for them to get a well-rounded and broad education.

VIRGO MAN
CAPRICORN WOMAN
The Capricorn may not be the most romantic woman of the Zodiac, but she's certainly not frigid when she meets the right man. She believes in true love. She doesn't appreciate flings. To her, they're just a waste of time. She's looking for a man who means business—in life as well as in love. Although she can be very affectionate with her lover or mate, she tends to let her head govern her heart. That is not to say she is a cool, calculating cucumber. On the contrary, she just feels she can be more honest about love if she consults her brains first.

The Capricorn woman is faithful, dependable, and systematic in just about everything she undertakes. She is very concerned with security and makes sure that every penny she spends is spent wisely. She is very economical about using her time, too. She does not believe in whittling away her energy on a scheme that is bound not to pay off.

Ambitious herself, she is often attracted to the ambitious man—one who is interested in getting somewhere in life. If a man with this temperament wins her heart, she'll stick by him and do all she can to help him get to the top.

The Capricorn woman is almost always diplomatic. She makes an excellent hostess. She can be very influential when your business acquaintances come to dinner.

The Capricorn woman is likely to be very concerned, if not extremely proud, of her family tree. Relatives are very important to her, particularly if they're socially prominent. Never say a cross word about her family members. She is likely to punish you by not talking to you for days.

As a rule, she's thorough in whatever she does. The Capricorn woman is well-mannered, well-groomed, and gracious, no matter what her background.

If you should marry a woman born under this sign, you need never worry about her going on a wild shopping spree. She understands the value of money better than most women. If you turn over your paycheck to her at the end of the week, you can be sure that a good hunk of it will wind up in the bank.

The Capricorn mother is very ambitious for her children. She wants them to have every advantage and to benefit from things she perhaps lacked as a child. She will train the youngsters to be polite and kind, and to honor traditional codes of conduct. She can be correct to a fault. But the meticulous Virgo mate will not find fault with the Capricorn mother's careful ways.

VIRGO MAN
AQUARIUS WOMAN

If you find that you've fallen head over heels for a woman born under the sign of the Water Bearer, you'd better fasten your safety belt. It may take you quite a while to actually discover what she is like. Even then, you may have nothing to go on but a series of vague hunches. The Aquarius woman is like a rainbow, full of bright and shining hues. She's like no one you've ever known. There is something elusive about her.

The Aquarius woman can be pretty odd and eccentric at times. Some say this is the source of her mysterious charm. You might think she's just a screwball, and you may be 50 percent right. The Aquarius woman often has her head full of dreams. By nature, she is often unconventional; she has her own thoughts about how the world should be run. Sometimes her ideas may seem weird, but chances are they're just a little too progressive. Keep in mind the saying: The way the Aquarius thinks, so will the world in 50 years.

She'll probably be the most tolerant and open-minded woman you've ever encountered.

If you find that she's too much mystery and charm for you to handle, tell her so and say that you think it would be best to call it quits. She'll probably agree without making a scene yet still want to remain friends. The Aquarius woman is like that. Perhaps you'll both find it easier to get along in a friendship than in a romance.

The Aquarius woman is not a jealous person and, while you're romancing her, she won't expect you to be, either. You'll find her a free spirit most of the time. Just when you think you know her inside out, you'll discover that you don't really know her at all.

She's a very sympathetic and warm person. She is always helpful to those in need of assistance and advice.

She'll seldom be suspicious even when she has every right to be. If the man she loves makes a little slip, she's inclined to forgive and forget it.

The Aquarius mother is bighearted and seldom refuses her children anything. Her open-minded attitude is easily transmitted to her youngsters. They have every change of growing up as respectful and tolerant individuals who feel at ease anywhere.

VIRGO MAN
PISCES WOMAN

Many a man dreams of an alluring Pisces woman. You're perhaps no exception. She's soft and cuddly and very domestic. She'll let you be the brains of the family; she's contented to play a behind-the-scenes role in order to help you achieve your goals. The illusion that you are the master of the household is the kind of magic that the Pisces woman is adept at creating.

She can be very ladylike and proper. Your business associates and friends will be dazzled by her warmth and femininity. Although she's a charmer, there is a lot more to her than just a pretty exterior. There is a brain ticking away behind that soft, womanly facade. You may never become aware of it—that is, until you're married to her. It's no cause for alarm, however; she'll most likely never use it against you, only to help you and possibly set you on a more successful path.

If she feels you're botching up your married life through careless behavior or if she feels you could be earning more money than you do, she'll tell you about it. But any wife would, really. She will never try to usurp your position as head and breadwinner of the family.

No one had better dare say one uncomplimentary word about

you in her presence. It's likely to cause her to break into tears. Pisces women are usually very sensitive beings. Their reaction to adversity, frustration, or anger is just a plain, good, old-fashioned cry. They can weep buckets when inclined.

She can do wonders with a house. She is very fond of dramatic and beautiful things. There will always be plenty of fresh-cut flowers around the house. She will choose charming artwork and antiques, if they are affordable. She'll see to it that the house is decorated in a dazzling yet welcoming style.

She'll have an extra special dinner prepared for you when you come home from an important business meeting. Don't dwell on the boring details of the meeting, though. But if you need that grand vision, the big idea, to seal a contract or make a conquest, your Pisces woman is sure to confide a secret that will guarantee your success. She is canny and shrewd with money, and once you are on her wavelength you can manage the intricacies on your own.

Treat her with tenderness and generosity and your relationship will be an enjoyable one. She's most likely fond of chocolates. A bunch of beautiful flowers will never fail to make her eyes light up. See to it that you never forget her birthday or your anniversary. These things are very important to her. If you let them slip your mind, you'll send her into a crying fit that could last a considerable length of time.

If you are patient and kind, you can keep a Pisces woman happy for a lifetime. She, however, is not without her faults. Her sensitivity may get on your nerves after a while. You may find her lacking in practicality and good old-fashioned stoicism. You may even feel that she uses her tears as a method of getting her own way.

The Pisces mother totally believes in her children, and that faith never wavers. Her unconditional love for them makes her a strong, self-sacrificing mother. That means she can deny herself in order to fulfill their needs. She will teach her youngsters the value of service to the community while not letting them lose their individuality.

VIRGO
LUCKY NUMBERS 2008

Lucky numbers and astrology can be linked through the movements of the Moon. Each phase of the thirteen Moon cycles vibrates with a sequence of numbers for your Sign of the Zodiac over the course of the year. Using your lucky numbers is a fun system that connects you with tradition.

New Moon	First Quarter	Full Moon	Last Quarter
Jan. 8 2 5 3 8	Jan. 15 2 6 1 0	Jan. 22 7 3 1 4	Jan. 30 2 5 9 8
Feb. 6 4 4 7 2	Feb. 13 2 6 8 3	Feb. 20 1 4 7 5	Feb. 28 8 3 2 7
March 7 0 1 5 9	March 14 0 2 6 4	March 21 7 9 7 0	March 29 5 4 9 3
April 5 3 7 2 4	April 12 8 6 9 7	April 20 4 7 2 1	April 28 1 6 9 4
May 5 7 8 1 5	May 11 3 6 4 4	May 19 7 2 1 9	May 27 5 8 3 7
June 3 2 9 4 2	June 10 2 5 3 6	June 18 1 9 6 0	June 26 5 9 4 6
July 2 4 1 0 8	July 9 2 9 3 7	July 18 7 6 2 4	July 25 4 8 3 5
August 1 8 7 1 8	August 8 8 2 6 5	August 16 1 4 8 3	August 23 7 9 4 6
August 30 6 5 3 6	Sept. 7 6 1 9 0	Sept. 15 5 8 3 7	Sept. 22 9 4 5 3
Sept. 29 9 4 7 2	Oct. 7 2 1 6 9	Oct. 14 9 4 8 0	Oct. 21 5 3 6 9
Oct. 28 7 1 5 4	Nov. 5 4 9 3 7	Nov. 13 7 2 4 8	Nov. 19 6 9 3 1
Nov. 27 1 8 7 3	Dec. 5 3 6 1 5	Dec. 12 5 7 2 9	Dec. 19 3 1 6 9
Dec. 27 7 5 8 9	Jan. 4 ('09) 6 2 5 3	Jan. 10 ('09) 8 2 6 1	Jan. 17 ('09) 0 3 7 8

VIRGO
YEARLY FORECAST 2008

*Forecast for 2008 Concerning Business
and Financial Affairs, Job Prospects,
Travel, Health, Romance and Marriage
for Persons Born with the Sun
in the Zodiacal Sign of Virgo.
August 22–September 22*

For those of you born under the influence of the Sun in the zodiacal sign of Virgo, ruled by articulate and quick-minded Mercury, this year promises to be one where the door of fortune can open wide in the area of creative ventures, speculative enterprises, and romance. Contributions to career aspirations can come to fruition through creating new opportunities and setting fresh projects in motion. This is a year when new business ideas and skills can be developed, positively revolutionizing employment conditions and daily routines.

Saturn, the measurer of effort, is in your own sign of Virgo throughout 2008. Saturn begins the year in retrograde mode and remains retrograde until May 2. Throughout this period delays can cause frustration if your timing is off or if strategic planning and proper preparation have not been carried out. Taking on more responsibilities, overcoming obstacles, and learning to delegate are some of the lessons and challenges augured by Saturn this year.

A rise in status can come through promotion, marriage, or a new career. At times you might feel lonely or isolated even when relating to others. Carrying the load that rightly belongs to a partner, teammates, or friends may be forced on your shoulders. Rewards will come by completing whatever you begin and applying sustained effort.

Consistent effort and sensitivity are especially important when interacting with touchy coworkers and service people. If you are self-employed or run an established business, this is not the year to rest on your laurels. Customers could be more unpredictable throughout 2008. If your commercial interests rely on repeat business, there may be an increased need to continue cultivating and providing extra good sales and service to maintain the loyalty of regular clients.

Changes are likely in daily routines and employment conditions.

You may decide to take a totally different occupational avenue. For some Virgos, alterations on the job could mean relocation or retirement. Singles might meet a new love in the working arena or experience a breakup with a lover. Both events could find one of you opting to leave your current place of employment. For other Virgos, an offer to return to a previous place of employment may be too good to refuse. An ideal scenario would be working with an intimate partner and realizing great benefits.

Jupiter visits all year in Capricorn, your house of love and romance. So Lady Luck will be smiling on you for most of 2008. This is the year you can afford to take a moderate gamble in both love and money. Virgos already in an established relationship might travel more extensively or find a leisure pursuit you and your partner can share on familiar turf. Passion makes its mark. Romantic relations should flourish for the Virgo who chooses to commit and consolidate. Although Virgos in happy unions might decide to walk down the aisle, there may be just as many of you who will play the field, have a good time, and postpone settling down until another year. Some single Virgos may begin a new romantic relationship while traveling for business or pleasure either abroad or within your own country.

Jupiter's influence extends to children, creativity, all forms of leisure interests, speculation, and spending. Spending on recreational pursuits could be an issue if you are inclined to overindulge or waste your hard-earned cash on trivial items. Virgo parents might be guilty of spoiling children or spending too much money on their entertainment. Discovering and immersing yourself in a new creative pastime can lead to much satisfaction. Major family celebrations may be a feature of the year, and the birth of a baby is a possibility.

The influence of Jupiter in Capricorn can be beneficial for Virgo finances. Building toward the future should be a priority. Many of you might decide to try your hand at speculation. As long as your investments are not high risk, gain is more likely than loss. Gambling might also hold more interest for you this year. The same rule applies. Gamble only what you can afford to lose, and you could have a few minor windfalls.

Uranus all year continues merrily through Pisces, your house of relationships. Uranus brings change and excitement to personal and business partnerships. Some Virgos will experience erratic conditions and thrilling surprises in your intimate and casual relationships, alliances, and affairs. Take care if considering entering into a business partnership. Do your homework first and go in with your eyes wide open. July through November, while Uranus is retrograde, presents a chance for you to review or reconsider issues concerning either a business partnership or an intimate union. Unexpected occurrences could affect your significant other or business partner.

Pluto is in Sagittarius, your sector of home and family, during January and from mid-June through late November. Pluto can bring major changes within the family circle that may impact your life. There might be beginnings or endings at home or in your personal life. Moving to another country or state with your parents to improve the lifestyle or for employment purposes is a possibility. Your housing situation could dramatically improve through upgrading or relocation. Carrying out major repairs, renovations, and refurbishing to improve living conditions could occupy a lot of time, effort, and money of Virgo home owners. Pluto is in Capricorn, your sector of leisure interests, late January to June and late November through year's end. With serious Capricorn there may be major negotiations in business, investment, or money earmarked for children. An alteration to belief structures could bring change to your home life. If you are a typical Virgo, you are a gifted and articulate communicator. This talent will be on display even more in 2008 as you argue for and defend the need for significant change.

All year Neptune is in Aquarius, your house of health. Health and hygiene are always a high priority on the personal agenda of Virgo, even more so now. Your strong interest in this area of life sometimes borders on the hypochondriacal. A healthy diet and exercise regime are usually easy for you to maintain. However, this year you could throw caution to the wind and indulge in some serious overeating, drinking, and partying. Virgos who have ongoing ailments or periodic issues with illness may seek an unusual or alternative method to promote healing and to recover overall wellness. Pacing yourself will be important, as bouts of illness could occur through fatigue or overwork. With fluctuating levels of physical energy, make sure to get plenty of vacation time, rest, and relaxation. And daily therapy in the form of meditation, yoga, massage, or physical exercise can reduce stress and anxiety.

With Neptune in Aquarius, many Virgos will begin or continue your interest in healing work of some type, possibly through alternative methods. You may study various aspects of health and medicine to prepare for a career. Difficult to diagnose or sudden nebulous changes in your health could bring confusion and worry. However, regular checkups can reduce any fears that you may have in this regard. May through October, while Neptune is retrograde, is a period when you should be extra cautious with medication, alcohol, and so-called recreational drugs. This period is good for Virgos trying to lose weight. Those of you trying to gain weight may find this task harder.

With Jupiter all year gracing Capricorn, your house of fun, social activities and special occasions are likely to be plentiful. However, take note when the Sun visits the signs of Leo and Aquarius. These are times when vacation should be scheduled and you should slow down to recoup and recharge your energy resources. Periods when you may be more accident-prone exist at the beginning and end of the year, and extra care is required to avert injuries. Virgos who participate in dangerous leisure activities should take extra care throughout the entire year.

The astrological cycles of the Moon and planets can highlight opportune times for you and provide advice as when to begin and complete certain projects. The New Moon phase is a perfect time to initiate something fresh, as this is the beginning of a new cycle. The Full Moon phase indicates the culmination or end of a cycle, and marks a significant change.

As your life ruler, planet Mercury is of prime interest. Mercury goes retrograde three times a year for approximately three weeks each time. In retrograde the planet appears to be moving backward. These Mercury retrograde phases mark a period when time and patience are required. Of equal concern, these retrogrades are periods when you can revisit, reexamine, and rethink plans, situations, and recent decisions. During retrograde periods travel and transportation can be delayed. Equipment, in particular computers, may be subject to problems or breakdowns. A retrograde phase is not an auspicious period to sign new agreements or to purchase major items. Avoid misunderstandings by issuing clear instructions and writing down important messages. Mercury is retrograde this year from January 28 to February 19, May 26 to June 19, and September 24 to October 15.

Good fortune in 2008 is foreseen for Virgos who can quickly adapt to changing conditions and who will happily learn new employment and life skills. The stars are with you in these undertakings.

VIRGO
DAILY FORECAST
January–December 2008

JANUARY

1. TUESDAY. Vibrant. Happy New Year. Virgo emotional contentment is high, the world looks great for you at the beginning of this new month and year. Your energy is elevated, so you might decide to continue celebrating or entertaining at home. However, a few challenging celestial influences lurking in the atmosphere warn against complacency or impulsive risk taking. Be careful with personal safety, especially when working around your home. In particular, pay careful attention when handling sharp or hot objects. Reckless Mars in retrograde motion while opposing intense Pluto discourages rushing around.

2. WEDNESDAY. Promising. Virgo vim and vigor remain high, providing the physical energy to work and play hard. A new opportunity looks promising for those with creative talent and flair. On the negative side, open warfare could erupt between family members or work colleagues. Take care to avoid becoming caught in the cross fire. An accident-prone period continues, urging Virgos to remain vigilant. Drivers should proceed with extra caution and must guard against any involvement in road rage. If you are half of a couple beware a power play with your mate or partner. There is also strong indication that single Virgos may begin a new romance or pick up where a former relationship was broken off.

3. THURSDAY. Stimulating. Mercury, your life ruler, is currently transiting the sign of practical Capricorn, which highlights your house of romance, children, leisure activities, and artistic projects. Creative ideas are likely to come pouring forth. Determination to create a desired environment is strong. Plans and designs based on reality can be inspirational and could even prove life-changing. Impatience is still in the air, advising against any impulsive action. Take it easy on the roads if driving or cycling, If walking, don't run. It is vital to discern between fact and fiction in all dealings with other people.

4. FRIDAY. Encouraging. Virgo enthusiasm is at a peak and will remain that way even though you may encounter a few upsets throughout the day. Early morning focus on writing, teaching, or sales is favorable. Midmorning the Moon slips into Sagittarius, encouraging you to enjoy time off with family members. You may even extend your hospitality by entertaining friends or neighbors. Real estate or home matters are highlighted. You could be taking time to inspect new residences with an intention to purchase or rent. Do a household check to ensure that all appliances are in good working order. There are indications that minor hazards could exist and need correcting.

5. SATURDAY. Varied. Make this a low-key day. It is time to nurture yourself, especially if the last few weeks have been a constant round of hectic visiting and socializing. If you have been spending most of your leisure time entertaining other people, make this a happy family day, relaxing at home. Spend time with close loved ones. Cook a favorite meal or order takeout. Soak your stress away in a nice relaxing bath. If venturing out this evening you should enjoy the chance to shine in a social setting. Singles might encounter an interesting romantic potential who looks promising.

6. SUNDAY. Surprising. Very diverse vibes prevail. You need to spice up your life in order to experience an enjoyable day off. Staying in bed as long as you want can be a positive beginning to the day, and better still if you can convince someone to serve you a healthy breakfast in bed. If you are half of a couple, be prepared for a lack of passion and romance over the next few days as love planet Venus challenges serious Saturn. However, the Sun is getting together with erratic Uranus, creating possible surprises and unusual happenings. Children could bring additional worries or responsibilities for their Virgo parents.

7. MONDAY. Carefree. Even though it is off to work for many Virgos, this should be an easier day than yesterday. A hectic pace is likely as your social world continues to open up and your focus begins to shift toward health, work, and daily routines. Your ruler, intellectual Mercury, moves into quirky Aquarius, emphasizing your employment sector. Look for possible changes in work methods, in conditions, or in staff. Creative energy is strong and should be released into projects geared to financial rewards and emotional fulfillment. A couple of super social invitations may come your way, adding excitement and nervous anticipation.

8. TUESDAY. Inspiring. Today's trends indicate an upsurge of positive energy. Your happy mood is sure to be contagious, evoking an enthusiastic response from other people. A New Moon in Capricorn accentuates your solar sector of self-expression, allowing your creative energy and imagination to flow freely. Focusing on your artistic dreams and working toward achieving these aims should lead to success. If you have been working hard lately, it is time to give yourself the evening off from routine obligations so that you can have fun with loved ones. There is a strong likelihood that the solo Virgo will cross paths with a potential new love.

9. WEDNESDAY. Changeable. Upsets and excitement mark the day. Don't allow annoying details to upset you or slow down positive progress. Coworkers could cause frustration and upset, but your energy would be better spent in some physical activity to keep both body and mind occupied. Changes taking place in the office could also prove unsettling. Midmorning is a period when you may lack detachment or objectivity, so postpone important decision making until later in the day. Conditions are favorable for those involved in marketing, assessing the public mood, or plotting demographic trends.

10. THURSDAY. Uncertain. Irritating issues are likely to crop up this morning, disrupting your schedule. Make the necessary adjustments to ease pressure and reduce stress. If you are not sure where matters relating to a health issue are heading, it may be wise to wait until you have more information. Unexpected upsets in your romantic relationship are likely over the next few days as Venus, planet of love and money, challenges erratic Uranus. An opportunity for a new love affair could arise for singles. Although exciting, it is apt to be short-lived. Take care with money and assets and avoid any type of speculation.

11. FRIDAY. Active. Taking action is the key to the day. If you experience any form of restlessness, get moving and do something to reduce that agitation. Physical exercise could be of benefit. Jog to the gym, climb aboard the treadmill, or go for a bike ride. Later in the day the Moon visits Pisces, your solar house of relating to people. The Pisces Moon encourages Virgo to enter into a spirit of cooperation and compromise if required. When it comes to business matters, make sure you have all the pertinent facts and figures before jumping to conclusions. Your judgment may be skewed. Social activities are likely to be unusually exciting and anything except boring, so enjoy.

12. SATURDAY. Variable. Take a flexible approach and endeavor to be on the ball throughout the day. Otherwise changes or surprises are likely to catch you off guard. An unusual situation that urges you to assist a friend could have unanticipated consequences. Shopping could appeal, but control your spending. The inclination to splurge could do great damage to your bank balance. A romantic encounter should be full of excitement for the unattached Virgo who prepares for the sudden or unexpected. If you are looking for a new friendship or just to have a good time, this evening should provide super experiences at a party or nightclub.

13. SUNDAY. Tiring. It might be difficult to get really motivated because both your mental and physical energy will be sluggish. However, by nightfall you should be raring to go. If you have certain chores to perform, best results will come by prioritizing and sticking to an agenda. Resist the urge to perform tasks that require heavy manual labor or will last a long time. Ultrasensitivity to the needs and moods of those in your daily environment as well as your significant other could become overwhelming. It would be a good idea to allow more emotional freedom in your romantic relationship. Use the day to relax by watching television or indulging in a favored hobby.

14. MONDAY. Difficult. The Moon traveling through aggressive Aries increases Virgo energy and motivation as the new working week begins. However, your patience could be a little lacking. An inclination to be confrontational could find you involved in an argument or dispute with someone at home, a partner, or coworkers unless care is taken to avoid this possibility. You should gain comfort and support from people who share your thoughts and future aims, especially those relating to partnership issues. If you have been waiting for additional funds to be made available, news regarding this may finally be received.

15. TUESDAY. Tricky. Remaining focused could be a challenge as this new day begins. If you become distracted by the antics of other people your progress will be minimal. By midmorning you are apt to be touchier than usual. You might find people more annoying, seeming to encroach into your territory or interfere with the way you handle tasks. You may be on edge for no apparent reason. Others are likely to notice this moody approach unless you make a supreme effort to remain friendly and upbeat. Happier vibes arise later in the day. Singles might discover a romantic attraction in the workplace.

16. WEDNESDAY. Suspenseful. It depends on your current environment as to how this day unfolds. Because positive as well as unhelpful influences prevail, changes and adjustments will need to be implemented to existing plans and schedules. Your artistic sense is heightened and will need a constructive outlet to make use of the flowing energy. Put off arranging a social activity or other large event because an element of strain indicates plans may not come together smoothly. If you are offering advice or assistance, don't be disappointed if your efforts are unappreciated or unnoticed. Listen to music, dance, or go to the movies as a way to unwind this evening.

17. THURSDAY. Disquieting. Frustrations and dissatisfaction could cause anxiety. Pay attention to other people and do your best to communicate as clearly and as calmly as possible. Work pressures could take a toll on your health and patience, increasing stress and the likelihood of arguments with family members as well as with those you work with. If you have been considering traveling or returning to school, this is a positive period to take your goals one step closer to reality by exploring various options. Be prepared to resolve an issue involving long-distance communication with relatives living out of town. Business transactions dealing with family concerns or property require utmost attention.

18. FRIDAY. Demanding. A slight edginess to the day is likely, although feelings of restlessness should be easy to control. There may be some interesting ideas presented. You could discover a novel or alternative approach to solving a perplexing problem and then progressing forward. You might have to deal with an older relative or someone who doesn't grasp whatever you are trying to convey. Try to remain patient. Be mindful of the generation gap and what can and cannot be freely discussed. Virgos traveling for business purposes may encounter a few obstacles and delays, frustrating those who become easily stressed over minor problems.

19. SATURDAY. Stressful. If your enthusiasm is low, make an effort to achieve a more positive attitude. This could be a tough day for Virgo, as warrior Mars currently dueling with saucy Venus will escalate the chances of conflict. Steer clear of touchy neighbors, colleagues, or relatives because finding a suitable compromise for any disagreement that arises is unlikely. Relations and communications with loved ones might be strained due to the amount of time you are spending on the job, away from family responsibilities. Endeavor to alter your routine and find a better balance for everyone's sake.

20. SUNDAY. Reassuring. Relations with loved ones will still be a little shaky as the day begins, then will improve later. Today the Sun, the giver of life, enters the sign of eccentric Aquarius, joining your ruler Mercury and Neptune there in your solar house of health and employment conditions. The Sun visits Aquarius until February 19. So for the next four weeks the focus moves to your daily routines and the more practical things of life. This is an excellent period to examine how you use your time and energy, with an eye to improving efficiency, effectiveness, and productivity. If you haven't started a new health regime, now is the time to begin. Implementing healthy changes to work habits, diet, and exercise can be successful now.

21. MONDAY. Beneficial. Look forward to making steady progress. Gains can be made by pushing ahead with both personal and professional plans. Important discussions, decisions, or changes made now increase the chance of adding more balance and stability in your life. Jupiter and Saturn are happily linked together, providing an opportunity to overcome fears and to expand in a positive manner. This energy encourages you to take love and commitment more seriously, which could find some Virgos deciding to enter into a permanent union. Attached Virgos are likely to feel a resurgence of devotion to their mate or partner. This is an excellent time to organize or prepare for a large social occasion.

22. TUESDAY. Sensitive. Your sense of peace and contentment could be slightly disturbed as emotions and sensitivity begin to run high. Today's Leo Full Moon could arouse concerns or unexpected developments concerning a health or employment issue. Go easy when dealing with coworkers because disagreements could quickly erupt, adding tension to the air. Endeavor to detach yourself from emotional situations by steadfastly going about your daily routine. Ensure that all communications are discreet. Be especially careful when chatting or e-mailing with friends. Repeating gossip or innuendos could strain a friendship or damage your reputation in some way.

23. WEDNESDAY. Useful. Creative juices are flowing, although you may be inclined to isolate yourself from other people. For the sake of your health, this is a good time to schedule a medical or dental checkup or begin a diet that you have been putting off. Follow any professional advice you are given. There may be some hidden issues behind the scenes, advising Virgos who work for a large organization or institution to remain silent about current conditions even if this is difficult to do. Take extra care this evening. There is a possibility of arguments arising with someone at home or who used to live with you.

24. THURSDAY. Arousing. Celestial influences conveyed from love planet Venus can make a huge impact on Virgo people today. Before dawn Venus enters Capricorn, your solar house of creative self-expression, play, and romance. Venus here adds the right amount of encouragement to turn a casual lover into a permanent companion. Her blending with passionate Pluto over the next few days will increase your desire and emotional drive but also jealousy and the potential for possessive behavior. If a current partner is not fulfilling your emotional needs, don't look for greener pastures. Instead take the initiative to turn things around so your fantasies can be fulfilled.

25. FRIDAY. Auspicious. The feminine, nurturing, changeable Moon glides through your own sign of Virgo today, possibly increasing moodiness but also instilling a sense of happiness. Spoil yourself with a few tasty treats, a long relaxing bath, or a beauty treatment. Tonight Pluto, planet of regeneration and transformation, enters Capricorn, your solar house of special interests, children, and love affairs. If you have been waiting for a long time to further develop a special hobby or leisure pursuit, put energy into this now. Children's activities could become more important for parents. Just take care not to exert undue pressure for them to conform or perform.

26. SATURDAY. Opportune. Creative activities remain emphasized. Your special talents and skills can be a wonderful way of generating extra income over the next few years. Your love life is likely to be passionate and intense. Beware being tempted by lust and infatuation rather than love. Remaining in a committed union is the prime choice. An opportunity for new romance could surface for Virgo singles and should work out very nicely. Avoid any tendency to gamble or to speculate in risky ventures. Watch your finances if socializing this evening. Ego or an overly generous attitude could find you overindulging or picking up the tab for everybody else.

27. SUNDAY. Pleasant. If you maintain a healthy balance of give-and-take, this should be a relaxing day. As a Virgo you are naturally inclined to be careful with your money, and this is a day to stick to those principles. Aim to increase rather than decrease your bank balance. Using your creative abilities is one way that the talented Virgo can generate more revenue. Don't allow other people to take advantage of your good nature or your inability to say no to favors, especially if you are not comfortable with the nature of the request. Your ruler Mercury is slowing down, which advises the use of clear and concise discussions when talking to those who share your home.

28. MONDAY. Significant. Tricky Mercury, your Sun sign ruler and the planet responsible for communication, information, and transportation, goes into retrograde motion today and will be retrograde until February 19. Brace yourself, Virgo. Be prepared for delays involving work projects, technical breakdowns, and disagreements with coworkers. Totally unexpected misunderstandings and thwarted plans are also likely. It is up to you to make the decision to go with the flow without becoming stressed and anxious, rather than allowing frustration to overwhelm you. The upside of this celestial phenomenon is that the opportunity is now present to renegotiate, revisit past decisions, and conduct research.

29. TUESDAY. Diverse. A bevy of cosmic trends ensures that this day will be anything but boring. Love and loyalty are featured. For many Virgo singles their love affair will be moving closer to a permanent commitment. For Virgos who enjoy writing and putting thoughts down on paper, this is a great time to document ideas, plots, plans, dreams, and themes. This could even lead to generating more money to enhance your bank balance. If you feel like gambling, and if bets are hedged and stakes are small, you might come out a winner. Realistic investment made now should bring future gains. Just recognize and respect your limits.

30. WEDNESDAY. Helpful. Expect delays, postponements, or cancellations to travel or other prearranged plans. Dynamic Mars moves forward in the sign of Gemini now, which helps to ease any impatience and also to remove obstacles you may be experiencing in regard to a career project or job proposition. Take advantage of any opportunity to make changes in your home and personal life that will increase comfort and security. Money matters should begin to look up, with the possibility of a promotion or pay raise. Virgos who present workshops or lectures for a living can expect to convey the message that the audience wants to hear. Spend quality time with your mate or partner tonight.

31. THURSDAY. Lucky. A social atmosphere prevails now and over the next few days as Venus, planet of the good life, meets up with abundant Jupiter. This is a time to expect luck to come your way in the guise of increased opportunities. Talk about your dreams for the future with a loved one. A social gathering planned for the weekend should be enjoyable and happy. Just make sure you are not overspending or overindulging with regard to lifestyle, romance, or leisure pursuits. A new social venue could be a potential meeting place for singles looking for love as well as good times.

FEBRUARY

1. FRIDAY. Positive. Another happy day greets Virgos as this new month gets under way. There is, however, a need to be careful when it comes to money matters. Generosity toward family members could tend to go over the top if discretion is not enforced. Mixing business with pleasure should prove successful for the self-employed. This is an excellent time to take off on an interstate or overseas trip for pleasure or for business reasons. Legal action currently pending should produce positive results. Currently unattached Virgos should be on the lookout for a new romantic potential, possibly with a friend of a family member. Couples can share happy rapport tonight.

2. SATURDAY. Enthused. The energy that surrounds you is one of inspiration and imagination. Don't hesitate to exploit your creative talents in a constructive manner, which can be a means of improving income. Mental concentration for routine activities may be lacking, so defer activities that require strong focus and attention to detail. Be very cautious with decision making. Read the fine print before signing any important document. Virgo shoppers should watch expenditure because it can be very easy to go on a spending binge. A special family celebration should be successful, giving you the opportunity to kick up your heels and have a great time.

3. SUNDAY. Relaxing. This enjoyable day highlights romance and creative activities. If you find yourself with time on your hands, seek pleasure by researching a new hobby interest that might one day become a passion. If you have been working hard and are feeling stressed, find some time for activities that provide total relaxation. Entertaining and socializing with other people can be a source of enjoyment for many. A new love might be just around the corner for the unattached Virgo who is seeking a new romantic relationship. Partnered Virgos hoping to increase intimacy and affection with that special person should pull out all the stops to create a romantic scene for both of you to enjoy.

4. MONDAY. Satisfying. Have fun and do enjoy yourself even if you are on the job. Make the most of enhanced social skills by spending time with people who may be able and willing to support your progress. Mixing business with pleasure continues to be a plus, especially as a way to increase profits for the business oriented. Virgo parents might need to spend extra time with an unhappy child. Making a concerted effort to understand the difficulties that a youngster is experiencing can go a long way toward resolving the issue in a positive way. An art show, a visit to the movies, or a painting class might keep you pleasantly amused.

5. TUESDAY. Constructive. It could be time to choose a new hobby. If seeking an interesting pastime consider a creative activity that also has a practical application, such as pottery, knitting, or writing. Singles and any Virgo who is lonely could consider purchasing a pet. A small animal can provide a wonderful source of love and affection. This is a favorable time to complete outstanding chores around the house or office. Your motivation for routine tasks is at a high level. Participating in a sports event or physical exercise can be a relaxing form of pleasure. Challenge a friend or a coworker to an indoor game of tennis, handball, or Ping-Pong.

6. WEDNESDAY. Refreshing. An abundance of celestial activity lights up today's sky. Your ruler, intellectual Mercury, and the golden Sun meet up, which will increase your enjoyment in performing work that you take pride in. If you need to raise cash to complete a work project, draw up a business plan and have it ready to present to the bank or other financing agent. Your verbal skills are enhanced, providing the opportunity to speak clearly and concisely. Later tonight an eclipsed New Moon in the sign of Aquarius can aid your effort to establish new practices concerning work, health, or daily routine. There could be positive changes to the way employment duties are performed.

7. THURSDAY. Pleasant. Life is bound to be both busy and pleasant. You are apt to be seriously concentrating on work and career matters, pondering the best way to move forward so that goals can be established and cherished desires reached. Someone in the employment arena may be willing to impart some useful advice, so take the time to listen to ideas and thoughts. Weight watchers need to apply discipline if dining out or socializing because there will be a tendency to overindulge on some of the finer things in life. Use your talents to create a harmonious and pleasing atmosphere.

8. FRIDAY. Fair. There should be no major problems to contend with apart from a couple of minor irritations. However, just because it is the end of the working week it is not the time to slack off. Stay in touch with all that is happening in your environment and remain alert. Not everything is as cut-and-dried as it may appear, so reserve judgment and don't jump to conclusions. Resist any request to lend a large sum of money to a coworker. Even though you may be repaid, it might not be within a reasonable time frame. Take your mate or partner out this evening to a healthy eating establishment and savor spending quality time together.

9. SATURDAY. Foggy. If you wake up feeling a little lost, getting away from everyone and everything could restore some perspective. Over the next few days your head may be up in the clouds and your thoughts and emotions may be slightly foggy. If you are not scheduled to work over the weekend, this is an excellent period to spend time at home resting and relaxing. Or retreat by taking a spontaneous trip for two out of town. Try to bring more fantasy and inspiration into your world. Be creative and consider ways to turn some of your cherished ideas into reality. Young Virgos heading out to a club or party should avoid areas where drink and drugs are commonplace.

10. SUNDAY. Disconcerting. Confusion continues to hamper progress except if you are engaged in creative pursuits. Avoid activities that require focus. In particular, steer clear of working on important paperwork because errors are likely to be made or something crucial may be overlooked. This is not a very good day to interview a prospective roommate. You could be taken in by their promise of assistance with household duties that later turns out to be false. If alarm bells go off in your mind, do some investigating regarding shared financial responsibilities. Make sure everyone is pulling their weight when it comes to mutual monetary matters. Outings today favor museums, the movies, art shows, or concerts.

11. MONDAY. Mixed. Watch out for a couple of minor upsets throughout the day. Issues involving credit and tax matters may need to be put in order to restore peace of mind and avoid potential problems with authorities. Self-employed Virgos should give high priority to overdue business payments or collections, past promises, or important decisions. This is not the time to allow the opinions of other people to alter your course of action or change your mind unless doing so also gels with your current views. You may be looking forward to socializing but there is a possibility that a party, outing, or other prearranged activity will be canceled.

12. TUESDAY. Diverse. It looks like a promising day ahead. Problems that you may be experiencing within a significant relationship require a different approach before a satisfactory resolution can be found. Matters relating to an elderly relative or in-law could come to a happy and successful conclusion. Virgo students taking an exam or completing a training program are likely to be very contented with the final results. If you are waiting on news from an overseas contact or someone living at a distance, information received tonight might not be exactly what you had hoped to hear.

13. WEDNESDAY. Manageable. Keep one step back from the line of fire in the employment arena. Examining and reevaluating your position can help to expand your knowledge and broaden your horizons. Virgos who are the romantic type but haven't yet made plans or booked a restaurant to celebrate Valentine's Day need to get a move on now to avoid missing out. If you will need a babysitter call a family member who owes you a favor. You want to be able to enjoy an evening alone with your mate or partner. Curb the tendency to take on too many employment duties or to make unrealistic promises which are bound to increase your stress level.

14. THURSDAY. Invigorating. This should be a fun Valentine's Day as you combine excitement and good times while remaining practical and responsible. If you have been uncharacteristically unorganized or just plain slack and did not make reservations for this evening, do so first thing this morning. Otherwise all the best venues are apt to be full. Professional matters or dealing with people in authority can produce successful results. By taking the initiative without upsetting colleagues or superiors, you will be moving another step forward toward a special career or vocational goal.

15. FRIDAY. Challenging. It is a good day to take action to advance your career and business aspirations. Communication with your partner or an associate could become a little heated around lunch time. If you must speak your mind, try to be diplomatic and tactful. This might be in regard to the challenges of combining employment responsibilities and the demands of your home life. If upsets threaten to become overwhelming at any point, slow down, reassess your approach, and try to adapt to changing conditions. Getting some fresh air or exercise can also help clear your head and cool your emotions.

16. SATURDAY. Problematic. Issues with a child or with your lover may mar morning activities. Examine the situation to identify the reason this is occurring. A loved one might be displaying bad behavior due to feeling alienated or neglected. Power issues could erupt within a group or organization that you are affiliated with. This might lead to a need to scrutinize the current level of your involvement and commitment. Problems are likely to arise if you are socializing with friends, especially those who are immature. Try to choose responsible, more mature friends to have fun with this evening.

17. SUNDAY. Empowering. Venus, goddess of goodies, visits eccentric Aquarius, your solar sector of work and health, from now until March 12. This is an excellent period to create a more harmonious working environment by updating the office decor, negotiating improved employment conditions, or seeking a pay raise. Work-related duties and responsibilities might change due to new technology and procedures, which should be a positive move that increases job fulfillment. Treating yourself to a small luxury that doesn't break the bank can give you a great reason to smile. Unattached Virgos should be prepared to find love on the job.

18. MONDAY. Rejuvenating. You are likely to prefer your own company rather than socializing or working with a group of people. Take care with whatever you are doing. Keep alert for mistakes. Minor errors picked up now can lessen problems escalating and causing future difficulties. You now have the chance to see past recent setbacks, confusion, and frequent breakdowns. Your ruler, fleet-footed Mercury, is now no longer in retrograde motion, so delays with employment projects, paperwork, or leases should begin to ease. Office equipment that has been causing distress due to failing at inappropriate times should now work as expected.

19. TUESDAY. Bright. The Sun now begins the annual trek through sensitive Pisces and stays there until March 20. Sun in Pisces accentuates your sector of long-term relationships. Cooperation and renewing connections with other people will be important. However, throughout the next four weeks also be prepared for some periods of confusion, when it may be better to let things unfold in their own good time. This is an excellent period to become involved in a team project since your preference will be to work with others rather than alone. Rewards will come if quality time is spent with those you love the most. Singles looking for a relationship should enjoy success if effort is expended in socializing away from work.

20. WEDNESDAY. Stressful. You need to go with the flow over the next couple of days. Emotions heighten due to tonight's eclipsed Full Moon in your own sign of perfectionist Virgo. If nervous tension and anxiety begin to build, it will be imperative to work off steam in a constructive manner. This can put considerable stress on partnership matters as well as showing you just where things stand with the other people in your life. If you have been having difficulties with a client or associate you can now begin to make good headway resolving the situation to everyone's satisfaction. Don't put off attempting to sort out a legal concern.

21. THURSDAY. Varied. There is no way that you can please everyone all the time, so it is futile to even try. Professional and personal relationships could be less than pleasant. Other people will respect you more if you stand up for yourself. You should feel strong and be ready to face whatever challenges are presented. The Moon is gliding through your own sign of Virgo, which accentuates your sense of self and your personality. You could meet or become involved with someone who works in an unusual business, opening your eyes to an area that you never have considered as a potential career choice.

22. FRIDAY. Lively. The working environment livens up due to changes that are occurring. Be on guard when working as part of a team. Avoid bringing up touchy subjects that could add tension to the employment environment. Stay aware of your own body language in case someone should misunderstand your intentions. This is an excellent time to confer with a health consultant or practitioner. Take care of your physical body and overall well-being by pledging to only eat food that is good for you. Tonight listen to music or spend relaxing time in the company of people you enjoy.

23. SATURDAY. Chancy. As the Moon moves into Libra, your solar house of finances and personal values, the potential for positive monetary opportunities increases. Simultaneously, the tendency to spend more than you should also increases. It might be hard to resist going on a shopping spree, especially if you are out and about with your significant other. Endeavor to control impulse purchases if this is against the express wishes of your mate or partner. Increased intensity between you and your loved one is likely to cause some difficulties and possible resentment if you do not openly express your emotional needs.

24. SUNDAY. Disquieting. You need to find a healthy balance between work and rest. Virgo vim and vitality could be lacking. Try to conserve your physical energy. Don't worry if other people call you a lazy stick-in-the mud if you opt not to go out with them. You might prefer to remain true to your normal weekend routine, which will provide the sense of emotional security that is required right now. Partnered Virgos could experience a loss of direction in regard to where your relationship is heading, but hang in there. This is a short passing phase and things should become clearer in time.

25. MONDAY. Reassuring. Don't waste any of your valuable time worrying about matters over which you have little control. Grab today's energy and run with it. Celestial trends indicate that you should have an easier day than yesterday. If you have been expecting to receive a sum of money over the past few days, funds should finally arrive. Your ability to communicate on a deeper level is an attribute that endears you to other people and assists your star to rise. Virgos employed in planning weddings, other social events, and large public functions should have a productive day. If single and seeking to improve your love life, you could find romance at a local community event.

26. TUESDAY. Expansive. On this positive day there should be nothing to burst your bubble. Your mind could be itching to get out and explore new vistas or experience new activities. Business-oriented Virgos can make steady progress by working hard to increase sales and thus improve the bottom line. Employees with an ax to grind regarding working conditions or current pay should be given a fair hearing by those in authority. The unemployed might receive encouraging news about a favorable recommendation supporting a recent employment application. Today offers the opportunity to be more talkative with your nearest and dearest. Tell those you love just how much you care.

27. WEDNESDAY. Deceptive. Misleading trends prevail this morning. Beware of door-to-door salespeople or you could be sold something that is extremely overpriced or is just a dud. Be prepared for disappointment. You might wonder how you could have trusted a coworker or relative so completely after learning that they have let you down. Appointments and interviews are unlikely to convey a sense of security or contentment. Virgos in charge of arranging a staff meeting or study group might be wise to defer the session. Unless discipline is strict, the outcome could be very unproductive, with a lot of talk but very little being accomplished.

28. THURSDAY. Distracting. Not everything is likely to go according to plan. This is a day to be prepared to make changes and alterations without becoming stressed or agitated. Home and domestic concerns may be your first priority. There is a possibility of a disagreement with someone within the family unit. Ask other people to back off if you feel their inference is hindering rather than helping a situation. If you are firm, your wishes should be respected. A situation involving land or property requires that an agreement or arrangement be made sooner rather than later. A romantic relationship with a coworker or employee could hit a bumpy patch.

29. FRIDAY. Fulfilling. You should be in a fine mood. Take comfort in familiar and supportive surroundings and with people you trust implicitly. Join forces with your significant other to create more elegance and ease in your lifestyle and surroundings. Home decorating projects should fare well. Your ability to coordinate color, furnishings, and fabrics is enhanced. An eye for quality also assures that you will keep within a set budget and won't be tempted by fad themes. Someone close to you could spring a surprise later in the day that proves upsetting unless you are on the same wavelength.

MARCH

1. SATURDAY. Unsteady. Practice patience because you are prone to flying off the handle. Delve into a situation and get to the bottom of it. Time alone at home or socializing with family members can recharge your spirits after a busy working week. You might need to obtain extra funding to follow through with a real estate venture. A close relative may be able to provide a short-term loan. Guard against getting into a dispute with a male coworker. A new romance that begins now has a very good chance of progressing into a more serious and possibly permanent relationship.

2. SUNDAY. Romantic. The Moon gliding through your Capricorn sector of love invites Virgo to be more romantic than usual throughout the day. Begin by having a leisurely stay in bed with the Sunday newspaper. Top this off with a late breakfast or brunch at a local restaurant with friends. Over the next two weeks Mars will be opposing Pluto. This planetary aspect warns you to be more vigilant about your personal safety. You are likely to come up against people engaged in power plays and are unlikely to respond well to these types of situations. Nor will it be easy to deal with anyone intent on dominating or getting the upper hand.

3. MONDAY. Unpredictable. A number of minor lunar aspects bring possible changes to your schedule, which might be a blessing. Boredom with everyday routine is a recurring theme as your mind yearns for excitement and greener pastures. Continue to be on guard during this accident-prone period. To avoid domestic and work-related accidents, be extra careful and watch every step. There are apt to be moments of personal revelation as well as confusion. You may crave romantic contact, which could result in crossing paths with an interesting person very different from anyone you have ever been attracted to in the past.

4. TUESDAY. Encouraging. With five planets gathered together in Aquarius, your sector of working conditions and service, your reliability and hardworking traits are now in focus. A new employment situation or connection could be the opportunity you've been waiting for. You are likely to be working extra hard on the job, which could clash with social arrangements and home duties. This is an excellent day to be more active in regard to your health and exercise regime. If you are dining out tonight, avoid foods that have the potential to upset your stomach. And don't stuff yourself or drink too much.

5. WEDNESDAY. Guarded. Dynamic Mars is visiting the sign of Cancer until May 9. Mars in Cancer impacts your friendship circle and accents your cherished desires. Club activities will feature. You can find emotional fulfillment by joining with people who share your interests. Mars is not always happy in the watery depths of Cancer, so be careful with your physical resources because you could run out of steam more quickly than usual. Don't give in to anyone's whims or to anyone who won't supply helpful answers to your questions. You could get a lucky break at work and make a great impression on a higher-up who can provide assistance and support.

6. THURSDAY. Opportune. Enthusiasm and luck are at a high level, increasing your determination to turn ideals and ambition into reality. You may harbor a strong desire to learn as much as possible about your field of expertise. Expanding horizons and increasing knowledge will benefit from teaching a class, taking extra courses, or training that hones your current skills. You may not be very practical when it comes to health, working environment, or finances, so this is not the best time to make any decisions regarding these matters. A new opportunity is likely to arouse increased excitement. This is a good time for endeavors of an artistic nature because your Virgo imagination and creativity are enhanced.

7. FRIDAY. Mixed. The current celestial trends indicate a good day but one on which you should proceed cautiously. Be careful when traveling to avoid an accident. Don't rush into any situation without gathering facts and figures beforehand. Sort out problems as quickly as you can. Dealing with male friends could be tricky, especially at a social function. If possible, steer clear of people who tend to be moody, cranky, or quick to fly off the handle. The dawn of a New Moon in peaceful Pisces provides a chance to experience deeper intimacy and to move closer to your mate or partner. If you have been experiencing difficulties with a business associate or client, take a chance designed to cultivate a more harmonious working relationship.

8. SATURDAY. Stimulating. This should be an easygoing day, although you may be in an unusual mood. As a Virgo you are normally very practical and grounded. Today, however, you might feel restless and out of sorts. If you don't need to be anywhere in particular, do something exciting and out of the ordinary. Your mate or partner is likely to be restless and inconsistent, although only for a short period. Add variety to your activities and take a trip out of town together, or explore parts of the city that you have not visited for some time. Choose stimulating friends to socialize with this evening.

9. SUNDAY. Expressive. Luck and opportunity surround Virgo people. Your life ruler, talkative Mercury, merges with dreamy Neptune, encouraging you to put your best foot forward. At the same time there is a warning to be aware of possible deceptive forces. Expressing yourself with clarity and conviction might not be easy, so refrain from taking part in important discussions that need clear, logical thinking. Virgos who engage in risky leisure pursuits or play a contact sport should be extra vigilant to follow all safety measures. This is not a good time to participate in any high-risk activity, especially if you are a novice or are out of shape.

10. MONDAY. Productive. Consider your next vacation destination if it has been some time since you last went on a trip. Talk to the boss about taking some time off, drop by a travel agency, go online to see what is available. Be discerning and don't believe all that you read in travel brochures. Advertising can make any place sound fabulous. Educational, cultural, and trade-related activities may proceed better than planned and could produce greater than expected financial gains. A love affair is highlighted. Virgos who have a lover living some distance away could receive a surprise visit that is full of passion and romance. Don't settle for words alone when it comes to expressing your feelings.

11. TUESDAY. Constructive. This is another excellent day to plan a real or even a fantasy vacation. Obtaining necessary travel documents, arranging an itinerary, or applying for a passport should proceed without a hitch. If setting off on a business or pleasure trip you can expect a trouble-free journey. A legal matter can be resolved in your favor thanks to expert representation. Don't hesitate to ask tricky questions or challenge anything you do not agree with. If you have considered returning to the classroom either on a part-time or full-time basis, examine various ways to turn these plans into reality. Philosophical or religious topics could be of special interest tonight.

12. WEDNESDAY. Eventful. There are plenty of cosmic vibes to keep you guessing. From today until April 6, Venus, the planet of love and values, visits Pisces. Venus in Pisces will focus your attention on partnership matters and cooperation with others. Virgos who are in business can expect an increase in new contacts and clients, helping to amplify profits and sales. If a new commercial partnership is under consideration, complete your research as soon as possible and begin putting plans into place. For currently single Virgos there may be a new romantic interest to make the heart beat a little faster.

13. THURSDAY. Favorable. A career change or another major event you have been waiting and hoping for could at last develop, putting a smile on your face. Sexy Venus and intense Pluto harmonize together, making this a great day to find new love or, better yet, to adore the one you are with. Deepening of affection is likely to improve your current union. Be open to try something new. Marriage or an engagement might be on your agenda. Lust, love, sensuality, and sexuality will be the motivating forces behind most of your action and reaction now. Settling a legal matter out of court or working out a financial agreement in your favor is a pleasant possibility.

14. FRIDAY. Happy. Influential people should be more accessible, assisting your career or business efforts. Your ruler, communicative Mercury, now joins the Sun, Venus, and Uranus in Pisces, your relationship sector. While Mercury is in Pisces, Virgo thoughts regarding a personal or professional partnership are apt to consume much time and attention. Avid discussions and interesting concepts are likely to be aroused during conversations with close associates or partners. This is a time when you can allow other people to open doors for you and to lead the way. Love and romance remain intense. A marriage proposal could create a most memorable weekend ahead.

15. SATURDAY. Diverse. A mixture of vibes prevails. Your powers of reason are superior right now, aiding your ability to think through any problem to a logical conclusion. Digging beneath the surface to investigate and follow up with more research can be a constructive use of this energy. Just be wary of probing into areas that are none of your concern. If you feel that discussions with someone have been very superficial up until this point, inaugurating an in-depth conversation can be revealing and helpful. Noisy social activities are unlikely to appeal. Turning a leisure pursuit into a group activity may be more pleasurable and an inexpensive way to find relaxation and amusement.

16. SUNDAY. Loving. Amorous trends should help to sweep away any bad feelings conveyed by yesterday's influences. A happy union between dynamic Mars and sultry Venus is likely to make both partnered and solo Virgo a magnet to other people. Current conditions favor your efforts to seek a fulfilling and loving relationship. If you are contributing to the reputation of a group and have been overlooked for special acknowledgment, don't be shy in talking about your considerable contributions and efforts. With Virgo popularity on the rise, opt to socialize with a crowd through the daylight hours. After dark you will prefer to spend time alone or as part of a twosome.

17. MONDAY. Low-key. The manner in which you look at life can determine what you see. Today you might have your blinkers firmly in place. Avoid making any decision that involves an intimate or business issue. Your thinking is likely to be uninspired and unenthusiastic. If you are not happy with a particular aspect of your personal life, now is not the best time to look for solutions. Charitable activities are favored. Sharing your blessings and offering to assist other people can help keep your spirits from falling. However, endeavoring to raise funds for a good cause is likely to fall on deaf ears, so it may be better to leave this work until tomorrow.

18. TUESDAY. Bright. Even though you might prefer to have a quiet day enjoying solitude and peace, this is unlikely to happen. As a Virgo your mental processes are usually enhanced. And today your ruler Mercury links with Mars to put you at your intellectual, energetic, and talkative best. Be prepared for other people to rely on your expertise and wide-ranging knowledge. You will be able to provide assistance on a vast array of topics. Salesmanship is also an area where you can excel. This is an excellent period to get your message across via the written word, an advertising campaign, or public speaking.

19. WEDNESDAY. Excellent. As you greet the dawn, the Moon has already slipped into your own sign, bringing a renewal of energy. Virgo personal magnetism increases. You should feel more comfortable and at home in your own space. Your ability to communicate remains strong, a significant boost if you need to speak to or deal with a large group or organization. You might feel the urge to buy something frivolous to boost your confidence. This is a great time to revamp your wardrobe, alter your hairstyle, or consider cosmetic surgery. A self-improvement or self-growth course can also be a powerful way to enhance your self-esteem. Gaining a new language skill can be a positive learning experience.

20. THURSDAY. Promising. Virgo folk now welcome the spring equinox with the movement of the glorious Sun into the sign of impulsive Aries, which is one of your financial sectors. The emphasis now shifts to long-range financial planning, assessment of your future security, and formulating strategies to achieve goals and ambitions. Payment and collection of debts might need more attention so that you can eventually achieve financial independence. Make a concerted effort to pay off any loan that has been outstanding for too long. This is a period when compromising is not easy but can be vital in successfully revitalizing a stagnant relationship.

21. FRIDAY. Stressful. Powerful energies between the Sun and Pluto collide today, warning that tact and diplomacy are necessary to ease strain and reduce tension. You might put considerable pressure on yourself, which could be the motivation that forces you to challenge other people. It is important not to come on too strong unless you won't mind alienating a loved one or a business partner. Guard against adopting an ambivalent attitude toward authority figures. There is also a focus on monetary concerns, as the Libra Full Moon puts your personal and joint finances under the microscope. This is apt to reveal problems that can no longer be ignored.

22. SATURDAY. Problematic. You are likely to lurch from one crisis to the next. Anxiety about your financial security may seem overwhelming, especially if all you have been doing lately is spending money rather than saving it. Shoppers should try leaving credit cards at home for a change to reduce the temptation to purchase items on sale. If expecting visitors or entertaining guests with children, ensure that valuable personal possessions are out of reach of prying little hands. Otherwise accidental breakage of a treasure could be upsetting. Take an inventory of what you need to do now to improve a significant relationship.

23. SUNDAY. Demanding. Avoid contact with quarrelsome people, and refrain from apologizing if it is not necessary. Practice saying no to those who demand more of your time and attention than you can afford to give. Conflict is possible regarding your spending habits or those of your mate or your partner, especially if you have just moved in with someone new. Sit down together and work out a budget so you each know where money needs to be spent and how much. A child's leisure activities could be straining the budget. You might need to examine alternatives to ease the money crunch.

24. MONDAY. Positive. Communicating is very important today. Listen and observe the reactions of other people, seriously considering their comments as they may see things that you miss. Positive developments could result. This is a good day to clear your desk and get up to date with all outstanding paperwork, especially if you will be going on vacation soon. Someone may be interested in discussing an item you own that is for sale. Make sure it looks its best. If buying or selling a motor vehicle you should be happy with the outcome. Even though it is a Monday, don't hesitate to socialize and relax in the company of other people tonight.

25. TUESDAY. Variable. Mixed celestial trends must be dealt with today. Communicating your thoughts to other people should proceed without any trouble as long as you are not overly analytical in your approach. Satisfaction can be derived from meeting deadlines and challenges. Put your best foot forward and you will reap emotional and financial rewards. Use ingenuity and insight when dealing with partnership problems. Be sure you have a consensus of opinion before making concrete decisions. Social plans with friends are likely to change without much notice, which may work in your favor because you could prefer the thought of a night spent at home.

26. WEDNESDAY. Moderate. It will be wise to take life at a more moderate pace since your energy is apt to be lower than usual. Steer clear of friends or coworkers who tend to be on the aggressive side. Conflict between other people could arise. Even though you are not directly involved and don't feel inclined to become involved, you might be expected to take sides. Don't leave unpaid bills lying around. If you can afford to pay them, do so right away. Otherwise you might forget and incur a late fee. Paying extra money on your home mortgage is a good form of compulsory saving.

27. THURSDAY. Surprising. Mischievous Mercury, your ruler, will make this anything but an ordinary day. Mercury clashes with erratic Uranus but harmonizes with fortunate Jupiter. Unexpected news might cause an initial panic in the household, but a happy outcome is likely. Partners or close associates could feature in a sudden surprise. You will need to wait until things become clearer before moving ahead with any major decision. Buy a lottery ticket with an Aquarius or Sagittarius friend, and luck could smile on you from the sidelines. Any form of buying or selling should keep you on your toes and your bank balance in the black.

28. FRIDAY. Fortunate. Life is definitely going your way, with Lady Luck by your side. Thoughts of love and romance may be on your mind regardless of your age or personal circumstances. The currently unattached could form an unusual relationship that not only takes you by surprise but has the potential to become a lasting union. If you are half of a couple, consider surprising your mate with a weekend retreat or a candlelight dinner for two. Take advantage of today's romantic vibes to strengthen your loving bonds. Moderation is needed if socializing this evening. Resist an inclination to overindulge in the good things of life. Don't let anyone talk you into anything.

29. SATURDAY. Lively. Yesterday's positive and lucky trends continue. Virgos who have recently fallen in love at first sight are apt to linger in a dreamy mood, unable to focus on the simplest of activities. Artistic and creative pursuits are highlighted. You will obtain emotional fulfillment following your own imagination rather than resorting to other people's inspiration or ideas. Wait awhile longer to hold out the olive branch or give in. If you have been at loggerheads with a particular friend, this is not the day to make peace. The more you try to compromise and get along, the worse the situation might become. Spoil yourself with a special dinner tonight.

30. SUNDAY. Playful. You may feel like playing rather than taking care of routine chores. Patience might be in short supply, signaling that it is time to rest, relax, and be kind to yourself. Don't become involved in any risky recreational pursuit. Be extra careful if participating in a sports activity. A massage, sauna, or long soak in a hot tub could be an enjoyable way to nurture yourself and relieve pressure and tension from your body and mind. Partnered Virgos could feel a strong need to share intimate feelings and moments with that special person. An hour or two in the garden or a local park might make you feel more attuned to nature and in touch with the simpler things in life.

31. MONDAY. Manageable. An easygoing mood is likely even though this is the first day of the new working week. Getting plans off the ground will depend on your presentation and how your ideas and concepts are sold to other people. Speak up if you notice ways to improve the work site or office environment. Even if someone grumbles, more than likely they will agree with your assessment and assist with the changes. A new exercise or diet regime should proceed smoothly if you are committed to making positive changes to enhance your overall health and lifestyle. A romantic relationship with a colleague could begin to blossom.

APRIL

1. TUESDAY. Accomplished. You are capable of achieving a tremendous amount on the job if you look at the larger picture. Don't let yourself become bogged down with minor details. This is a good day to fill in forms, tackle red tape, or establish a more efficient way of handling routine chores. Be restrained with your diet. Drink plenty of fresh water and incorporate a moderate amount of exercise in your day to enhance general wellness. An hour at the local gym or a friendly tennis match after work can be a pleasant way to work out. Finish off the day on a high note by stimulating your palate this evening with a healthy, delicious meal.

2. WEDNESDAY. Active. Significant cosmic energy provides plenty of activity today. Virgos who work independently should experience favorable conditions with employees, service providers, and vendors, increasing productivity and potential financial gains. Discussions may take a serious turn regarding a business partnership or another type of joint venture. Your ruler, busy messenger Mercury, is now visiting Aries, one of your financial sectors, and creating plenty of discussion about shared resources and partnership assets. Hidden desires and secrets could be revealed, causing embarrassment if you have something to conceal.

3. THURSDAY. Interesting. Establish priorities early this morning in order to accomplish a fair share of the workload. Pluto, planet of transformation, went retrograde yesterday in Capricorn, your solar sector of romance and leisure. As a result changes you were hoping for could be stalled. However, a former investment of time, talent, money, or energy could now begin to pay off in a positive way. Friends or associates may have interesting ideas or stimulating possibilities to be considered. You are apt to be more thoughtful and intense than usual. It would be wise to keep your thoughts to yourself, at least while you are out and about in public.

4. FRIDAY. Guarded. Leave home in plenty of time if punctuality is important this morning. Confusion, delays, or mix-ups could hinder progress. A significant other might need more attention than you have been giving. Spend more quality time as a twosome, and sort out any issues that you have been avoiding. Virgos with work-related worries should discuss problems fully with a trusted and respected colleague to gain another perspective and to increase trust. An urgent matter regarding your financial affairs might require a quick solution. Set aside quiet time to concentrate on this worry, which is apt to be more complex than paying overdue accounts or balancing bank statements.

5. SATURDAY. Rewarding. Today's New Moon is the chance for renewal and to begin new projects. This New Moon culminates in Aries, the sign of initiative, giving you a chance to begin something new as well as test possible improvements by trying new techniques. Information you received recently regarding a joint financial or legal matter may not have been helpful at the time but could now be clarified, with a more positive outcome likely. Take stock of your financial status. Consider combining a number of small loans into one larger loan with a smaller repayment. Also check mortgage rates and review all of your insurance coverage.

6. SUNDAY. Auspicious. Venus now visits Aries, joining the Sun, Moon, and Mercury here in your sector of love and money. Virgo thoughts are focused on gain. A financial plan or scheme could be taking good shape, but sit back and think clearly rather than rushing into anything right away. Over the next few weeks love and passion are likely to become very steamy. A number of romantic encounters are more than likely for the solo Virgo. Venus tonight will clash with Pluto, which can cause dramatic upheavals and altered circumstances. Consider removing household items and general clutter that you no longer need in order to add energy to your personal space.

7. MONDAY. Supportive. A loved one who is experiencing problems with money management needs your expertise to help sort out problems. If you have something important to convey involving family property, finances, or an estate matter, a one-on-one discussion conducted in private will be more successful than speaking to several family members at one time. Reach out and contact someone living at a distance, especially if it has been some time since you caught up with their news. Virgos interested in learning more about the stock market should consider enrolling in a course.

8. TUESDAY. Low-key. A slow start will help you ease back into work routine. Confusion is likely to reign throughout much of the day. The pleasant Taurus Moon sailing through your solar sector of spirituality can relieve some of the pressure. However, irritating situations could make you tend to let off steam or become overly stressed. Paperwork is likely to pile up, and you might have to deal with bureaucratic hassles that demand more time and attention that you can afford to give. Plan to spend leisure periods doing whatever lifts your spirits. If you can convince someone to take you out for dinner or to cook at home, all the better.

9. WEDNESDAY. Manageable. Today's slightly restless atmosphere can be reduced by incorporating fresh air and exercise into your schedule. Accepting any responsibility that comes your way in the working arena is one way to be noticed. Someone in authority is apt to be watching your performance. If you are the one carrying most of the weight at home, this is a good day to reorganize a list of chores or make arrangements with those you live with regarding who will be handling domestic responsibilities. If conflict exists with a loved one over money, work to resolve your differences in a positive manner.

10. THURSDAY. Challenging. Expect a demanding day. Try not to exaggerate or blow anything out of proportion. There is a tendency to only see things your way. If someone you have to deal with seems a little cranky or irritable, give them a wide berth. Find another way of handling the situation, or let things slide for the time being. You might be in the mood for some retail therapy, but make sure you don't go over the top and blow the budget in one shopping spree. Although you are bound to be in the mood for romance, be careful not to spoil the moment by being contrary or too demanding.

11. FRIDAY. Pressured. Something you thought had been cleared up may need additional clarification. A number of problems are likely, forcing you to put on your thinking cap to seek unusual solutions to resolve these matters satisfactorily. If you need to conduct research for a special project or homework assignment, gathering appropriate information may be a struggle. It might be wiser to concentrate on revising your notes instead. Virgo students taking exams are also unlikely to find the going easy. Friends may call or drop by and ask you to join them in a social activity, which can be a great way to unwind after the busy week.

12. SATURDAY. Good. A thorough approach is needed before you take any action. It would also be wise not to accept anything at face value. Virgo entrepreneurs can make good progress by setting priorities and eliminating nonessential duties. A number of small achievements can add up to something much bigger by the end of the day. Expanding your friendship circle should be easy. Energetic Virgos might decide that going for a hike, playing a sport, or entering a marathon would be a pleasant diversion. Those with less interest in active pursuits might prefer to join a group of like-minded people to discuss a book or critique a play.

13. SUNDAY. Revealing. Your creative ability is heightened, allowing you to enjoy exploring your talents and assessing your expertise. An imaginative friend might invite you on a fantasy adventure that takes you all over the world, stirring creative juices and the artist within you. This is a starred time to examine the past or to review an old situation, even if just to see how far you have advanced. You might want to consider returning to a project, practice, or hobby that you haven't devoted much attention to lately. Make time for rest and relaxation. If you are having any health problem, consider meditation, yoga, or an alternative therapy. Be sure to go to bed early and get plenty of sleep.

14. MONDAY. Creative. This is another day when artistic potential is written in your stars. Do not hesitate to act on creative impulses more readily than usual. Judgment regarding concrete matters might be a bit foggy, however, so it is advisable to delay making any important decisions. Your ruler, intellectual Mercury, is forming an easy link to whimsical Neptune. So you might believe that just because you want something it will automatically happen. This is a positive time to follow your dreams, as long as they are based on reality. A desire to enhance romance and affection can assist Virgos in a committed union to go all-out in an effort to strengthen the bonds of love.

15. TUESDAY. Energetic. Increased energy and stamina should be readily available to Virgos today. Keep advancing your special plans and personal schemes. New and positive happenings could eventuate, with the Moon gliding through your own sign. You should be in an optimistic and sunny mood, ready to soak up any exciting experience that comes your way. It might be time to update your wardrobe and introduce a new style and image. If you are romantically attached, don't go overboard in any way. It would be wiser to plan an evening at home as a couple. Sharing time with friends could result in unnecessary tension between you and your loved one.

16. WEDNESDAY. Active. As the Sun and your ruler, thoughtful Mercury, come together in your financial zone, your attention turns to getting rid of debt and increasing financial stability. If you missed the deadline for filing taxes, today's cosmic influences can assist concentration and help you get through this job quicker than usual. Sorting out an insurance problem or obtaining a quote to cover personal possessions should be a breeze, providing competitive prices that you are willing to pay. If your bank is not giving the kind of service you want and deserve, consider changing financial institutions.

17. THURSDAY. Variable. Some people in authority might be irritable or touchy throughout much of the day, adding tension to the air. Your ruler, quick-witted Mercury, darts into Taurus this afternoon, and will turn your focus toward education and travel matters. Virgo students could find that this energy helps you to learn. Your mind will slow down, allowing you to absorb more facts and information. If you are planning to take a vacation, this is an excellent period to do some research and check out destinations that you find appealing and suitable for family requirements. Virgo business owners should look to foreign markets for import and export opportunities.

18. FRIDAY. Expressive. Mercury now is happily linked with stable Saturn and intense Pluto. Your mind should be focused, particularly on practical matters. It will be hard for other people to divert your thoughts away from responsibilities or the tasks at hand. Your ability to totally concentrate on work or personal obligations can help you with jobs that need meticulous attention to detail. This is not the time to become involved in a situation where you are required to make quick decisions. It would be wise to assess things thoroughly, analyze, and carry out your research first. Insight and profound thoughts are apt to surface, and you will not be afraid to have your say.

19. SATURDAY. Expansive. The world might seem to be much more interesting now that the Sun is moving into Taurus and joining your ruler Mercury there. Sun in Taurus encourages Virgo people to take a wider view and to expand horizons. This is a perfect time to plan a long vacation, to organize a business trip overseas, or to return to formal classroom study. Money matters feature in the day. You need to remember that you have a budget limit that must be adhered to in order to meet a number of your goals. Treat the family to diverse new cultural or culinary experiences that will whet their appetite for more.

20. SUNDAY. Bumpy. You might want to rest and recover from recent strenuous activities that have kept you occupied. Take a little extra time in bed this morning, then treat loved ones to brunch at a favorite restaurant. If tension exists with a sibling or other relative, try to steer clear or remain in the background. The Scorpio Full Moon can increase the potential for bottled-up emotions to pour forth, causing a scene or a clash of wills. Be careful when making decisions or judgments. If possible, delay coming to any final conclusions. An in-law could issue an invitation that proves to be life changing.

21. MONDAY. Easygoing. The pressure of the last few days should ease somewhat, enabling your focus to return to long-term goals and aims. Although there may be important changes taking place in your life, you have the self-discipline to utilize this energy constructively. General communication and dealing with authorities are likely to feature, and the outcome should have a positive effect on your progress. Read as much as you can. Virgos with an inclination to write might decide to keep a journal of experiences or begin writing a book that could serve to help other people. Make sure thoughts are recorded in your own words to avoid any hint of plagiarism.

22. TUESDAY. Eventful. Keep your schedule simple and flexible to ensure getting through the jobs on your agenda before tedium takes over. An attraction to the unusual could find you crossing paths with people you have not seen for a long time. Contracts and legal concerns feature, and you should be able to sort out any minor glitches quickly. Virgos should perform very well in any interview or audition. If you are looking for a change, check out the help-wanted advertisements. Refrain from impulsive action; however, a well-calculated risk could lead to successful achievement.

23. WEDNESDAY. Suspenseful. An affair connected to either love or money is about to experience change or new developments. Venus, the love goddess, is out on a limb, clashing with both testy Mars and giant Jupiter; these planetary aspects will boost drive and emotional desire. A craving for excitement could find the unattached Virgo mingling in different circles while seeking love or a romantic involvement. Finding a happy balance may not be easy. Partnered Virgos in a contented arrangement can expect to enjoy the passionate influences conveyed now. These of you going through a rough period might find that differences are highlighted even more.

24. THURSDAY. Tricky. More challenging trends are sent by the universe today. Jolly Jupiter and warrior Mars go head-to-head, which warns Virgos not to take risky action or overestimate personal abilities. Guard against making promises that may be difficult to keep or are not within your direct control. Mothers-to-be may get interesting news about upcoming childbirth. If someone is being offered or given special treatment that you feel is undeserved, this is not the day to take up the challenge. Gather more facts before speaking out. Opportunity may come through friends or a social occasion. Examine a recurring dream to figure out its message.

25. FRIDAY. Sparkling. A bevy of celestial forces beams down again today, giving Virgos a tendency to daydream. Remaining focused on routine work might be a challenge, because the Moon is transiting your Capricorn house of leisure and pleasure while Venus in Aries and Neptune in Aquarius are harmonizing with each other. Creative activities are favored. Imagination and inspiration are on a high, urging you to take the day off and let artistic juices flow. Music, painting, and poetry are art forms that could especially appeal to you. Flights of fantasy can stir the romantic side of your nature, setting the scene for love with your significant other.

26. SATURDAY. Empowering. Virgo parents might feel slightly overburdened by responsibilities regarding youngsters, especially if their recreational pursuits are straining the household budget. If they are old enough to understand the value of money, it might be time to discuss options and then choose what activities can be cut in an attempt to reduce expenditures. Taskmaster Saturn and transformative, Pluto are working in unison to bring constructive change into your personal and romantic life. Positive advances can be made that will impact your life in a meaningful manner. Consider learning a discipline such as yoga or meditation to reduce stress and increase overall wellness.

27. SUNDAY. Excellent. Enjoy this happy and fortunate day. Your mind is sharp and your imagination is lively. No serious work should be allowed. Variety and a change of pace are required, and there will be plenty of time for routine obligations and responsibilities during the coming week. Foreign, bizarre, or original themes are likely to arouse your interest. You can find an unusual solution to just about any problem you confront. By day's end you might welcome new challenges, which will provide insight into how you are handling issues and dealing with other people. It is time for a family get-together or dinner with friends to break away from your usual Sunday evening entertainment.

28. MONDAY. Uplifting. Communications with those living overseas should be successful, assisting Virgo entrepreneurs or those who need to contact foreign agencies or companies. If you are considering long-distance travel, this is a great time to make final plans and organize your itinerary. Virgos who are already on vacation can look forward to happy travels. There is also a high probability that solo Virgos may enter into an overseas love affair. Artistic types could find their talents reaching new heights. It is a fine time to further expand your creative imagination, even if this requires breaking away from old traditions or methods.

29. TUESDAY. Misleading. There are elements of delusion or deception at work today, suggesting that you need to carefully examine everything in detail before leaping in. This is not a good time to approach your boss for a favor. Virgo employees considering asking for time off should defer doing so because the request might be refused, especially if you have used up all of your vacation days. Even though your mental capacity is sharp, take care when passing on messages. Issue clear and concise instructions to guard against confusion and misunderstandings with coworkers. Verify information received since important omissions or distortions are possible.

30. WEDNESDAY. Peaceful. Happier trends prevail, with the likelihood of good fortune arriving on your doorstep. Goddess Venus enters her own sign of Taurus, joining the Sun and Mercury. This opens up even more opportunities for Virgos involved in foreign activities, traveling abroad, or getting a degree. Those of you taking part in a legal challenge should experience a more positive outcome than envisioned. Dealing with people abroad is still a major focus and a potential source of financial gain. Social affairs are likely to be enjoyable. You could meet influential people who can help you reach a special goal.

MAY

1. THURSDAY. Loving. Romance is in the air as you enter this new month. Seductive Venus and controlling Pluto are more than happy to put extra love and passion into your love life. Virgos traveling abroad could fall very quickly for a temporary companion. Even if this is not your eventual soul mate, the memories you make will be remembered forever. If there are any legal issues hampering your enjoyment of life, this is the day when you can arrive at a positive solution. New opportunities could provide future financial gains if you are able to spot them now.

2. FRIDAY. Opportune. Communications are highlighted. You could receive some important news. Accomplishments will add up thanks to your mental agility and sharp thinking, which increase from now until July 10 while your ruler Mercury is visiting Gemini. Gemini, the other sign Mercury rules, represents your solar house of vocation and business activities. Improved business and financial deals are possible. This is a good period to lay the foundation for a new beginning. Your analytical ability will help you find the solution to a prolonged issue. Don't be shy about speaking up. Colleagues in the working arena are likely to be impressed by what you have to say.

3. SATURDAY. Significant. You are apt to be very conscious of today's sluggish atmosphere which will limit and restrict your activities. Your ruler, tricky Mercury, is challenging both serious Saturn and powerful Pluto. This warns Virgo folk to move slowly with plans, deals, or financial negotiations. In addition, this is not the best day to purchase a new vehicle or to take a driver's test. Late last night Saturn turned forward in your sign of Virgo. Saturn here will give you increased energy and motivation, boosting your staying power. A business meeting might be mandatory but not very productive.

4. SUNDAY. Serene. Make the most of this very positive day to express innermost thoughts to your nearest and dearest. If the weather is good, enjoy relaxing and communing with nature. Walking, hiking, visiting a park, or spending time in your own garden could appeal. A pleasant interlude might also be found experiencing scenic vistas and a special social scene. Your mind is ready to open up to what exists outside your immediate environment. This is an excellent day to make overseas travel plans or arrange a family vacation closer to home.

5. MONDAY. Renewing. This morning's New Moon in Taurus opens up the highway to broaden your outlook and widen your horizons. Learning, legal matters, overseas contacts, or distant travel will feature in the day. Positive developments are likely in one or more of these areas. Look ahead and set a course for future progress. Include further education as one of your goals, even if this involves part-time classroom study, workshops devoted to a hobby interest, or a training course to enhance your employment skills. In the romance department, try not to overanalyze everything that occurs. Instead, just go with the flow.

6. TUESDAY. Uncertain. An authority figure on the job could be on the warpath, so make sure to put your best foot forward and stay under the radar. Although this may mean you do not have the freedom you'd like, at least you will avoid bringing trouble down on your head. The outcome of a difficult decision that was made recently could prove much more positive than you first anticipated. Include art galleries, cathedrals, and historical buildings in your vacation itinerary if jetting off overseas in the next few weeks. If socializing this evening guard against an inclination toward decadence or an overly generous attitude toward other people you barely know.

7. WEDNESDAY. Problematical. You are apt to experience extremes of emotion, from buoyant to frustrating. Concern regarding an overdue task could put you in a position of responsibility. Enjoy the surge of power that is likely to come from this. At the same time, do not take on more than you can handle within the allocated time frame. If you have to confront a troublemaker in the workplace, utilize all of your powers of tact and persuasion to bring about a satisfactory resolution. This afternoon you should be ready to shake off the shackles of conventionality and do things your own way.

8. THURSDAY. Revealing. Virgo is the sign of service to others, but sometimes you may not do enough to nurture yourself. Make time for yourself today. Consider all of your achievements so far this year. If you are not advancing toward your goals fast enough, rethink cherished desires and devise new strategies to help you move forward at a quicker pace. A friend who asks for an honest opinion could put you in a difficult position. You might need to consider whether it will be better to tell the unvarnished truth or whether to sugarcoat it. Even if a major purchase is needed, select it with care. Find a companion to share your interests and ideas this evening.

9. FRIDAY. Important. From today until July 1 dynamic Mars visits Leo, your twelfth house of private affairs. Mars here gives you a chance to slow down and work on plans in solitude. Although Mars always tend to provide more energy and enhance the need for power, while Mars is in Leo you should conserve your resources. Be more aware of signals from your body that could indicate a health problem. Use your good Virgo intuition to avert or work around opposition that comes from outsiders. Focusing on developing your creative skills can pay future dividends. Feelings of closeness are likely to significantly increase toward those people you trust completely.

10. SATURDAY. Soothing. Set aside time for extra rest and relaxation this morning. Let your probing Virgo mind wander and reflect on important insights. Yesterday Jupiter, planet of wisdom, started to go retrograde in Capricorn, your solar sector of creativity, children, and leisure interests. Jupiter retrograde here until September 8 gives you a chance to review your relationships with a lover or with young people as well as on what you choose for entertainment and education. For today make sure what you pick for amusement does not tire you out. If you are feeling run-down or stressed, a gentle workout will relieve aching muscles and joints. And be sure you are following a balanced diet.

11. SUNDAY. Gratifying. Today's mood should be lively but not hectic. This is another good day to slow down and avoid rushing through tasks. Take the time to satisfy your inner needs and recharge your batteries. Creative projects or your spiritual life might be your choice of activity to occupy leisure time in a productive manner. Going all-out to splurge on yourself or loved ones is fine for those with money to spare but not if you are on a limited budget. A desire to help the needy is admirable and can provide emotional satisfaction, but don't allow an overly generous approach to lead you into debt.

12. MONDAY. Lucky. Although you might feel like being alone for the first half of the day, this is not the best time for solitary activity. Sun and Jupiter, two of the powerbrokers in the zodiac, are happily linked. So a perfect opportunity is presented to tap into luck, love, and all the good things of life. Think positively, and if you need help ask for it. Write out a wish list to attract more abundance into your life. Virgo singles should find the possibility of love in all sorts of unique places, especially for those on vacation at home or overseas. Mixing business and pleasure can produce gains. Traveling for commercial purposes can be particularly profitable.

13. TUESDAY. Variable. Good luck continues. The Moon in your own sign shifts the focus to personal growth and accomplishments. Diligence and strenuous effort on the job or at school are likely to be noticed and rewards may be forthcoming. Reinventing yourself by altering your appearance, style, and manner of communicating can be beneficial and will be recognized positively by other people. If something private needs attention, now is the right time to focus on it. Virgos currently in a romantic relationship should be careful because a third party could play a major part in creating a rift between you and your mate or partner.

14. WEDNESDAY. Mixed. A few difficulties are likely to arise. Energy and efficiency may be at a low level, causing lethargy and reducing motivation. However, with the right attitude you have a good chance of getting what you want and making some progress. You may have delusions or high expectations about current working conditions, a homework assignment, or even a love affair. Avoid discussing issues of a controversial nature, especially religion, politics, or beliefs because general conversation could escalate into a heated debate. Your judgment may be clouded, so this is not the best day to make concrete decisions.

15. THURSDAY. Vague. Minor confusion continues, indicating that caution is needed in all financial matters. You are apt to be indecisive about what might be considered a luxury purchase, so defer buying. Instead create a new household budget that adds financial security. Ask your partner or another household member to help if you cannot decide which expenses need to be trimmed. You could feel that your self-esteem is lower than it should be. Consulting a professional counselor could provide beneficial advice that helps to restore your self-confidence and self-esteem. Getting to know other people depends on being willing to apply effort.

16. FRIDAY. Successful. Meetings could keep you busy. You need to focus on career priorities if you hope to get ahead. Let domestic responsibilities take a back seat, at least for a short while. Use morning energy for important decision making, negotiations, and financial dealing. This is also a good day to check creative pursuits and projects that you are considering. Patience is required midafternoon. Those of you working later may be inclined to disagree with the boss or another authority figure. It would be advisable to hold your tongue and think twice before saying something that could cost you dearly.

17. SATURDAY. Changeable. Ask other people to share domestic chores if you are usually the one left to carry the whole load. Virgos facing speaking in public or presenting a seminar need not panic. As long as you pay attention to detail you are bound to excel. If you are required to work today you should experience increased productivity. This is an excellent time to network or to be involved in a public relations event. A long walk will do wonders if you are seeking a pleasant way to get some physical exercise. Lack of self-confidence could hamper Virgo singles in the romance department this evening.

18. SUNDAY. Romantic. Luck and love mark the day. Excitement and variety are a plus for those looking for love and romance. Virgo couples can use positive energy to strengthen loving bonds. Singles should search for a romantic potential in an unusual venue. Don't be surprised if you are fascinated by someone who doesn't fit your usual type. Even if love doesn't last long, you can enjoy the experience and the emotional rewards. Control an urge to splurge. There is a tendency to be drawn to expensive luxury items. This is a great day for those hosting or attending a party because you should be at your most charming and sociable.

19. MONDAY. Sensitive. A bad-tempered atmosphere may prevail today, making many people both grumpy and disagreeable. An intense Full Moon in Scorpio is likely to strain personal relations. You and those in your immediate environment might be inclined to take comments too much to heart. Avoid being drawn into a discussion that could cause friction, particularly involving politics, the environment, or religion. A problem with an older relative needs to be sorted out quickly. Try to take care of their needs without neglecting your own personal responsibilities. Money might flow out as fast as it comes in.

20. TUESDAY. Helpful. Today's bevy of cosmic influences is all good for Virgo people. New horizons are likely to open up on the career front. Beneficial opportunities could arrive as the Sun moves into quick-witted Gemini, your career and business sector. Your motivation increases to take important action that will positively affect your future. The effort you apply could attract the notice of someone in a position of authority. Imagination and creativity are enhanced, and you may even be inspired to produce a masterpiece. Virgo lovers should take off those rose-colored glasses and realize that some promises are unlikely to ever be fulfilled. Trust your good instincts when it comes to romance.

21. WEDNESDAY. Fortunate. Even though there could be some tension regarding career or business matters, generally the mood should be upbeat and optimistic. Luck and expansion are the key to making this a positive day. Don't be surprised if a number of happy coincidences occur. Time spent negotiating for your future security can be very constructive. Matters relating to children, travel, sports, or speculation are under favorable aspects. An evening at home with family members or good friends could be fun. If eager to offer hospitality, plan a dinner party. A small gamble could pay big dividends.

22. THURSDAY. Pressured. Expect a demanding day. Your patience is likely to be tested by people and situations on the job. There might also be some criticism and objection from work colleagues, associates, or an authority figure. Remain cool and calm. This influence will pass tomorrow, so try not to push yourself too much. Motivation might be at a low ebb. Adding some variety to your routine could spice up the day and help overcome lethargy. Be sure to research creative projects and possibilities thoroughly before progressing too far. This is not a day to take speculative risks, including commercial operations.

23. FRIDAY. Flexible. Try to devote part of the day to children or to your significant other. You might think that you do not have time for your own problems let alone to give loved ones the attention that they deserve. However, consider spending quality time instead of quantity time. This is not a favorable day to stick your neck out in a business or financial venture. Virgos traveling for business reasons could encounter a few obstructions and delays that are aggravating unless you remain cool, calm, and in control. Those without family responsibilities could get involved in a creative project that is not only enjoyable but potentially a reputation maker.

24. SATURDAY. Auspicious. Venus, planet of beauty and style, now moves into Gemini, the sign of the thought processes and your solar house of vocation. Venus visits Gemini until June 18. Career or professional matters will feature prominently throughout this period. Many Virgos are likely to be on the move. Traveling, mixing business with pleasure, or hosting a social function to sell special products can be profitable. Those involved in promoting beauty, artistic, or feminine goods can expect a large increase in business. Commercial retail outlets started now should fare well. Teaching, lecturing, and writing a novel are other areas where Virgos might expect to excel.

25. SUNDAY. Useful. With the Moon slipping through Aquarius, your health house, ask yourself whether you need to change your lifestyle in any way. Physical exercise, whether a gentle sport or lifting weights, will help strengthen you physically, mentally, and emotionally, adding resilience when life becomes tough. Tone down possessive and jealous tendencies or you risk losing the respect of other people. Even if all you are seeking is the best for loved ones, stifling their independence is not the way to show you care. If people who you perceive as powerful make you feel uncomfortable, perhaps it is time to reestablish your own power base.

26. MONDAY. Tricky. It is Mercury retrograde time again. Your ruler will appear to be moving backward in the sky from now until June 19, causing irritating delays and mix-ups. You could experience the most frustration with career and business matters, so it would be wise not to begin projects, sign an important lease, or draw up contracts throughout this period. Defer purchasing major business equipment and keep computer data backed up. To establish a healthier you, aim to correct any bad habits. Reorganize your desk and filing system. Ideally it would be better to avoid making travel arrangements, especially if this is for employment purposes only.

27. TUESDAY. Confusing. Keep a low profile if possible. Other people may seem more irritating than usual, as if nothing is good enough or they do not know what they really want. There could be a battle of wits with those on the job, or issues with a competitor. You might feel that you can't work in your usual efficient style. Try not to take on more than you can comfortably handle, and make sure that others carry their fair share of the workload. Delusional Neptune is going retrograde in Aquarius, your health and work house. This makes for an unrealistic attitude, confusion, and deception. Disappointment is foreseen when an overly optimistic plan falls through.

28. WEDNESDAY. Encouraging. This will be a fair day, although some areas of life might not be as good as envisioned. Burying your head in work is the best option. You can get along well with other people in completing a special job or project. Inspiration and motivation come with new ideas and concepts. Be prepared to look outside of the square and to break with tradition. Welcome originality and a different approach to old problems or situations. Spend some time reducing clutter from your environment. Discard household items and clothes no longer needed, donating them to a worthy local charity or planning a garage sale.

29. THURSDAY. Productive. This is another day when the cosmos sends difficult vibes. However, steady effort can equate to achievement if you apply yourself. Look into obtaining credit or a loan as the way to get through a short-term financial problem. Do the research but wait until your ruler Mercury moves forward before signing important paperwork. Do not allow other people to pressure you into overlooking the risky aspects of a business or commercial deal, especially if you are not comfortable about the possible outcome. A minor issue could lead to trouble in your romantic paradise this evening unless emotional content is removed from a discussion and views are stated calmly.

30. FRIDAY. Unsteady. Romance and your emotional life are in the spotlight. Expect some ups and downs to upset your equilibrium. Tension or disputes with your mate or partner over money matters might develop, especially if leisure expenses are spiraling out of control. Don't let these ruin any chance of saving for a major purchase. Restless urges are likely and could be your downfall unless moderation is exercised. A special dinner for two could help smooth over a romantic relationship that has been experiencing problems. Take care that self-indulgent pleasure doesn't ruin your evening or frighten away potential romance.

31. SATURDAY. Favorable. If you have no choice other than dealing with business matters, accounts, or tax issues, be sure to go over every detail carefully. Expect to make adjustments to your entertainment budget if your finances are not stable. You might benefit from discussing with your mate or partner the joint budget, and you may be surprised at their offer of the cooperation to reduce expenses. A better understanding of joint goals can also follow. This is a favorable day to engage in romantic pursuits. You should be closely attuned to your partner's thoughts and needs. Singles could try something different when seeking pleasure and new faces tonight.

JUNE

1. SUNDAY. Vexing. Expect some disconcerting influences as this new month gets under way. Communications from someone at a distance are likely to upset your day. Make sure you have a fully stocked fridge because you might be unexpectedly hosting an overnight visitor. Further insight, enthusiasm, and understanding can be gained by exploring religion, philosophy, or other interesting topics. Visit your local library, browse the nearest bookstore, or surf the Web to find out more about a subject of interest. Virgo travelers should double-check reservations before leaving home. If sending out special invitations, be sure that spelling and punctuation are correct.

2. MONDAY. Perplexing. Positive happenings are likely. However, you are apt to encounter numerous delays and obstacles before reaching your ultimate goal. Keep your eye on the final prize as a way to keep motivation high. Issue clear instructions to coworkers to avoid mixed messages and confusion. Travel matters are likely to feature strongly in the day. Conditions might be challenging, testing your resolve particularly through the morning hours. Virgo business owners should get out where the action is, talking, selling, and making new deals. Profits will increase based on your personal effort. Don't delegate work you do better than anyone else.

3. TUESDAY. Renewing. There is a good chance that a fresh idea is coming from the New Moon's influence. Today this energy arrives in the sign of Gemini, focusing attention on your house of career and business activities. With four planets also clustered in this area, you may have a strong urge to change your employment. Now is the time to implement plans to turn this goal into reality. If this is also balanced by personal aims, you will obtain an enormous amount of satisfaction and achievement. A long-standing issue involving a colleague can finally be satisfactorily resolved. Fill out important paperwork correctly in order to avoid last-minute hassles.

4. WEDNESDAY. Accomplished. This is another day when your ability to initiate new projects, schemes, and ventures is heightened. Situations that require leadership and competence will benefit from your shrewd and astute thinking. If you have something important to say, express your views succinctly. Other people are more willing to listen with an open mind. You should have additional energy providing enough physical vitality to improve a sports or exercise performance. Virgos engaged in a secret love affair need to make a decision regarding where the romance is heading. Continuing to keep your relationship quiet may not be possible much longer.

5. THURSDAY. Stimulating. You will not relish being stuck with routine activities and chores. Get out of the rut by adding variety to your day in order to overcome boredom. Virgos on the job will not be satisfied doing the same old things over and over again. Offer to take on different duties or experiment with new procedures. Act on a flash of brilliance, converting original ideas into concrete plans. Stay busy and active even if someone offers to take over for you. Financial gains are likely to come from enterprising projects that put you ahead of the competition. Friends may rally around, increasing confidence and demanding your charming company. Recreational activity this evening can release built-up tension.

6. FRIDAY. Mixed. Hidden influences are at work. You need to stay alert by using your good Virgo intuition and powers of perception. It may be hard to avoid or escape entirely from an argumentative situation. Just do your best to keep the peace, and don't do anything that would inflame a dispute any further. A personal connection could open the door to new career options and business leads. Mixing work and pleasure can work to your advantage. Couples have the chance to share magic moments. Romance can flourish if you remember the little things that matter to your mate or partner.

7. SATURDAY. Stable. Even though it is the weekend you will be in the mood for practical discussions, especially about employment matters. This is also a good time for artistic creativity and self-expression. If you are about to start a new job that is a change of direction, you can expect some concern as to whether you have made the right move. Don't worry. This is a chance to advance toward your long-term goals. You might get inside information about a profitable investment that could give your bank account a nice boost. Popularity rises, and you should have a good time at a party or other social function.

8. SUNDAY. Starred. Lightning-fast thinking and a mind that you have trouble turning off will energize the day. If you are engaged in a debate, presenting a public lecture, writing a special assignment, you can expect a particularly productive day. This is also a lovely time for Virgos who are planning a wedding, engagement party, or special anniversary celebration. The unattached heading off on a blind date can look forward to an exciting experience. If you are seeking entertainment, treat yourself to tickets for a concert, theatrical performance, or sports contest. Socializing is likely to put you in a romantic mood.

9. MONDAY. Cheerful. Monday is the Moon's day, and she is currently sailing through your own sign of Virgo. You will want to look and feel your best, so wear an outfit that will wow colleagues or clients. A job interview or buying and selling wholesale may keep you on the run, so be sure to have a healthy breakfast before starting that day. An advertisement in the newspaper might lead to a career or business opportunity. Strong feelings for those people who are most important to you are likely to emerge. For Virgo singles, a new relationship that begins now has a good chance of being long lasting.

10. TUESDAY. Guarded. If you are dieting, make moderation your motto. Find a healthy balance to overcome a tendency to overindulge in food or drink or in spending on a restaurant meal. A special relationship with a colleague or associate needs to be handled with care, especially if you are romanticizing about this person. Reserve major financial decisions until later in the month unless you are considering renegotiating a loan or a home mortgage. Explore your own talents thoroughly and you could find a latent skill that you have not yet made constructive use of. Just don't judge your early efforts too severely.

11. WEDNESDAY. Chancy. This is another day to practice moderation. Also watch the purse strings. Talking to a knowledgeable friend could help find positive ways to reduce financial worries. An older or more mature friend or relative would be the best adviser. Prepare for a shake-up in your career or when dealing with an authority figure. The social circuit could be claiming a lot of your valuable free time. Having to go out again tonight may be the last thing that you feel like doing. If staying home is your preferred option, consider skipping a work-related social function that is unlikely to be much fun.

12. THURSDAY. Diverse. Over the next few days your energy is likely to be scattered. You will need to apply effort and push yourself. Today love planet Venus collides with erratic Uranus, bringing a restless attitude to the fore. You may want to break free and do your own thing rather than settling into routine obligations. Virgo singles may have a number of romantic possibilities to choose from, including a longtime friend. However, discerning who you are most attracted to may be a problem. Refrain from rushing into a serious romantic affair because feelings of love and lust could disappear as quickly as they blossomed. A lucky break in regard to finances is highly likely.

13. FRIDAY. Uncertain. Lots of action is expected, and none of it is likely to be directly connected to the date. This is another day when agitation needs to be kept under control in order for progress to be made. Nothing much will happen unless there is input from you. Love and romance might again occupy your thoughts. However, before you rush out and do anything rash, stop and consider the possible consequences of your actions. Although new ideas and schemes could stem from group discussions, teamwork is unlikely to be productive. The combined dreamy and restless atmosphere makes reaching a definite decision almost impossible. Defer meetings until next week.

14. SATURDAY. Changeable. This should be a pleasant day if music or creative art is included in your agenda. Keep an eye on trivial matters in order to avoid troublesome situations. If you need to reach a conclusion, be patient. You are apt to make a wrong move if you hurry. If it is essential that a decision be made, talk it over with a friend or a close relative. Pluto, planet of regeneration, is revisiting your Sagittarius house of home and family, which gives you a chance to review decisions and current situations in this sector of your life. If something is not working well, consider making changes to inspire more emotional fulfillment.

15. SUNDAY. Encouraging. Establish and act on your priorities early today. Otherwise progress may be hindered as friends flock around, which could be a nuisance or at least a distraction. Frustration might occur because of the chores or responsibilities that you need to carry out alone. Set aside some time for fun, and ask visitors to abide by your timetable. Virgos with a creative flair could find that extra effort applied now marks a turning point in getting a project ready to be put on display for sale, as a gift, or for personal use. Nervousness is likely if you are involved in a public meeting, but everything will proceed smoothly.

16. MONDAY. Useful. Expect an ordinary sort of day. In some areas you should experience some success, while in others it might be difficult to make much progress. The sensible option is to work on projects and tasks that are not likely to cause any problems. Be prepared for someone to let you down. Or there may be a change or cancellation of arrangements. If there are disagreements concerning home and employment responsibilities, try to resolve these sooner rather than later. Otherwise the stress may be ongoing for some time. With creativity still enhanced, make sure you maintain control of projects that need an artist's touch.

17. TUESDAY. Fair. Virgo ideas are flowing freely. If you have the feeling that something could be done better or should be given another chance, go with your instinct. Business plans or negotiations may be continually plagued by errors or holdups. Be patient. Ongoing problems and delays should not last much longer. Over the next few days sweet Venus duels with intense Pluto, creating power struggles with colleagues and family members. Dramas and personal issues are also likely if a sense of emotional detachment is not maintained and your ability to analyze a situation objectively is slightly diminished.

18. WEDNESDAY. Sensitive. The summer sky is dominated by a bevy of celestial influences. Artful Venus starts to visit Cancer, your house of hopes and wishes as well as your friendship circle. Cherished dreams and goals could become easier to obtain while Venus transits Cancer until July 12. Family and working relationships could be pressured and tested under today's Full Moon in expansive Sagittarius. Opposition from feisty colleagues or a loved one might make life more difficult. Be on guard when dealing with those in authority so that issues of power and control don't emerge. Partnered Virgos should tread warily in the love department or the relationship could become a little tense.

19. THURSDAY. Distracting. Watch your temper this morning. Irritation due to the actions of other people could cause you to fly off the handle, leading to regret later on. Partnered Virgos may have to deal with issues of possessiveness or emotional manipulation within a relationship. There may not be a pleasant outcome unless jealous tendencies are kept under control. Single Virgos should proceed slowly and with care if starting a new romantic affair. A community get-together can provide a chance to display a talent or expertise, boosting your social standing in the process. Your ruler, skillful Mercury, is now in forward motion, reducing the likelihood of delays, misunderstandings, and machinery breakdowns.

20. FRIDAY. Exciting. The summer solstice arrives today with the entry of the Sun into family-oriented Cancer, which represents your sector of hopes and wishes. Virgos will be energized to pursue long-term goals, spend more time with friends and loved ones, and even to create a personal masterpiece. Turning a pleasurable hobby into a group effort can be a fulfilling experience. The Sun is also challenging Pluto today, which warns you not to become embroiled in a drama not of your making. If discontent with the amount of time your mate or partner is spending on the job boils over, find a way to ensure that there is plenty of time for togetherness.

21. SATURDAY. Variable. Ambiguous influences mark this day. You may not have as much energy as usual, so treat yourself gently. A sensitive attitude could lead to overreacting to the comments of other people. Think before you lash out. You may be tempted to say something that you later wish you had kept to yourself. Take care if you are out on the water fishing, boating, or swimming. Be extra choosy when selecting food and drink. Love and marriage are under favorable trends. This is a great day for celebrating an engagement, wedding, or anniversary. A long-term investment could soon pay excellent dividends.

22. SUNDAY. Challenging. Be alert because there is an element of dishonesty floating around. Don't waste money on useless items. Avoid purchasing large household or electrical appliances; you could pay too much or end up with a lemon. Guard your personal possessions if mingling in a crowd, being especially alert for pickpockets. Someone intent on relieving you of your hard-earned cash may have an eye on you. A new recreational pursuit could have all sorts of positive effects including new friends or even a new romance. Today is the perfect time to host a barbecue for friends and loved ones, putting your flair for catering on display for them to enjoy.

23. MONDAY. Helpful. Revise your approach if you feel you are stuck in the same boring routine. Pay attention to diet, increase exercise, and consider reducing the amount of coffee or soft drinks you consume. Include more fruit and fresh water in your daily intake to improve general wellness. Be warned that becoming involved in a romantic office attraction could end up with one of you required to depart the scene. It would be wise to confront an issue that you are worried about rather than trying to keep it a secret or cover it up. Compromise is important as long as it is not always one-sided.

24. TUESDAY. Smooth. You should be feeling sociable, preferring to spend leisure time with family members and friends. If you need mutual aid and support from a business partner or team, you will have more success during the morning hours when an atmosphere of cooperation exists. Your ability to communicate on many levels will help other people to understand your reasons and motivations. When it comes to technical issues, however, stop and listen to those who have more knowledge and experience than you do. Extra precautions need to be taken if you are driving, handling sharp tools, or serving hot dishes.

25. WEDNESDAY. Favorable. Discipline and tenacity are heightened, and these traits should be used to your advantage. Leadership skills come to the fore. Your ability to overcome obstacles and to give a stalled team project a new lease on life can raise your profile considerably. Bask in group recognition, and acknowledge your role in the successful outcome. A verbal agreement with a friend or coworker might not be enough protection if you are considering a joint venture. Obtain legal advice to better safeguard your interests. To avert potential problems, communicate openly and honestly with children. A committed relationship might need a dash of spice and variety.

26. THURSDAY. Uneasy. A celestial shake-up occurs today. Uranus, planet of radical ideas and disruptive influences, begins backtracking in Pisces, your house of personal and professional relationships. Uranus retrogrades here until November 26. Restlessness and an overly stimulated mind are likely at least for a short period of time. Try to combine ingenuity and creativity as a way to release stress. Choices await you. You have the chance to pick where you want to go from here in terms of a committed or business partnership. Once you realize that most problems you are currently experiencing are of a temporary nature, overcoming negative emotional feelings will be easier.

27. FRIDAY. Promising. Investment and financial security are emphasized. If venturing out to shop leave your credit cards at home and refrain from extravagant or impulsive spending. An old debt could be repaid, much to your surprise. Resist the temptation to invest in a get-rich-quick scheme. An employment project might be shelved due to lack of funds, but don't despair. Your employer could have a better option in mind. Making money from a hobby is likely for the talented Virgo. Important decisions regarding business assets can be successfully finalized. Covering old ground may lead to new insights.

28. SATURDAY. Harmonious. Getting your point across and making valuable connections will be easy. Allow your flair for articulate communication to guide you through important negotiations, transactions, or decisions. The rediscovery of a creative pursuit that used to keep you amused could bring back happy memories and provide another pleasurable way to use your leisure time. Quiet periods spent with your significant other or with family members can be a valuable way to cultivate and strengthen loving bonds. Consider a romantic dinner for two, cooking up your specialty or a partner's favorite dish. Singles might prefer to go out with friends to seek possible romantic encounters.

29. SUNDAY. Comforting. Remaining in bed to recharge your batteries is recommended for those born under the sign of the Virgin.

Your restless Virgo nature can inspire you to book a flight to an exotic destination somewhere in the world that is very different from your usual vacation locale. Various family members are likely to be vying for your attention, possibly causing extra stress. Give them a fair hearing, but don't become overwhelmed by their demands or requests. Virgos with a problem that needs to be addressed should openly talk over concerns and inner thoughts to someone close. They are likely to provide valuable advice as to how to deal with whatever is causing your concern.

30. MONDAY. Energetic. Your drive and energy should be high. You are apt to feel a surge of excitement as new projects or plans flow into the working arena. However, confusion abounds, so be sure that other people comprehend exactly what you mean in all of your communications. Otherwise misunderstandings are likely. If in charge, don't assume that employees understand all requirements and techniques. Long-term goals could be questioned, and you may be unsure if they still have the same validity that they once did. It would be wise to examine your aims more fully next week when conditions become a bit clearer.

JULY

1. TUESDAY. Motivating. Virgo folk are charged up and raring to go, a great way to start this new month. Energetic Mars enters your own sign, bringing good vibes for personal action from today until August 19. Now is the time to tackle tricky tasks that you hid away in the too-hard-to-do basket. There are strong indications of a raise, bonus, or promotion at work. Fitting everything that you want to do into your schedule for the day might not be easy. There is also a tendency to go entirely your own way. Just be sure to avoid a head-to-head confrontation with someone in a position of authority.

2. WEDNESDAY. Good. This promises to be another good day sent by the cosmos. A fresh New Moon culminates in Cancer, your sector of friendship and cherished desires. Now you can set a new course. Teamwork is favored. As a Virgo you instinctively recognize and respond to the needs of other people. This energy can provide an opportunity to restore broken connections or reestablish a relationship that dissolved due to the passing of time or changing interests. You might receive an offer to earn money by using your technical skills. Increased responsibility and activity in your daily routine makes this a demanding but productive day.

3. THURSDAY. Happy. You are in the mood for serious fun, games, and relaxing, which is terrific if you are on a summer break. However, if you are on the job, keep alert to be sure your boss is not watching if you decide to slack off. The planets of pleasure, Venus and Jupiter, are currently at odds with each other. So this is not the time to neglect your own well-being. Avoid excessive food or alcohol. Otherwise, you will undermine efficiency both at home and at work. If you are intent on venturing out, refrain from social extravagance or your wallet is likely to suffer. Be ready to smooth over an argument if entertaining or visiting friends. Problems could arise and put a damper on social activities.

4. FRIDAY. Quiet. The Moon is heading through Leo, your solar twelfth house. The Moon here suggests that you seek a less strenuous form of amusement even while celebrating the holiday. Privacy and solitude might be your preferred option rather than mingling with a crowd. A quiet day with close family members or friends could best satisfy your social needs. Or you might decide to take off to the beach or take a picnic lunch to a favored spot out of town. Virgos who are resting at home could spend some time finishing tasks that are close to completion. You may also choose to sort through your wardrobe to discard outfits that now don't fit or are no longer trendy.

5. SATURDAY. Interesting. This is not the time to allow extraneous situations to upset you. Mix-ups and changes to plans are more than likely, so you will need to go with the flow. Let the day slowly evolve at its own rate. Your ruler, communicative Mercury, will add tension to the atmosphere by challenging unpredictable Uranus. This is likely to cause some unexpected situations but also add excitement and spontaneity to the mix. Outdoor activities are favored as a way to provide a break from routine. Visiting new vistas and different venues is sure to be relaxing. Your mate or partner might overlook some risky factors, so be doubly alert and watchful.

6. SUNDAY. Surprising. With today's array of planetary aspects you can expect conditions similar to yesterday. Saucy Venus is happily linking with unpredictable Uranus, causing chaos and excitement. Anything and everything will be possible, particularly when it comes to love, money, friends, and a partner. A search for endless pleasure could put you in contact with people whose moral values are very different from yours. If you have time to spare, consider volunteering with an organization you admire. Creative projects can provide recognition and possible financial gain.

7. MONDAY. Mixed. Although there may be a few glitches throughout the day, you can gloss over these fairly quickly and still maintain harmony at home or on the job. This is a good day for personal accomplishments. Tackle hard chores or those that have been left on the back burner for some time. However, don't try to complete everything at once or your achievement is apt to be negligible. No matter how much you might want to purchase something that costs a lot, patience is needed. Wait a little longer and it could go on sale. A quiet night at home offers the most fun for partnered Virgos. Singles are unlikely to meet anyone who sparks a second glance.

8. TUESDAY. Opportune. You may experience a few difficulties as the day unfolds. Turn off negative thoughts, especially this morning. Keep in mind that you don't have to agree with everything a family member or associate says or does. There may be changes to your routine without you realizing what's happening. Fortunately these should be for the better, improving both efficiency and effectiveness. There is apt to be an influx of opportunities to choose from. Virgos who are unemployed or seeking another job can get off to a flying start by applying for an advertised position that offers increased salary as well as improved benefits.

9. WEDNESDAY. Uncertain. Friends could be a little contrary and might surprise you with their impulsive actions. Be careful to stay out of power games, and distance yourself from people who are prone to this type of behavior. Communication with someone in authority might not lead to desired results as an official decision does not swing in your favor. Remain calm and keep your cool if a verbal contest becomes heated in a team meeting or group discussion. Important matters may cause some confusion or disruption in business finances, so be alert for the sudden or unexpected. Prepare for extra expenses if socializing is on the agenda.

10. THURSDAY. Testing. Your ruler Mercury provides the flavor of the day. Mercury duels with powerful Pluto, then enters into the home-loving sign of Cancer. These influences could make it difficult to maintain a balance between personal and domestic life, as you struggle to fulfill career and home responsibilities. Clashes are expected, particularly in your working environment if annoying issues have been building. Your significant other could be argumentative, and a major power struggle might be brewing on the home front. Expect to receive a flood of information as well as some unfounded rumors concerning home affairs and business contracts.

11. FRIDAY. Tiring. On the job you may feel that time is not on your side as you rush around trying to handle urgent chores, make important phone calls, and run numerous errands. You might not actually have a heavier workload than usual, it may just feel that way. Your energy and enthusiasm could be in short supply. Although you won't actively seek conflict, criticism from a partner or associate is unlikely to go unnoticed and is almost bound to provoke a reaction. If you are not happy with the service or advice conveyed by a paid professional, it might be wise to obtain a second opinion before taking any action. Enjoy the company of mature people this evening.

12. SATURDAY. Revealing. Venus, the planet of love and attraction, moves into the showy sign of Leo, which impacts your solar twelfth house of solitude and personal limitations. This is a time to reflect on past mistakes made in the love department and to consider changes to be made in the future. Virgos in a committed union can share happier rapport if love and affection are openly and honestly displayed. Your creativity should be heightened. Keep a journal by your bed because you may experience vivid dreams that translate into inspirational ideas. Complications could arise for Virgos involved in a love affair that has to be kept secret.

13. SUNDAY. Varied. This morning's influences provide the best chance to obtain cooperation from family members. Later in the day unsettled feelings could upset your emotional equilibrium. To bring peace and harmony back to the home scene, spoil yourself and your loved ones with a well-prepared meal and a period of rest and tranquility. If entertaining at home, social interaction will be best prior to late afternoon. Take advantage if possible by making arrangements for a lunch date. If something is supposed to be a secret, make sure it remains that way. A confidential matter should not be revealed to anyone.

14. MONDAY. Energetic. Your stars offer plenty of vim, vitality, and enthusiasm. Let your mind wander and you could come up with new and original ideas and concepts. If you like the idea of the flexibility that comes from working at home as well as the potential for extra income and for being your own boss, spend time exploring options in this regard. Talking openly with someone you normally do not get along with can break down barriers and make interaction more comfortable in the future. Choose interesting and stimulating work to stave off boredom. Performing routine chores is likely to bring on a bout of restlessness that reduces efficiency and overall productivity.

15. TUESDAY. Diverse. Various forms of cosmic energy beam down from the sky, stimulating your emotions and thoughts. Mental focus is very strong, assisting those who need to concentrate on employment duties, household tasks, or school work. Self-employed Virgos who are behind in tax, debt, or credit matters can make excellent progress by putting forth more effort. You can get up to date very quickly. Virgo folk with a fetish for entering competitions or solving mysteries can excel now and are apt to get on a winning streak. Advancements can be made in areas of communication, selling, business, and computer-related operations.

16. WEDNESDAY. Helpful. Children or younger adults may request assistance with a special project. If you have the necessary skills, provide as much help as you can to steer them onto the right path. Although it might be difficult right now, you will be respected more by standing up for yourself than if you bow to the wishes and demands of other people and put yourself in the role of martyr. You are super sharp, making this a perfect day to look into new recreational pursuits that will keep you pleasantly occupied. For singles this might be an opportunity to meet new friends who could open up romantic possibilities.

17. THURSDAY. Positive. If you are eager to turn one of your more creative ideas into reality, you should receive support providing you know where to look. If unsure how to promote yourself or your ideas, check the Internet or ask an older relative for advice and assistance. Offering your services to baby-sit for a friend or family member will be appreciated and can be a good opportunity for Virgo parents-to-be to hone child-care skills. Your mate or partner might be surprisingly romantic, revealing a fantasy side that is deeply appealing but rarely shown. The unattached could find a romantic encounter exciting as well as amusing.

18. FRIDAY. Sensitive. Emotional drama marks the day. It would be wise to maintain an objective outlook and not get caught up in any demonstration of a sensitive nature. If feeling tired or experiencing some trouble on the job, it is essential that your main priority be your own health and well-being. If work is tedious and draining your energy you may need to make immediate changes. The Capricorn Full Moon emphasizes Virgo lifestyle issues, social activities, and romance. There could be some alterations or endings now. Saying good-bye to an adult child leaving the nest for the first time or a lover departing due to work reasons may cause some concern and misgivings.

19. SATURDAY. Manageable. For Virgos working today, disagreements with colleagues or subordinates should be handled with care. Any problems that need to be addressed would be better put on hold until next week. It is a good day to investigate new health treatments, exercise regimes, or a beauty makeover. Extra vitamins, food supplements, and increased physical activity might be just what you require to fight off a minor ailment. If a strenuous workout at the local gym is not something you aspire to, taking the dog for a walk, splurging on a massage, or riding the waves can also benefit those looking for a gentler way to keep fit.

20. SUNDAY. Confusing. Minor confusion could affect a member of your household this morning. If tempers become frayed, conserve your energy and walk away. Tension should quickly pass. If emotion is clouding an issue, concentrate on therapeutic activities such as gardening, cooking, or finishing off a do-it-yourself project designed to enhance living comfort and conditions. A family gathering could provide pleasure later in the day. Meeting up with loved ones can be an extremely enjoyable way to pass the time. Your magnetic Virgo charm can work wonders on other people of all ages and stages of life.

21. MONDAY. Slow. This is a day to relax and work around any obstacles. If you feel the weight of the world resting on your shoulders, spend time with people who are positive, supportive, and encouraging. Don't overload yourself with too many chores or attempt to do everything on your own. Sharing responsibilities promotes friendly relations and can ease your workload. A partner or close associate might be highly excitable or argumentative later in the day, forcing you to use all of your powers of reasoning to restore peace and calm. Be patient with friends because they may not be as attentive as usual.

22. TUESDAY. Eventful. Prepare for a busy day. Try to remain focused on details both small and large. The Sun enters the sunny sign of Leo and your twelfth sector of solitude. Sun in Leo for the next four weeks suggests that you maintain a balance between activity and take a more circumspect approach. This is an opportunity to slow down or to work on plans in secret. Just be sure that you do not become your own worst enemy with the way you handle problems. With your ruler Mercury happily linking with electrifying Uranus today, you will like nothing better than mixing and mingling with people you find exciting and stimulating.

23. WEDNESDAY. Fine. Sometimes it is good to act on impulse, but today this type of action could cause minor or major problems. You need to take extra care with joint finances. If you don't have the money in the bank, this is not the time to go on a spending spree. You may be inclined to rush in and buy instead of taking the time to think about the budget. You might have to visit or call a government tax office, accounting firm, or real estate expert. Even though this may be a nuisance in the short term, financial gains are more than likely. If you are involved in a personal dispute or a legal skirmish try to negotiate a win-win settlement to save time and money as well as restoring peace of mind.

24. THURSDAY. Accomplished. Structure your time carefully. Today you have the energy you need to get your financial life back on track. Resolve to pay growing debts, increase insurance coverage, and check your credit report. A business partner or associate might clue you in about a lucrative deal. However, be sure that your nest egg and financial future are protected. For Virgo singles, enjoying the company of family members can be a good way to unwind. For coupled Virgos, being with that special person is ideal. Emotional insecurity could be the reason that you choose to keep outgrown possessions instead of discarding them or donating to a worthy charity.

25. FRIDAY. Hectic. You are apt to be late with everything you do, resulting in very little time to spare. This may be due to becoming stressed or too sidetracked to make good use of your time. It would be wiser to proceed slowly so that you can carry out your agenda steadily. There is a possibility that you will be invited to go on a trip or to speak, teach, or lecture. The implied compliment is likely to be exhilarating as well as a cause of nervous anticipation. Concentrate a little harder than usual to ensure that all data and facts are correct. A problem regarding an in-law could require input from your mate or partner in order for it to be satisfactorily resolved.

26. SATURDAY. Pleasurable. Your ruler Mercury is now visiting Leo and joins the Sun and Venus there in your solar twelfth house. Virgos are bound to be more in demand with the party set. If you don't yet have any plans to go out and socialize, it won't be long until you do. If your phone is not ringing, make the calls yourself to plan a get-together with friends, coworkers, or loved ones. You do not have to upset the budget in order to have an enjoyable time. Choose food and entertainment that is inexpensive but still will provide a fun day. Beachgoers should pack plenty of fresh water and sunscreen to protect their skin and to guard against dehydration.

27. SUNDAY. Bountiful. If you have been working long hours on the job and need some time off, consider making plans for a trip you have been dreaming about but putting on hold. If money is a problem take a conservative approach. Check the Internet for special last-minute package deals that would suit your needs. Seeking a low-interest bank loan might be an option providing you don't go overboard with spending. Even though you may be inclined to withdraw from a noisy gathering or crowd, continue to get out and about to meet and greet other people. Going to bed at an earlier hour than usual should provide the necessary vitality to face the new working week.

28. MONDAY. Constructive. Job interests should go very well. You can expect to be busy and on the go for most of the day. There may be an opportunity to work on a project that is actually more fun than work. Ask a colleague to provide support, and you can both enjoy a very productive day. Virgos who are employed in areas where there is a lot of paperwork to handle or forms to fill out are likely to run into some problems. These can be kept to a minimum if you double-check your work before signing off. Whatever you do at the end of your shift, take time for yourself or to be with your significant other if you are half of a couple.

29. TUESDAY. Promising. A bevy of celestial influences indicates that you will be as busy as a bee and probably running around for much of the day. This is an important period for Virgos who have a career or business decision to make. Clarity of vision will make this process easier. Seeking the knowledge required to achieve your goals should be successful. Much can be learned by asking other people about their experiences and challenges while moving up the career ladder. Be unpretentious if invited to show off your talents. Enjoy a touch of luxury with your special companion this evening while still maintaining a conservative approach to the budget.

30. WEDNESDAY. Encouraging. You need to remain flexible, which is generally not a problem for those born under the sign of Virgo. There may be changes or unexpected developments regarding your social arrangements with friends. Spend time reviewing your hopes or wishes for the future to be sure you are still on the right track. Talk over any problems you have at work or at home with someone trustworthy. Sometimes other people have a clearer perspective when a problem is considered from an outsider's vantage point. There may be unexpected developments that affect your love life, forcing you to take another look at an issue you thought had been resolved.

31. THURSDAY. Guarded. As a Virgo you recognize that patience is a prime virtue. Today, however, that patience will be put to the test. Get an early start to avoid immediate overload. Plan the day with care, including occasional periods of relaxation. Talking about the weather or your favorite sports team can be a good emotional release. Offer congratulations and praise for work well done, but don't brag about your own recent accomplishments. Get outside yourself and away from what has been bothering you. A decision over which you have no control probably won't be made until next week at the earliest, so try not to dwell on the matter.

AUGUST

1. FRIDAY. Purposeful. Virgo folk begin the month with good intentions. If you're hoping to turn a long-cherished dream into reality, devote time to this aim over the next two weeks. An eclipsed New Moon in creative Leo aids your efforts to turn in a new direction to achieve your goals and wishes for the future. This is not the time to fear failure. Even if you are facing the unknown, trust your good Virgo instinct and intuition. Quiet time with an interesting book or project can help keep your energy level at a peak. Spending time outdoors is a great way to maintain a healthy glow as long as the weather is not too hot and humid.

2. SATURDAY. Fair. Remain alert. You may not be given correct information, particularly if you ask tricky questions. Your ruler Mercury is in an agitated state with Jupiter today. The best way to handle this planetary energy is to establish priorities and stick to them, especially if you have important tasks to act upon or a deadline to meet. Don't make promises that are difficult to keep just to show other people what a good person you are. Your star will dim quickly if you let them down. Take extra care with personal or business dealings, alert for a touch of rivalry. Things improve later today when the Moons enters your sign.

3. SUNDAY. Beneficial. Now the Moon is rising in your sign of Virgo, so today should be far more productive than yesterday. The desire to withdraw from social activities or from friends and family members will ease somewhat. You should be looking forward to time away from home. Going to the beach or on a picnic would be a cheap alternative to more expensive entertainment and can provide stimulating interaction. Be careful that a secret is not accidentally revealed. Also guard against putting your foot in your mouth and saying something you later regret. In the romance department, dreamy possibilities that provide captivating moments are possible.

4. MONDAY. Arousing. Avoid arguments this morning, and eventually other people will come to understand your points of view. A small but important obstacle could bring a job to a halt. Avoiding this possibility requires a measured, slow approach so that you can be sure every detail is covered and nothing has been overlooked. As a Virgo you are generally not comfortable with lots of emotion in a romance because it can make you feel awkward. Right now and over the next few days, however, you are likely to change your mind as sexy Venus and intense Pluto team up. This becomes the perfect opportunity to get up close and personal with the person who means the most to you.

5. TUESDAY. Promising. If you are in a business or an intimate partnership, take time to review everything related to joint finances. This should pave the way toward a more stable future together. Love and passion reign supreme once again. Virgos who are in a clandestine relationship might find it becoming even more intense and hush-hush, leaving you to wonder if this is really what you want. Venus is about to make her gracious presence felt in your own sign of Virgo. Venus in Virgo will heighten your ability to attract whatever you now need in your life. Your social popularity is about to soar. Creating a good impression on other people will become second nature.

6. WEDNESDAY. Tricky. Challenging celestial aspects could have you hopping. Allow your innate logic and powers of reason to guide you. It is usually wiser to sidestep contentious issues, but today you are apt to be in the mood to meet these head-on. If you decide to handle issues directly, be prepared for eruptions to arise. You may find it hard to concentrate. To avoid an accident Virgo drivers need to proceed with extra care. Your mind may stray, dwelling on everything but what you are supposed to be doing. If you experience problems balancing your checkbook, blame the stars and defer this task until later in the week.

7. THURSDAY. Mixed. Focus might still be a problem for Virgo, with drifting thoughts causing a myriad of possibilities to surface. Most of them will be good. It is a fortunate day for self-expression. Contemplating your own creative skills can be a productive use of time and energy. If you yearn to write you could find words flowing easily, so don't waste the opportunity to put pen to paper. A past situation that transpired with friends might recur and will need to be dealt with quickly. If you learned well from previous experience, you should have little difficulty handling the situation in the best way this time around.

8. FRIDAY. Challenging. If you feel a little stymied in your current occupation, you may be lacking sufficient mental stimulation to make the job satisfying. Your powers of judgment may prove faulty, making you prone to unrealistic thinking. Dealing with other people, particularly with coworkers, may be a chore because you are severely lacking patience and tolerance. You may be exposed to untruths. Trying to figure out why people bother to lie when you are aware of what they are doing could be a hard dilemma to solve. With three planets in your sign of Virgo, this is the time to work on revamping your personal style and image.

9. SATURDAY. Accomplished. Having a fulfilling purpose ensures that your energy will be focused in the right direction. Problems with mental concentration are not likely now. Your ruler Mercury connects constructively with profound Pluto. You are now more magnetic than usual, and your ability to mesmerize other people with your charisma is heightened. This is an excellent day to initiate a new public relations campaign, present an address, or sell something of value. Your mind should be working overtime. Just be careful about making any impulsive purchases. These are apt to be a waste of time and cash, and could mean that you run short of money to pay other commitments.

10. SUNDAY. Hopeful. If you have lost or misplaced something of value, recovery is very likely now. Take a few minutes to get busy looking for your missing treasure. Even Virgos who are not usually very talkative will be more communicative in the period coming up. Clever Mercury, your thought-provoking ruler, starts transiting your sign of Virgo from today to August 28. With Mercury, Mars, Venus, and Saturn all in Virgo right now, your tendency to strive toward perfection is heightened. Focus on the details without losing the big picture. You have plenty of stamina and endurance to complete chores that have been neglected or too hard to do before. Those of you who engage in meticulous work can make tremendous progress over the next three weeks.

11. MONDAY. Ordered. You are in a methodical and organized frame of mind, making this a great day to work through red tape, fill in forms, file, or write a report. Take advantage of any opportunity to talk with a boss or other superior. You should find that the content of such a discussion is very interesting, informative, and in your favor. Later in the day doing your own thing without restrictions can lead to good output. A focus on home activities might be the signal to attend to routine household chores, including mowing the lawn, weeding the garden, or getting repairs and routine maintenance done personally or by a hired professional.

12. TUESDAY. Rewarding. Positive thinking will pay off. Even if the day is a little difficult, remaining positive and optimistic can help reduce stress. Formulating a business assessment in regard to your own creative talents could be a smart move, especially if you are considering marketing what you make or do. A focus on romance assists singles to visualize perfect love, although meeting up with this vision might not happen today. The secret is to be patient and keep looking. Spending a few hours with a favorite book or movie might be the preferred option if you are intent on relaxing in the comfort of your own home tonight.

13. WEDNESDAY. Fruitful. Your practical and sensible approach will propel ideas and projects initiated now. If you are currently in the process of updating your self-image, further progress can be made. For those who have been planning a wedding or other ceremony, this is a great day to finalize last-minute details. For single Virgos this is a dynamic time to seek love that has the chance of lasting forever. Artistic Virgos could find special pleasure in creative expressions. With perseverance your earnings could increase through selling your wares on a part-time basis. Don't undersell yourself or what you make.

14. THURSDAY. Leisurely. All work and no play can make you very stressed out, so be sure to include some fun and games in your agenda. A child may be of major concern for Virgo parents if the lines of communication haven't been kept open. Guard against an overly protective approach toward those you love, allowing them space and independence and keeping worries to yourself. It might be wise to stock up on snacks and wine. Unexpected guests could arrive this evening, expecting to be fed and entertained. Creative activities are favored, so use your imagination and enjoy leisure time relaxing with a favored pursuit.

15. FRIDAY. Lackluster. Although motivation and enthusiasm may not be in abundance, some form of physical activity should be helpful. Keeping on the move will reduce a sluggish attitude. Removing clutter that you have accumulated over time will purify your personal space and serve as excellent decorating. If you now want to entertain and cooking is one of your talents, invite a few friends for lunch or dinner and display your excellent skills. Consider making an appointment for a medical, dental, or eye checkup that you have been putting off. Don't forget to include a session with a podiatrist or massage therapist if you think it would be helpful.

16. SATURDAY. Beneficial. This promises to be a lucky day, although there could be periods when you might doubt the truth of that statement. Saucy Venus, goddess of goodies, positively connects with abundant Jupiter, which can lead to a winning streak through sport or a game of chance. Try to be tolerant of the moods of other people. The eclipsed Full Moon in Aquarius increases sensitive emotions. If you are typical of your Virgo Sun sign, you have a health-conscious attitude. Now you have the chance to follow up in areas that would benefit from more attention. Don't start new projects. Instead, tie up loose ends at home or at work.

17. SUNDAY. Erratic. A wide variety of influences makes this an unpredictable day. Luck and good fortune abound, with Jupiter plus your ruler Mercury happily linked together. Sports-minded Virgos should be on the winning team. A small wager could enhance your bank account. However, fiery Mars is squaring off with dark Pluto, indicating that a power struggle or challenge could spoil the party. Maintain your cool if required to do battle with someone close. Take extra care because you are in an accident-prone period that could result in a minor injury, strain, or bruise. Caution is required if using hot or sharp objects.

18. MONDAY. Empowering. The people around you could benefit from your abundant energy. However, if you feel stressed it is imperative to work off steam in a constructive manner. A session at the gym, a brisk walk around the block, or a bike ride to work or the grocery store could reduce pressure if you have been burning the candles at both ends. Treat yourself to some pleasure this evening. Be sure to include your mate or partner, especially if your romantic relationship has not been going as smoothly as in the past. Discussions with your significant other can be productive, more so if you reach into your heart and allow your loved one to know how much you care.

19. TUESDAY. Tense. Toil and trouble at home or on the job might impact early starters, with ongoing irritation making it tough to bite your tongue. The day will not seem to get much better as it wears on. Underlying tension within relationships might create a number of unpleasant encounters. Do your part to maintain the peace by keeping sarcastic remarks to a minimum. Aspects from the cosmos are not all negative, as hardworking Mars visits your Libra sector of personal finances until October 4. This transit can increase your motivation to put plans in place that will generate extra income.

Gains will come if you are prepared, put more energy into your duties, and remain alert for opportunities that are coming your way.

20. WEDNESDAY. Trying. The current planetary aspects continue to apply pressure and increase frustrations. Take control in order to keep moving toward personal goals. Finances are in focus. Money will come through advance planning and increased effort. Virgos who are in an intimate or professional partnership should review mutual aims. Make sure that both of you are on the same wavelength in terms of where you are heading and how you intend to proceed. Remain firm without defiance in the face of criticism. If you are being unfairly targeted, give as good as you get but in a calm and articulate manner. Very few people can match your power of speech.

21. THURSDAY. Bright. A positive mood permeates your environment today. Virgo leadership abilities are to the fore. You certainly won't want to take a backseat or limit yourself in any way. If something is worth doing, let everyone know that it is worth doing correctly. Sharing a confidence or private pleasures with the one you love should be high on your agenda. Love is not out of the question for singles. Mulling over investment matters might lead to some important decisions regarding shared assets or personal possessions. You can act with more assurance of success.

22. FRIDAY. Auspicious. Happy birthday, Virgo. Your annual celebration now begins along with the need to shine. As a Virgo you are known as picky, pedantic, and perfectionistic in everything you aspire to do. With the Sun now visiting your own sign until September 22, you may notice that this attitude is accentuated over the next four weeks. Performing jobs that no one else can or wants to do is your forte, and for this reason you may be more in demand. Set yourself the goal of working toward what you believe in. Self-confidence is soaring, and making your mark in the world will become easier. Your energy rises and requires a healthy release. For the health-conscious Virgo physical exercise is always an excellent option.

23. SATURDAY. Unpredictable. A bolt of lightning may strike as swift Mercury and lover Venus challenge disruptive Uranus and foggy Neptune. These planetary aspects trigger issues with the other people in your life. Impatience with routine may create a restless and reckless attitude. Don't be too shocked if you react in a surprising manner toward clients, associates, or your partner. Money may be a problem at the moment. Limited financial resources will not help the situation if retail therapy is your way of feeling better or overcoming stress. Go easy on the others in your life. The tendency to display quirky behavior could be difficult for them to understand.

24. SUNDAY. Imaginative. Be watchful because deceptive trends prevail. Being cautious will not dampen your imagination. Virgo creative urges are strong and can be put to constructive use, especially if you enjoy leisure pursuits with an artistic flavor. Involvement in a project that appreciates inspiration and flair can be relaxing. The talented Virgo currently surviving on a shoestring budget could find success applying for a loan or grant to finance a new creative venture. Lock up your home securely if going out. Double-check that doors and windows are locked. Guard personal items if in a crowd.

25. MONDAY. Prickly. A number of irritations could upset your day. Steer clear of situations that reduce your optimism, which would only drag you down. A planned group get-together might present a dilemma. However, with a little more planning you should be able to quickly resolve the situation and get it back on track. Doubts and insecurities in regard to business finance might emerge. Reexamine where you are now, where you are heading, and where you eventually want to be. If you don't like what you find, changes might be urgently required. Although this could mean altering your schedule as well as extra work and responsibilities, doing so should be worthwhile in the longer term.

26. TUESDAY. Manageable. Be open to progressive new concepts. You might become involved in a project that can raise extra money and give your bank balance a big boost. A female friend could be a blessing if you need to vent your present frustrations in a secure environment. However, exercise restraint and discretion around the office. Only concern yourself with what is necessary. Avoid gossip or the next target of rumors could be you. Involvement in a group pursuit might lead to a romantic encounter for currently unattached Virgos, or at least a new and exciting friendship.

27. WEDNESDAY. Demanding. Carefully monitor all communications to avoid hurt feelings, conflict, or unpleasant repercussions. Your ruler, tricky Mercury, duels with intense Pluto. This aspect will heighten your powers of persuasion and ability to investigate but also creates a tendency to speak sharply. The impetus to push ahead with long-term plans and to expand your horizon can lead to actively seeking new goals. With a firm eye on financial resources, selling a business plan should be easier. Business owners can reap rewards by networking more and providing an improved customer-oriented approach with goods and services. Romance presents a mixture of allure and understanding that can sweep you off your comfortable perch.

28. THURSDAY. Quiet. Many Virgos may be protective of your privacy today as the Moon slips into Leo, your solitude zone. Spend time in self-reflection. Don't allow other people to intrude into your personal space. Follow your good Virgo intuition. An old concept could be a viable option for the future. Tonight busy Mercury will move into Libra, your zone of money. Mercury here gives you the chance to plan and to consider options in regard to personal finances and values. Retracing your steps could be the best course of action to restore financial stability. At day's end put a smile on your face and look forward to peace, quiet, and relaxation.

29. FRIDAY. Comforting. Although you might still prefer your own company to that of other people, there should be plenty of energy to expend on whatever you love to do. A former love or someone who has been the cause of grief in the past might return. Making a decision regarding what action to take might make you very anxious. Rather than acting impulsively, consider all of your options over the weekend. Not everything that is offered or available needs to be acted upon by you right now. Strong connections and feelings of desire and passion stir for couples in a happy union. For singles, a potential new partner could be lingering nearby.

30. SATURDAY. Renewing. Love, lust, and desire remain today. Extra care is needed because possessiveness, jealousy, or power issues could arise if you are currently in a romantic relationship. Your personal finances will receive another boost with the entrance of Venus into Libra, joining Mars and Mercury there. If you are prepared to do something different, you are likely to experience positive developments that can enhance your bank balance. The New Moon in your own sign of Virgo begins a new cycle that favors getting projects off the ground and concentrating on your personal life.

31. SUNDAY. Rejuvenating. With energy to spare, irritations are only likely if routine obligations keep you from pursuing preferred personal interests. Renovate and rejuvenate your mind and body by putting health and daily routines squarely in focus. If necessary, revamp the way you perform everyday tasks. Now is the time to turn over a new leaf. A good place to start could be with your diet if your current food intake is not as healthy as you would like. Complete self-nurturing with a tasty meal that is tempting to the palate. A long relaxing bath or a deep tissue massage to soothe aches and pains could please you tonight.

SEPTEMBER

1. MONDAY. Beneficial. If you can capture your enthusiasm and put it to good use, there is a very good chance for a productive beginning to the month. A new home project begun now will progress in good order under the current stars. If stretching the household budget is currently challenging your resolve, don't waste valuable time and energy counting your small change. Instead look at overall expenditures, especially recurring bills. Work out where cost-cutting procedures can be implemented. Emotions this evening may be extremely sensitive and vulnerable, warning Virgos to steer clear of situations where feelings could be easily hurt.

2. TUESDAY. Rewarding. With four planets currently gracing your Libra house of personal money and possessions, this is another day when taking stock of your financial situation can be a great benefit if you are trying to build up savings for a rainy day. If there is a need to economize, now is a perfect opportunity to work out how to do so. If you already have a budget don't be so tough on yourself that you're totally unrealistic. As a discerning Virgo you realize that some things are worth paying a premium price in order to obtain quality or service. Innovative ideas with a practical application are likely and can be put to good use immediately.

3. WEDNESDAY. Variable. Feelings of insecurity and a drop in self-confidence might perturb you, but this is only a passing phase. Self-assurance is bound to increase as your family and friends place you in the center of attention. You have plenty of self-discipline, making this a perfect time to tackle almost completed projects languishing on the back burner. Talking with someone knowledgeable may help you resolve an ongoing problem. An older person is most likely to steer you in the right direction. Virgo couples will share happy rapport and can find a renewed sense of love and emotional fulfillment.

4. THURSDAY. Lucky. Most things are likely to go your way, adding a cheerful and optimistic atmosphere to the day. This current phase of empowerment includes exciting possibilities for change that can see your reputation positively expand. Past endeavors are likely to pay off at long last. Good fortune is smiling on you. If you have an important meeting to attend, making a good impression should be easy. This can lead to support from those in authority regarding one of your pet projects. You might benefit from a financial windfall. Because you are feeling lucky the temptation to make a modest gamble can pay off.

5. FRIDAY. Disconcerting. As a Virgo you are usually canny and shrewd, but these qualities are not apt to prevail now. Before being tempted to spend on an exclusive and luxurious item, consider whether you can afford the payments and the large hit to your bank balance. Messages could be misinterpreted, making it very tricky for anybody who is trying to follow your instructions or understand your views. By being attentive to all particulars, no matter how petty they may appear, you shouldn't end up overlooking anything important. Get in touch with friends even if you only have time for a hurried cup of coffee or a quick message on the computer.

6. SATURDAY. Active. Today's go-get-'em mood means that you will not want to sit around and be dormant. Working around your home base could be a preferred option. You might be in the mood for a general cleanup around the house, yard, or car. Increased satisfaction will come if you can bear to throw away some of the accumulated clutter that you have gathered over the years. If contemplating a change in residence, this is a good day to personally check properties that might suit your present and future requirements. Home entertaining can be a relaxing way to socialize with family members or friends this evening.

7. SUNDAY. Mixed. Fiery Mars and bountiful Jupiter argue in the skies, bringing a need to rein in your spending and take a more moderate approach. If there is a simple and economical way of getting things done, choose that rather than a more extravagant method. Be flexible. Prearranged plans might need to be changed in order to accommodate the needs of an elderly relative or family friend. You are well situated to confront any problem that crops up and should be able to resolve the situation quickly. Tonight Jupiter, the planet of grace and expansion, begins moving in direct motion, which will enhance your enjoyment of romance, children, and creativity.

8. MONDAY. Energetic. There's lots of action in the sky today. Your ruler Mercury and warrior Mars merge, which will heighten your mental skills and wit. Take care in any discussions or general conversations. People can all too easily make remarks that cause irritation. Be careful that you do not place overly lofty expectations on yourself. Treat yourself with gentle kindness, especially when unwinding at the end of the working day. Tonight passionate Pluto starts to move forward in Sagittarius, your sector of home and family, which will ease the pressures that have been causing angst and stress. If your domestic situation hasn't been all sweetness and light recently, things should now begin to change for the better.

9. TUESDAY. Spirited. A challenging day greets Virgo individuals. But problems can be turned into profit. Your mind may still be moving at double-time, increasing your alertness as well as nervous anxiety. This is an excellent time to take on more responsibilities and duties that will boost your climb up the career ladder. Care is needed with your manner of speech. Arguments are likely to erupt without warning. Deciding you know what is best for a loved one could be the wrong way to retain peace and harmony at home. A sibling is likely to accuse you of being nosy or interfering. Feeling that you are currently lacking life's pleasures could bring on a bout of overindulgence and overspending.

10. WEDNESDAY. Pleasing. Shopping for bargains may appeal. You could find just what you are looking for, an item that will add style to your home decor. If this also adds to your investment portfolio, all the better. You might have to compromise if you are seeking a perfect gift for a loved one but the purchase price is more than you can afford. Don't miss out on an opportunity to let your hair down and have a good time, especially if you have been putting in long hours on the job. If you want company tonight, invite extended family members or a few friends for dinner and cook up a banquet that you can share together.

11. THURSDAY. Enjoyable. Excellent developments are likely. If you have been considering applying for a new job, update your resume and fill out an application or make an appointment today. Success is likely if you are aware of everything that is happening around you. If there are elements of your domestic or employment routines that need to be altered or upgraded, applying more thought and effort could help you come up with the answers. As a result your job will ultimately be less time consuming and more efficiently handled. Opportunities for romance or to begin a new relationship are everywhere and will put a smile on your face. Enjoy the good times.

12. FRIDAY. Exhilarating. Let loose and go with the flow. The urge to act completely out of character can be a wonderful release providing this is not totally crazy. Include plenty of variety in your routine to avert boredom. Strike a balance between what makes you happy while still remaining considerate of the needs of other people in your life. Follow up with your medical adviser to get answers to questions or concerns regarding your health. Reaching an important decision about your working life should be easier now because your insight and understanding are enhanced. Unusual or different amusement will make this evening very memorable.

13. SATURDAY. Productive. Restless tendencies continue to prevail. If you are on the job today, you will probably work better as part of a team than alone. So ask the boss for tasks for two. Offering help and services to other people can be extremely satisfying, and they are sure to appreciate your caring attitude. Virgos who are temporarily unemployed can make great strides by putting in the required effort and actively seeking fulfilling work. Get up early and scour the help-wanted section of the newspaper, send out applications, and make some phone calls. Avoid arguments with your mate or partner by choosing an inexpensive leisure pursuit that is fun but doesn't break the bank.

14. SUNDAY. Distracting. Escapism aptly describes today's energy. Utilize your time and talents in productive daydreaming. Allow inspiration to take hold. Beware martyrdom and the tendency to let other people use you as their listening post for negativity. After routine chores have been completed, associate with positive folk. Spend the day in pleasant pursuits that happily engage your mind. Keep monetary matters simple so that you retain control of your resources. Singles are apt to be in a dating mood. Use your exellent powers of communication to meet and impress a potential romantic partner.

15. MONDAY. Sensitive. Feelings run high today, making everything seem more important or problematical than is actually the case. Don't let this hothouse atmosphere become overwhelming, or your emotions might seem to be spinning out of control. The early morning Pisces Full Moon accentuates your relationships with other people, which is bound to lead to a few disagreements or heated words. Even practical Virgo may wish to escape from reality if just for a short while. Treat yourself kindly this evening. Read a good book, go for a walk, or soak in a relaxing bath full of your favorite aromatherapy oils.

16. TUESDAY. Revealing. Plunging into the deep recesses of life can enrich the mind and open up other avenues to explore. It can also reassure you that you are being proactive regarding future possibilities. Have facts and figures at hand because you may be called to take part in a survey or testify in a legal matter. Be prepared for emotional and impulsive action when it comes to your love life. A romantic encounter could be exciting for the unattached Virgo but will probably be a case of opposites attracting. As a result a long-term love affair is unlikely. Enjoy the romantic vibes while still keeping all of your options open.

17. WEDNESDAY. Rousing. The universe is sending a vast array of cosmic action today. With inspirational energy prevailing, plans for an upcoming celebration can be made with flair and vision. Make sure you plan your travels carefully due to the price of gasoline. If you have to do lots of running around to finalize preparations, stay calm and in control. Secrets have a tendency to generate controversy, especially if these become public now. Take care with what you reveal in order to avoid problems or embarrassment. Life may seem filled with possibilities for the finer things, including romance and affection. Be open to love and let yourself experience the joy.

18. THURSDAY. Fruitful. Virgo intuition is strong. Inspirational ideas continue to flow. This will be a particularly productive period for Virgos involved in creating imaginative products and giving form to what started out as a dream. Study and travel may be on your mind. Investigate educational courses or travel brochures and you will come up with ideas that suit your requirements. Clashes of beliefs or ideals could interrupt what should be a generally favorable day, so it would be wiser to remain silent rather than initiating a debate that might become heated. Precise delivery of a public speech can easily convince the audience of the merits of your views.

19. FRIDAY. Resourceful. Creative flair can provide a touch of class to just about anything you get into today. Don't just talk about inspiring plans and aspirations. Develop fantasy into a realistic and practical form. Procrastination or indecisiveness could be an issue, hindering productivity. If involved in an overseas business venture you might need to rethink plans to find a more cost-effective way of handling shipments and orders. Romantic possibilities are starred for Virgos as your ruler Mercury makes beautiful music with stirring Neptune. Don't say no to a special suggestion.

20. SATURDAY. Uncertain. Today's atmosphere might not be as tranquil as yesterday's. Responsibilities at home or at work could increase. A power struggle may interfere with what should be a happy situation. If you can suppress anger toward other people and release it in a positive way through sports, dancing, or other physical exercise, you should come through this tense period relatively unscathed. Disagreements could arise with authority figures. Incorrectly believing you are a victim may produce a negative outcome. Steer clear of dangerous venues and locations. Take extra care with electrical or household products. A power failure or fault could cause inconvenience or an accident.

21. SUNDAY. Problematic. Peace and harmony might be jeopardized by the possibility that warring cosmic forces still surround Virgo folk. You can get through the day without too many hassles if you avoid voicing strong opinions. Also refrain from displaying a bossy or domineering approach. You can be honest about your feelings as long as you exhibit a calm demeanor, even if this is not how you actually feel. Tasks other people should have completed might be left up to you, causing anger and feelings of impatience due to the overload of your schedule. Perhaps you just need to get out of the house and spend the day with congenial companions.

22. MONDAY. Opportune. The fall equinox brings the Sun into the pleasant sign of Libra, encouraging Virgos to think about priorities and the values that rule everyday life. With four planets now gracing your Libra finance sector, money matters are bound to occupy much of your thought, time, and energy. Over the next few weeks consider making some sensible investments that can set you up for life by increasing financial security. Money could flow in, even an inheritance or other small windfall. Developments in a close relationship should make you feel on top of the world as your lover responds positively to your every word, action, and desire.

23. TUESDAY. Harmonious. Happy trends exist, although you may encounter a tricky situation that tests your patience and resolve. Luckily for Virgo individuals, Venus will skip into Scorpio tonight. Venus here will enhance passion and affection. Communication with other people may become more intense and emotional, assisting Virgos who need to connect on a deeper level. You will want to get along well with everyone you meet, so this is an excellent period to cultivate good relations with colleagues and clients. If your employment involves caring for others or being of service, you may have an increased urge to go beyond your usual responsibilities. Your love life should continue to look up.

24. WEDNESDAY. Useful. Now is the time to believe in yourself and your creative abilities. Take full advantage of an opportunity to participate in an ongoing project that you have never tried before. There is a first time for everything. Plan and prepare, but wait before actually beginning anything new. Not everything will go as planned because your ruler, tricky Mercury, starts another retrograde period today. Minor hassles are likely. Electronic gadgets and transportation could be the source of a few problems. This is not the time to sign a new lease, enter into a large financial deal, or purchase a car or a home. Order pizza, watch a movie, and relax tonight.

25. THURSDAY. Quiet. Your preference may be to be left alone with your own thoughts. With the Moon navigating through Leo, your house of solo activities, this is a time to unwind and recoup your energy. Delays in reaching goals are likely right now. However, if you have been trying to complete a project, this is the time to go into action. Entering a competition is apt to be pointless because you are more likely to follow than to take the lead. Defer updating computer software or hardware until after October 15 when your ruler Mercury once again heads forward. Avoid socializing in a crowd because quiet entertainment will suit you better.

26. FRIDAY. Reassuring. The early morning trends favor study and solitude. Good progress can be made by hitting the books, especially for Virgo students and researchers. Although your mind may be preoccupied with financial interests, don't become obsessed by a materialistic attitude. By noontime the Moon begins rising in your sign of Virgo, which will start bringing personal plans and issues to the surface. Difficulties within a romantic relationship that you have not tackled earlier can benefit from a practical, down-to-earth approach. You should be feeling great as the workday closes. If you are going out to socialize tonight, make sure you look your best.

27. SATURDAY. Lively. A desire to express can bring out the best in you. Today you bask in increased self-assurance and confidence. You might be spending extra time thinking about your current circumstances. Focus on how you can attain cherished desires, especially if you sense that through lack of effort these may be slipping out of your grasp. Meditation, a sports activity, or any type of physical exercise can help clear your mind and maintain your figure. Get together with a few of your favorite people. Consider organizing an outing where you can have plenty of fun and enjoyment.

28. SUNDAY. Sociable. Today's planetary configuration produces mixed influences. It is time to loosen up a little and have fun. If entertaining at home and worried about the menu, keep it simple. If you go overboard, anxiety and a lack of time to socialize with your guests can spoil enjoyment of the day. Self-employed Virgos might be wise to defer paying bills or handling paperwork. You could make mistakes and then have to redo the whole job. Take a middle-of-the-road approach in regard to finances. Reject any so-called surefire investment proposition.

29. MONDAY. Positive. This promises to be a very productive day. Money will be the main concern as a fresh cycle in regard to finances begins. There is a New Moon in your Libra sector of personal resources and material possessions. Set aside time to think about how you allot your money and whether you are frivolously spending more than you are saving. If this is the case, you now have the willpower and opportunity to cut back expenses and stick to a budget. It is important that you analyze your own actions as well as question other people's. Be on guard for someone who might try to pull the wool over your eyes while you try to help them.

30. TUESDAY. Fortunate. The general tone of the day is cheerful and positive. With this renewed vigor, increased productivity is more than likely. Finding love or friendship on the Internet can open up a whole new world. Providing you take care and don't believe everything you are told, this can be an enlightening experience. You can make financial gains through long-term conservative investments. However, guard against a tendency to only take an interest in what has monetary value. That outlook can be a very limiting experience. Allow yourself time to dream about what may not now seem realistic or practical, and expand your horizons.

OCTOBER

1. WEDNESDAY. Buoyant. Your energy and vitality peak as this month begins, so make the most of it. If you want to reshape your body, start a new diet, or restart an exercise program, you should have ample physical stamina to instigate a healthy fitness regime. Taking a few risks is fine right now as long as you guard against an inclination to be careless. You may forget a person's name or let things out of the bag that would be better kept to yourself. Payment you have been expecting for services rendered should finally arrive. Passion and desire are not in short supply, so plan a romantic evening with the love of your life.

2. THURSDAY. Soothing. On this promising day you could come up with a number of very inventive schemes and plans. Experimenting with different ideas can be a fun way to utilize your time and mental energy. A conversation could click your imagination into gear and provide important clues about where you are heading. Consider if changes need to be made to improve some areas of life. Go visiting. Enjoy sharing a cup of coffee and a chat with a close friend or neighbor while at the same time catching up on community gossip. Playing a game or going for a brisk walk in the fresh air this evening can produce unexpected insights and deeper understanding.

3. FRIDAY. Confrontational. Morning influences might not be gentle. Unstable tensions build in the cosmos, bringing change and delays. Avoid in-depth shared conversations because it might be difficult to see with clarity. Save your energy for this evening, when you can enjoy being with family members. If in the mood to give someone a helping hand, taking an elderly family friend or neighbor on a shopping trip can fulfill the need to be of service to others. Late tonight Mars will enter intense Scorpio. Mars in Scorpio will enhance your ability to communicate and to present ideas articulately as well as forcefully.

4. SATURDAY. Disconcerting. Although delays could be wearing you down, try to be patient for a little longer. In the meantime finish off or review old projects to see if these should be abandoned or if it would be worthwhile applying effort to complete them. It could be all too easy to blurt out something at the wrong time or offend someone with a careless off-the-cuff remark. An older family member may make a tactless comment that arouses upset feelings. It would be wise to keep tension at bay and just ignore sarcasm. Home and family may need more attention than usual. If you have a hectic job, consider taking a few days off if possible and putting your Virgo compassion to good use.

5. SUNDAY. Beneficial. The heavenly aspects cast a magical spell today, with the benevolent presence of Venus and Jupiter harmonizing happily together. If celebrating a special occasion with family members and friends you can expect to have a most enjoyable time. You are apt to be feeling more loving than usual, so romantic plans made with that special someone will be especially pleasurable. Virgo shoppers need to curb excessive tendencies. Control an urge to splurge on all sorts of merchandise. Even if these items are needed, the price could be unaffordable right now. Take control of your own emotional responses tonight or you might end up having trouble sleeping.

6. MONDAY. Stimulating. With an abundance of cosmic influences beaming down, this is a day to pay close attention to the voice of inspiration. If offered a leadership role or the opportunity to do something different, grasp the chance. Let other people see exactly how capable you are. Your primary symbol, Mercury, aligns with the Sun, which ensures that you will know exactly what should be said and how to say it. Submitting a sales report, teaching a class, or writing an essay are activities where you can excel as long as a litany of facts and figures is kept to a minimum Romance and friendship blossom under current celestial trends.

7. TUESDAY. Supportive. An overdue haircut or coloring could work wonders for your appearance and self-confidence. If your mate or partner has been feeling out of sorts and not as enthusiastic as usual, you can both receive a boost of spirits from a surprise night out to a new restaurant or local club. If this doesn't appeal, a relaxing night shared at home could be a pleasurable option. Singles can sweep away anxiety by launching into an exercise routine that increases heart rate and fitness level. Practicing a technique such as meditation or yoga can also help relax nerves and reduce stress. A new relationship that begins under current cosmic trends has an excellent chance of becoming permanent.

8. WEDNESDAY. Stressful. Tempers might become frayed. A tight schedule, an indecisive boss, or too many chores to act on in a short space of time could make you feel pressured and anxious. Calm down by working off nervous energy in a therapeutic and constructive manner. At home you could clear out the fridge or a closet as a way to calm your nerves. If at work, organize your desk or files. Virgos are always interested in health matters, so if you are not feeling up to par consider making an appointment for an alternative therapy, acupuncture, or medical treatment.

9. THURSDAY. Improving. Virgo health and vitality are on the upswing. You should feel as if nothing can stop you. However, don't be tempted to participate in a strenuous activity in order to test how much your fitness level has improved through exercise and diet. Go easy and pace yourself. This is a good day to go on a job interview or audition. You are likely to receive good news concerning a future change of position. Don't worry if a work project seems too large to tackle. If you have the knowledge and expertise, getting through the experience should not pose any insurmountable problems. For a capable and organized Virgo, significant gains can be made.

10. FRIDAY. Challenging. Beware of dispersing your energy too far and wide. Your biggest problem is knowing when you are overextending yourself so much that your health may suffer. A periodic checkup to assess your physical condition can determine if you need to slow down. Someone could be personally confused, making it risky to believe what they say. Even if they are not deliberately attempting to deceive, that could be the final outcome unless you verify all information with an outside source. If you are planning a vacation and need to board a pet, ask a friend or relative first. If they can't help, check out a boarding facility that comes with a recommendation from someone you know.

11. SATURDAY. Rewarding. Artistic projects are apt to be original and inspired. Keep an open mind when it comes to your love life. It might be time to do something different. With feelings very close to the surface, now is a good time to express heartfelt sentiments. Connecting with that special someone can be easily accomplished. Tell loved ones how wonderful they are. Display your affection because actions speak louder than any words. However, if you discover that someone has not been truthful, you are likely to go on the warpath. Virgo social life should be active. Enjoy going out to dinner with a favorite companion or sharing a home-cooked meal.

12. SUNDAY. Edgy. Restlessness can get you off track. Your energy can be utilized constructively if you participate in activities that provide stimulation and pleasure. It could be all too easy to speak out of turn or accuse someone of some type of transgression. However, it would be better for all concerned if you remain calm. Find a relaxing pursuit to ease anxiety. Being in and around nature can help you unwind and recharge your batteries. Consider going for a hike or planning a trip into the country. If you have been working hard to accumulate a stash of cash, you won't be very happy if your mate or partner decides to go on a shopping spree.

13. MONDAY. Uneasy. Although as a Virgo you are not usually noted for being overly emotional, today you are more sensitive than normal and inclined to overreact to the slightest hint of criticism or reproach. If you can remain detached you will save yourself significant upset. Think first, then speak. This is not the day to apply for a business or personal loan or to request an extension of your credit card limit. For most of the day your thinking might be flawed and not up to your usual analytical best. Defer thoughts of entering into a new business partnership until you have given it further consideration and have weighed the pros and the cons.

14. TUESDAY. Intense. Mixed vibes prevail. This is another day when major decision making should be deferred. Your vim and vitality could also be lower. You and the people around you may be in the grip of some very intense emotions as the Full Moon culminates in the fiery sign of Aries. Financial matters now take prominence. Virgo parents may have to take a hard stand in regard to loaning money to an adult child. Before saying yes or no, realize that you are unlikely to be repaid in full. You could now be placed in the happy position of making the last payment on your home mortgage or on a long-term loan. Opt for a relaxing night at home engaged in a favored creative pursuit.

15. WEDNESDAY. Promising. Your ruler Mercury has been moving retrograde, but now Mercury turns forward. As a result you should find that life becomes easier. Whatever has been causing delays should be revealed, allowing advancements to be made in required areas. As a Virgo you always take pleasure in giving your brain a good workout, and today you can do that by entering a competition, completing a crossword puzzle, or playing mind-stimulating games. A topic that you have never considered before might prove fascinating enough that you decide to do more research.

16. THURSDAY. Successful. Far-off people or places play an important role in today's activities. In your current mood this is an excellent day for any form of study, teaching, or school assignments. Get an early start if you are going to a conference or leaving on a long journey. Headway can be made by sending a manuscript off to a publisher, organizing a product to be patented, or signing up to take a course or to teach one. A current situation might leave you feeling a little disappointed or annoyed with yourself. Rather than engaging in self-pity, take decisive action but don't be too hard on yourself.

17. FRIDAY. Sparkling. Pay extra attention to career matters. If you can see a way to improvise, fine-tune, or adapt new methods, don't delay. The chance to make such changes could move you quickly up the professional ladder. There is a wonderful romantic glow, so use your imagination and enjoy the moment with the special person in your life. Socializing is favored in the employment environment. This is a good time to plan a morning staff meeting, a group lunch for employees, or an after-work get-together. Introducing more fun into the workday can give everyone a lift, and they are sure to appreciate your efforts.

18. SATURDAY. Testing. Professionally, it may be a challenging and hectic day. Be nice to other people if you hope to remain in their good graces. Glorious Venus moves into Sagittarius, your family zone, which shifts your focus to home and domestic life. Cooperate and bestow more attention on family members and on those who need your love and support. Making changes in the domestic scene can enhance the comfort of your living conditions. This is a starred time to spend money and exert effort to make your world more beautiful. If you are ready to purchase new home furnishings or change room colors, this is the time to do it.

19. SUNDAY. Exciting. A tendency toward an extravagant lifestyle needs to be reined in if you are trying to cope on a shoestring budget. For Virgos with money to spare, this is a good day to go shopping with your mate or partner. Spending each other's hard-earned cash will be a pleasure. Household furnishings, rugs, lamps, paintings, or anything that glitters is likely to attract your attention and can make a pleasant difference to the appearance of your living quarters. A group activity could be a happy diversion. Communicating with people who enjoy uncommon interests and outlook will fascinate you.

20. MONDAY. Volatile. The influence from today's planetary rays leads to restlessness or anxiety for immediate results in anything you undertake. This could become overwhelming. Don't foil your aims by being impulsive. Relax and slow down to achieve the most worthwhile results. A group consensus can develop from brainstorming and sharing ideas. Unless working for a living is your ultimate goal in life, make sure you are not so overloaded with work that you have no time to engage in recreational pursuits. If involved in home improvements or renovations, projects should move along smoothly. Opt for the best supplies you can afford.

21. TUESDAY. Purposeful. Although you may be in a reflective and contemplative mood, physical drive and energy levels are heightened. A great deal can be accomplished with little effort because other people are willing to follow your lead. Enjoyment comes from doing something exciting and challenging. It will be very difficult for anyone to pull the wool over your eyes or trick you more than once. You have the ability to spot errors and will quickly make or demand appropriate corrections. It would be wise to cancel social arrangements that have already been made because mixing and mingling this evening is unlikely to appeal.

22. WEDNESDAY. Slow. It will pay to conserve your physical resources, especially if you are worn out or don't feel up to par. As a Virgo, you will be at your best if left alone to contemplate in peace, without anyone looking over your shoulder. The next four weeks are bound to be busy running errands, visiting, and going on numerous short trips. Interaction with neighbors and relatives is likely to increase as the Sun blazes through Scorpio, your sector of communications, from tonight until November 21. Entertaining and sharing hospitality will be the best way to enjoy the company of family members and friends and to increase your rapport with them.

23. THURSDAY. Fair. Until midday, while the Moon is still in Leo, being left alone will suit you best. It may be difficult to snap out of an antisocial mood and engage in socializing. Go back to basics if expenses need to be trimmed. If a chance comes along to take care of someone who is unable to fend alone, consider it a special opportunity. Lending a hand to a volunteer group or charity if you are not already participating in this type of activity can provide both satisfaction and emotional fulfillment. Anger or resentment regarding a past incident may be upsetting but cannot undo what has been done. Learn from past experiences, then move on.

24. FRIDAY. Helpful. The day will be rather constraining unless you take a flexible approach. A shift in an intimate relationship could be due to an irrational fear of being controlled by someone. Although you might have the urge to act in a compulsive manner, conditions warn against this type of action. Instead, relax and examine what issues you are harboring when it comes to distinguishing between self-assertion and domination. The Moon is rising in your sign of Virgo now, impacting your first house of personality. So your thoughts may be more self-involved and directed toward personal aims and ambitions.

25. SATURDAY. Solemn. Life might appear to be more serious than usual to Virgo. A problem you are grappling with might assume larger proportions than it deserves. This might bring on feelings of being overwhelmed by current events and circumstances. The trick is not to let this mood dominate the day. Take a step back and try hard to quit worrying, especially if there is nothing you can do now to change the situation. Be sure to keep receipts and file them carefully away because you might need to return purchases for refund or credit. Virgo drivers must obey every rule of the road and refrain from speeding. Otherwise a confrontation with law enforcement is very probable. Pedestrians, too, need to be more aware.

26. SUNDAY. Pressured. Speak and act with the utmost discretion. Giving way to rash impulse might have serious long-term consequences. As a Virgo you know that more flies are caught with honey than vinegar, so if necessary sugarcoat your words even when you're angry and know you're right. Tackling money issues can bring results. Focus on how to generate more income and reduce expenses. Also consider your values and priorities in life, and whether you are devoting enough time and energy to this. Don't go overboard if hosting a party for a child. Keep the menu simple, and the kids are likely to have a great time.

27. MONDAY. Superb. Life should be less stressful. Unavoidable inconveniences or difficult personalities will not annoy you as much as usual. Take stock of your current financial situation. If necessary, take action to increase economic stability and security. You might decide to put more money into savings each pay period, pay off a loan quicker, or eat out less. Expanding your mind by finding a new subject to study or completing a daily crossword puzzle are positive ways to increase knowledge. Exploring new depths of your spiritual beliefs can be a pleasant diversion.

28. TUESDAY. Auspicious. Life has plenty to offer during the next two weeks. As a Virgo you will be excited by the many prospects and opportunities that come your way. A New Moon in the sign of Scorpio brings good luck, especially with meetings, discussions, and interviews. The usually reserved Virgo could manage to speak up about something that you have wanted to say for some time. This is a good period to purchase a new computer, phone system, or other technology. Involvement in a local welfare program or a fundraising event could be the vehicle to raise your profile as well as give you great emotional satisfaction.

29. WEDNESDAY. Profitable. Part-time study might assist your career aspirations but take you away from family responsibilities. Explain to loved ones that your enhanced employment skills will be of benefit to all once classes are completed. Today is well aspected for making new friends, especially for Virgos who have just moved into a new locality. Mixing at a community center, school, or shopping outlet will soon lead to a number of new acquaintances. Do all that you can to expand your social circle. Work with changing conditions or new influences until you determine what these will actually mean for you.

30. THURSDAY. Stirring. Imagination runs riot through the next few days. You may be distracted by daydreams of new love or an upcoming vacation. Creative work benefits from heightened inspiration. You possess the strong discipline to turn anything into structured form. However, making informed and practical decisions is better left until next week. Money might not flow in as quickly as expected, so leave a little extra in your bank account to cover unexpected expenses. You don't want to run short of funds. Tonight you may be in the mood to spend time in the kitchen experimenting with a different style of cooking.

31. FRIDAY. Blissful. Bright stars prevail to help you celebrate Halloween. Routine tasks are unlikely to appeal and might seem incredibly tedious and boring. Unexpected news from a friend or partner can raise your level of excitement and cause a possible change of circumstances. Holding discussions, attending meetings, and running errands will keep you on the run. Your social life is likely to be in full swing. If you are heading out of town, the usual haunts may not be of interest. Instead, head to somewhere different, particularly a venue that is new and has just opened for business.

NOVEMBER

1. SATURDAY. Comforting. No matter how organized you are or would like to be, it won't matter. You can expect things to go wrong. By keeping your schedule flexible it should be easier to cope with minor frustrations and disruptions. This is a day to stay home, do the chores, and find comfort in the family circle. Eat a nourishing breakfast and refuse to get agitated about upsets that don't really matter in the larger scheme of life. Let off steam by going for a brisk walk or working out at the gym or health club. Dinner and dancing with that special person could round off the day nicely. A special family occasion or happy baby news might be cause for a celebration.

2. SUNDAY. Inspired. Your creative imagination is stimulated. This is a good time to get away from humdrum daily activities and do some exploring. Dropping by a local craft market or antiques store can be a pleasant diversion. Your love partnership might require a dose of extra attention. Don't allow minor issues to interfere with your loving relationship. As a Virgo there are times when you find it difficult to discuss personal matters with your nearest and dearest. Today, however, you should feel free to talk together openly. Inspirational Neptune begins a forward march in your health and work sector. If you have been suffering a problem with your immune system, you should be granted some relief now.

3. MONDAY. Disconcerting. Today's energy will not work against you but is rather sobering. Vixen Venus challenges serious Saturn and disruptive Uranus, causing testing times in the romance department. If your committed relationship has been getting stale lately, consider new ways to brighten up your love life. Well-timed, tactful suggestions to your partner regarding change and experimentation could provide a new lease on love. Virgo singles who are seeking a new love affair or who hope to revive a previous one need to release any expectations and just go with the flow. An organized sports event or concert to raise money may not be as popular as predicted.

4. TUESDAY. Variable. A variety of cosmic rays will influence the outcome of this day. Mercury whizzes into your Scorpio communications sector, bringing an increase in mental acceleration until November 23. You may receive an invitation to a special party or wedding, sure to add excitement within the family circle. Plan on purchasing a new trendy outfit, especially if you are currently unattached. There is good potential to meet a romantic prospect at a family gathering. Expect several delays, a confusing situation, or possible misunderstandings when you are only trying to be helpful. Follow up matters regarding a health condition. A message may be delivered but not passed on.

5. WEDNESDAY. Romantic. Romance is in the air. If you are typical of your Sun sign Virgo, the dream of perfection is never far away. This is especially true today. Whether coupled or single, your mind is apt to wander to what you envision as an ideal romantic relationship. You may start to get in the festive mood, providing inspiration to begin holiday preparations early. This will be particularly useful if you know that the next few weeks are going to be a busy period for you. If you need to purchase a special present for a loved one, this is a good day to track down the perfect gift. Cook your favorite food if expecting guests for dinner.

6. THURSDAY. Pressured. Expect a stressful day ahead. Virgo business owners could experience a downturn and loss of confidence in the economy if sales and business activities are slower than usual. If you hope to get in better physical shape in time for the upcoming holiday season, get out your training shoes or treadmill and begin an exercise program while there is still plenty of time. Patience and the dedication to maintain a steady fitness and diet regime are strengthened. Indoor sports activities can also be a great way to increase overall fitness. Avoid arguments at home and in the workplace, and steer clear of anyone who is inclined to be aggressive.

7. FRIDAY. Expectant. Things may not be happening fast enough, but stay calm and remain patient. Don't rush with a legal matter or other problem or you might overlook a vital bit of information. Focus on the normal events that are happening in your life. Proceed with research for a class that can help you earn a certificate or degree. Becoming fluent in a new language could be one way to improve your worth to an employer. If you have been renovating or refurbishing your home you should be coming to the period where you can enjoy the fruits of your labor. Add a special touch of romance to your one-on-one relationship tonight.

8. SATURDAY. Heartening. Mainly positive influences are in force. Any problem or unexpected eruption that does arise is apt to come from other people. You can choose to ignore rude behavior or to deal with it in your practical, cool, calm manner. If the perpetrator is your mate or partner, they may need to engage in some serious gift or flower buying or helping around the house before being allowed to reenter your good graces. For single Virgos, prospects of being noticed by a romantic potential are more likely in the early afternoon rather than later this evening. Accept any opportunity to socialize with friends, which is bound to increase the chance of romance coming your way.

9. SUNDAY. Opportune. New opportunities are foreseen. One of these, in particular, may offer interesting future financial potential. Consider all options thoroughly. If you have been ignoring unpleasant financial issues regarding an overdue insurance payment, tax assessments, or high mortgage interest rates, devote some time to getting your affairs back in good order. Although this may not be a pleasant way to spend a Sunday, reviewing the overall financial picture can pinpoint where improvements might be made. Amorous feelings and passions are likely to be strong, allowing you to strengthen affectionate ties with your significant other.

10. MONDAY. Invigorating. Wonderful energy beams down, although Virgos who are stuck in a boring job might feel restless and constrained. Good fortune and opportunity are featured. Do all that you can to increase the chance of good luck coming your way. Remain alert. Business dealings with powerful people can boost your confidence and might produce an interesting but testing challenge. You may have the opportunity to receive the gift of wisdom from an admired and respected mentor. Listening carefully can place you in a privileged position, providing the opportunity and opening your mind to exciting new concepts.

11. TUESDAY. Enlightening. Gather strength and determination and get ready for action. Your hopes and wishes are happily highlighted. With the bright Sun and stable Saturn in a productive aspect, obstacles that you have been encountering will begin to disappear, clearing the way for your dreams to move closer to reality. With a little more effort, strategies can be put into place to produce a successful outcome. Check out a financial option or possible investment that could be a good source of future financial gain. This is a favorable day for business borrowers to seek a loan. Children might need increased guidance from their Virgo parent.

12. WEDNESDAY. Passionate. Visions of faraway places and exciting leisure activity might be dancing in your mind, disrupting everyday thoughts and routine. You will not tolerate jealousy or possessiveness very well, although having to deal with this type of behavior is a possibility. Vivacious Venus merges with passionate Pluto, adding an extra intensity to all of your relationships. Venus also now swings into Capricorn, your house of romance, visiting there until December 7. Venus here promises plenty of fun, love, and good cheer. Singles attending parties over the next few weeks are bound to have a great time and might meet a potential partner.

13. THURSDAY. Varied. Mixed trends prevail throughout the day, although Lady Luck smiles on romantic relationships and financial speculation. Learning and expanding your knowledge of worldwide customs and cultures can be enlightening. Virgo emotions are at an all-time high. This morning's Taurus Full Moon will be raising more questions than you can find answers to. If possible, defer a long journey because everything that could go wrong is likely, from delays and lost luggage to being seated next to an overly talkative passenger. Students attending lectures should take along a recording device since Virgo attention span could be unusually short.

14. FRIDAY. Demanding. Luck still lingers. However, this is a day of tension because avoiding mix-ups will be difficult. Work could be demanding much of your time, keeping you away from your significant other and friends. Friction could be aroused due to the lack of romantic time. This problem needs to be addressed before it escalates further. You may be in a hurry and not want to wait around for other people. Virgos now making arrangements will need to be patient when plans do not fall instantly into place. You may feel obligated to attend a work social gathering. Although this could be inconvenient, it might be essential to please your boss.

15. SATURDAY. Favorable. New career or business prospects could cross your path, or you may receive deserved praise for your efforts on a recent job. A loved one might be blocking a particular ambition or making life so difficult that new strategies are required before you can make further progress. If your circle of friends has undergone a transformation, possibly due to your change of attitude, meeting new people could be on your agenda. Joining a new hobby group or social circle with like-minded individuals can put you in touch with a number of interesting people you might consider as potential close friends.

16. SUNDAY. Motivating. Your ruler Mercury makes several aspects with the power brokers of the zodiac today, so you can expect a number of happenings, all of which should be exciting. Your sociable, outgoing mood indicates that pleasure will come from mixing with other people. This is a delightful day to arrange to get together with those in your friendship network. Although you are still focused on practical applications, thoughts are less conservative. This will assist efforts to tap into intuitive and creative resources that may surprise even you. If taking part in a group effort, enjoy the feeling that you are contributing something worthwhile.

17. MONDAY. Manageable. Mars has now taken up residence in your Sagittarius sector of home and family. Fiery planet Mars in a fire sign can be a combative mix, so be prepared for the sparks to fly. Home renovators will have more enthusiasm and motivation to complete do-it-yourself projects, draw up new plans, or contact a reputable contractor to finish a job. Expect quarrels and conflict within the family circle. Your ruler, tricky Mercury, is not friendly toward nebulous Neptune. Because of this, astute Virgos should defer major decisions. Discerning fact from fiction could be fraught with difficulties.

18. TUESDAY. Tricky. Remain alert because deceptive trends continue. You will probably prefer to work alone, which could upset coworkers or associates. With the waxing Moon gliding through Leo, your house of solitude and secrets, it is time to take life slower, to reflect, to recharge your spiritual batteries. Someone from your past could reappear, which might make you uncomfortable even though you are aware that it is way past time to let go and move on. Experiencing a crisis of conscience could be disconcerting. This might be the catalyst for making a moral decision, which will not be as easy for you as envisioned.

19. WEDNESDAY. Active. If there are items around the house that have an unhappy association for you, consider getting rid of them once and for all. Gifts or possessions that you no longer use or want should also be discarded or donated to charity. A coworker's word could be deliberately insulting or controversial. This may just be a ploy to anger you, so it might be wise not to rise to the bait. Ignoring insults can quickly take the heat out of any tension. Other people might entrust you with confidential data. Make sure you don't let any secret slip out. Acting on inside information could get you in trouble with a governing agency.

20. THURSDAY. Lively. You should be full of energy and enthusiasm after the last few days. Focus, energy, and intuition become stronger as the Moon slips into your sign. Your sense of personal freedom is enhanced. You assertively stand up for your rights. Effort put into moving beyond negative aspects from your past and implementing ways to increase self-growth can produce positive results. Setting in motion a new scheme or idea could pay dividends. Act on the desire to renovate and repair. Grab a paintbrush or hammer and begin renovating to maximize the comfort of your home.

21. FRIDAY. Spirited. The pace quickens from today until December 21 while the Sun visits the happy-go-lucky sign of Sagittarius, your sector of home and family matters. A focus on home entertaining may find you now making plans to hold parties or informal gatherings for family and friends. Putting arrangements in place to host guests for the upcoming festive season could be the motivation you need to give your domestic environment a face-lift. A conservative investment made now will add to your asset base, generating gains in the future. Virgos in business can look forward to increased sales and higher profits.

22. SATURDAY. Vibrant. Regardless of your particular circumstances, an urge to be a free spirit colors your speech and behavior. A constructive aspect between the two planets of wealth creation and wisdom, expansive Jupiter and conservative Saturn, is in play now. This helps you remove obstacles that might be blocking present aims and long-term goals. Virgo is determined to move forward while still remaining true to important principles. You can maintain this motivating force if you believe in yourself. A lull in the day's activities could be an excellent time to straighten out personal money matters. Work out a budget that covers both the upcoming holiday expenses and the regular bills.

23. SUNDAY. Productive. With the party season getting closer, expect action around your home base to greatly increase. Your ruler Mercury arrives in Sagittarius, joining the Sun, Mars, and Pluto there. Mercury will amplify your focus on emotional life, family matters, and property affairs. Changes are likely as your home becomes the center of attention. Plans to redecorate the domestic environment can provide both renters and owners a thrill of exhilaration even though changes may require a large sum of money. Consider the cost a way of increasing potential resale value as well as improving current living conditions for all family members.

24. MONDAY. Challenging. Establish your priorities first thing this morning, especially if your schedule is crowded. Time can be wasted by scattering your energy, resulting in limited progress by day's end. Improvement in your overall financial picture is foreseen, although resisting the desire to spend money may remain a problem. Beware placing too much confidence in professional advice because there is a likelihood of receiving incorrect guidance. This is not the day to challenge a legal outcome or to take on a large project even though you expect a successful result.

25. TUESDAY. Auspicious. A happy and bright day awaits Virgos. Expect to be on the move more than usual, running errands and contacting people. This energy will suit your wanderlust tendencies. Getting out and about around town will seem like a day off rather than work. If you have time on your hands, investigating nearby points of interest that you have not visited before will help you remain stimulated and active. In the world of work a significant conversation with a superior or approaching an avid mentor who is willing to propose you for a new job could be the beginning of a new phase in your life.

26. WEDNESDAY. Social. Another active day is ahead for Virgo as your ruler Mercury continues to vibrate positively with the glowing Sun, significantly increasing your self-confidence and communication skills. A gregarious and sociable mood prevails. If you don't have plans for this evening, invite a neighbor over for coffee and conversation. Or arrange to meet your sweetheart in town for a romantic dinner date. Make a dent in your festive shopping list by beginning this huge task now. This is a good day to hunt down quality goods and gifts at bargain prices. Virgo singles could receive an unexpected invitation from a romantic admirer.

27. THURSDAY. Excellent. Your outlook remains positive as more delightful rays from the cosmos shine on those born under the sign of Virgo. Intense Pluto reenters Capricorn, increasing your focus on love and romance. Singles could meet someone who has an immediate impact. Even meeting your soul mate is a real possibility. This morning's New Moon falls in your solar Sagittarius zone, encouraging devotion of more time and attention to home and family life. Celebrate this Thanksgiving holiday in style. If you have been contemplating moving to larger commercial premises or moving to a new house, put more energy into this goal now.

28. FRIDAY. Diverse. For most of the day the smile should remain on your face. The main flaw in current celestial influences comes from your ruler Mercury merging with warrior Mars. This increases your mental facilities but also conveys a shorter fuse than normal. Conflict around the home front is likely to emerge. As a levelheaded Virgo you may be asked to mediate between family members. Emotions and feelings tend to be erratic and explosive. Your significant other could be full of pleasant surprises. Be prepared for a romantic evening enjoying entertainment that may be very different from the usual night out.

29. SATURDAY. Reassuring. If you have been too busy to allocate as much time as you should to your romantic life or to your significant other, today offers the chance to correct this imbalance. Time and effort devoted to the people you value most will increase your enjoyment of life. Take a loved one out to lunch, or purchase an inexpensive treat to show how much you really care. This is another great day to head for the shopping mall. There is little chance that the shrewd Virgo will waste hard-earned cash on superfluous items. Purchasing an antique or some other article that will gain value over the years is also favored.

30. SUNDAY. Playful. A lighthearted atmosphere prevails and life remains exciting for most of you. Fun, laughter, and children are likely to occupy leisure time for Virgo parents. For others, an abundance of social invitations from which to choose should keep you on the go and well entertained. The unattached Virgo could meet someone who has an immediate impact. Under current stars any romantic relationship that begins now has a good chance of going the distance. Couples will find that sitting down and having a serious chat about current concerns can be a positive way to establish or reaffirm mutual goals.

DECEMBER

1. MONDAY. Smooth. You can cruise along in easy mode as the first day of the new working week and of the last month of the year begins. Your optimistic frame of mind should not be wasted. A surprising bout of good luck could strike when least expected. However, avoid getting too carried away in all of the excitement. Excessive spending on an upcoming social event or on gift purchases could make a large dent in your bank balance. This is the time to dream big dreams and turn them into reality. Romance is in the air. Loving rewards can be reaped by being attentive and devoting time and energy to your significant other.

2. TUESDAY. Accomplished. Get better organized. Arrange your schedule to suit yourself. Focus on completing the simple things first before performing the more intricate tasks. Take one step at a time. A responsible attitude and proper time management ensures that all tasks will be completed on time. With the holiday season approaching, do your best to curb any unhealthy habits. Get back into healthy daily routines that may have slipped by. Your home is likely a hive of activity with people coming and going, so be sure your pantry is well stocked for catering to unexpected guests. Spend the evening with people who are lively, stimulating company.

3. WEDNESDAY. Pleasant. If yesterday was a bit demanding, today should be a lot easier. You will feel more relaxed and positive. You have ample energy and focus to begin or complete employment projects designed to increase earnings. Virgos who are in the throes of relocating house or business premises should find everything moving along swiftly. If planning to set up a home business, you can make good progress by organizing your office space and ordering necessary equipment. Don't neglect to let loved ones know that their love and affection are returned. Relax this evening with your nearest and dearest.

4. THURSDAY. Fine. On this fair day, you should begin to feel your energy and motivation rising. There is very little impeding progress. Virgos who are working directly with the public can expect significant gains. As a typical Virgo you feel secure when in charge of organizing an event. Make sure these talents are used to the fullest extent for the annual office or neighborhood get-together. Finalize all details early so there are no unexpected surprises or increased costs. Charismatic Virgo appeal is on display. If you don't have a date, mingle with friends this evening and you soon will be spending time with one special person.

5. FRIDAY. Cautious. The peace and quiet that reigned over the past few days will be shattered now as your ruler Mercury meets up with disruptive Uranus. This is a combustible combination, so be on guard. Take extra care if handling electrical items around the house. Other people may be in a grumpy mood and as a result could snap at you or criticize you unnecessarily. Energy and enthusiasm are at a high peak. Restlessness could set in as you seek additional challenges and responsibilities on the job or within your daily activities. Be prepared to compromise if another person's ideas or expertise is essential to successfully complete a project.

6. SATURDAY. Diverse. A variety of aspects take form today. Focus centers on a number of areas, from shopping to family obligations to minor household repairs. Avoid boring or unnecessary chores that might wear down your spirit. Although energy should be in abundance, at times a less than optimistic mood could threaten to take over. If you do become gloomy or despondent, concentrate on creative activities that offer excitement and stimulation. Romantically, Virgo singles can expect a fantasy evening. If partnered, revealing in words and actions how much you love your mate or partner will strengthen ties of affection.

7. SUNDAY. Pleasurable. If you do not have any important activities to attend to this morning, opt to stay in bed an extra hour or two. A good book, the weekend newspaper, or your significant other should be able to keep you very pleasantly occupied. Venus, the planet of the good life, moves into Aquarius, your sector of work, daily routine, and overall health. It is appropriate now to focus on these areas of your life. Returning to a previous place of employment is not out of the question, particularly if higher pay or more perks are hard to refuse. A colleague is likely to be attracted to you and you to them, making love on the job a real possibility.

8. MONDAY. Cheery. Getting along with other people should be a breeze for Virgos. You might discover important data which could make your day. Keep alert for hints regarding information that can be useful for your progress. At work an eagerness to break away from what's tried and true can lead to experimenting with new concepts that open new areas. Creative energy can be put to good use. Those in authority are bound to be impressed with your ideas and plans. A discussion with a financial expert may be very helpful, providing an idea of future trends. Well-deserved rewards may be in store for singles when it comes to love.

9. TUESDAY. Tricky. Current energy emphasizes travel and education, but both of these areas could be fraught with difficulty. This is not the best day to plan a trip or to set out on a long-distance journey. If you are unable to make changes to travel plans, everything should be fine once you finally arrive at your destination. If you are arranging an upcoming vacation, be sure to write everything down so there are no mix-ups later on. Before handing in an important assignment or report, ask a trusted friend, parent, or colleague to check details and look for errors just as a precaution. Defer applying for a license or loan unless you are confident of success. Otherwise you might waste both time and money.

10. WEDNESDAY. Disconcerting. In order to make it through the day without becoming stressed, remain calm and expect the unexpected. Be prepared for last-minute changes to arrangements and to your schedule. Allow situations to flow naturally while staying patient. A superior or client might make negative comments regarding your work performance or behavior. If this is constructive criticism, accept it with good grace and vow to make improvements in the future. However, if this is just someone venting anger, justify your actions and then move out of the line of fire. Although you might need to work swiftly to complete your responsibilities, maintain safety precautions and avoid rushing.

11. THURSDAY. Suspenseful. You might find yourself in a dilemma. Family matters could be less than ideal. Someone close might be irresponsible or be accused of an indiscretion. Assist where you can, but don't take on any guilt by association. An increased workload may cause your significant other to complain of neglect. If you allow the situation to get out of hand, an emotional outburst will put a damper on romance. Continued care with personal safety is essential over the next few days, particularly if you drive for a living. As far as your love life is concerned, good vibes remain steady.

12. FRIDAY. Erratic. A bevy of celestial influences makes this a very busy and tiring day, increasing agitation. Unexpected situations are likely to produce over-the-top reactions. This will not be helped by the Gemini Full Moon, which affects both your home and career plans. Other people are likely to be overly sensitive with tempers that quickly become frayed. If a plan or procedure is not working, don't hesitate to cut your losses and move on. Avoid beginning any new project. Instead, focus on completing outstanding home and employment work. Your cool, analytical approach is needed to arbitrate an emotional family matter. The entertainment world may appeal this evening.

13. SATURDAY. Offbeat. Today's energy might be a bit unnerving. Your ruler Mercury has moved into Capricorn, joining Pluto and Jupiter there. This increases your enthusiasm for the more playful things in life. You may long to break free from ruts and restrictions or, if this is not possible, at least add variety to your routine. An innovative approach can assist your efforts to make a leisure pursuit worthwhile by turning a profit and being fun all at the same time. Meeting an outlandish type of person might be the eye-opener you need to see life in a different perspective, particularly if you have been single-minded recently.

14. SUNDAY. Hectic. As long as you remain calm, this is a perfect day to finalize plans for your holiday celebration. Creative juices are flowing, arousing a touch of flair. As a Virgo, the sign of the perfectionist, you want everything to run smoothly and won't be content to leave anything to chance. However, don't allow preparations to overwhelm you, which could cause upset with other family members. Keep in mind that unrealistically elaborate plans and demands are likely to prove disappointing. If you haven't heard back from expected party guests, check that invitations have not gone astray.

15. MONDAY. Taxing. Impatience for new opportunities is likely. Slow down and take a step back from the line of fire. Examine where you are and where you have been. Despite ambitions and aspirations, today is marked by the need for a realistic attitude in order to get through the day's responsibilities. Your physical resources are likely to be limited, so you will need to pace yourself throughout the day. Last-minute shopping could lead to panic if you have no idea what to buy certain people or one person in particular. Consider purchasing a gift certificate. These are practical and the choice of a gift is then not up to you.

16. TUESDAY. Mixed. Complex influences are taking place today. You might long for peace and quiet for a short while, then crave action and excitement. A high energy level is unlikely, forcing you to pace your activities. Use the day to gain perspective on any situation currently confounding you. Don't get caught up in foolish little squabbles, and avoid making rash choices. Continued success with work can lead to respect and rewards coming your way. You should begin to realize that progress is not about luck but depends on hard work and effort. Call a professional to take care of needed repairs and maintenance around home base.

17. WEDNESDAY. Productive. A renewal of energy is likely unless you have been burning the candle at both ends, combining too many social activities with increased time on the job. The Moon enters your sign of Virgo before dawn, impacting your sense of self. The focus is now very much on you. If you can assess where you are in terms of personal aims, you will be positioned to implement procedures to further your cherished desires. Discover your needs and begin marching forward. Grooming and fashion may be priorities now. You could find yourself hitting the shops, for bargain clothes and accessories to carry you through the festive holidays.

18. THURSDAY. Busy. Virgo confidence could slip unless you engage in positive self-talk. A certain satisfaction can come from getting on with normal everyday tasks, which conveys a sense that everything is okay in your world. As a Virgo, being organized is a priority. You like the feeling of ticking things off your current to-do list. Keep your eyes and ears open for information that is to your advantage. Trouble with your mate or partner is likely later today unless you take steps to avert this possibility. If you are participating in some form of exercise, be careful not to push yourself so hard that you cause an injury.

19. FRIDAY. Bumpy. Remain cool and composed even as your patience is tested today, possibly by a person who exerts some type of control or power over you. Your mind may wander to the upcoming holidays if social plans or preparations are still to be completed. Shopping for special gifts is not recommended because your spending could go to the extreme. Although this is an expensive time of year, too much enthusiasm can lead to overdoing, particularly on pleasure and leisure pursuits. It is fine to enjoy yourself and have a good time providing you are able to cope with increased financial pressure when credit card bills roll in next month.

20. SATURDAY. Carefree. Finances are once again to the fore. Don't be a spendthrift. Think twice before splurging with your hard-earned funds. Money is apt to be burning a hole in your pocket, and not just when you are in the department stores. Browsing Internet auction sites is also likely to make you consider a purchase, whether this is needed or not right now. Virgos who are looking for full-time or part-time employment should not undersell personal ability and talent. You can be realistic and still realize your worth. If you are going on an interview or audition that is related to the arts or has a creative theme, you should excel.

21. SUNDAY. Stimulating. Virgo folk are about to become more social. The accent switches from your home and family affairs to your leisure and social activities. The Sun is now shining in Capricorn, your sector of pleasure. If there hasn't been much time to hit the party scene and enjoy yourself, expect things to change. Virgo thoughts are likely to have a very practical foundation. A fresh creative idea or venture that pops into mind could provide the chance to achieve one of your dreams. Romance has an extra dash of fantasy. Singles can expect an exciting encounter, possibly leading to long-enduring love.

22. MONDAY. Intense. Right now you may feel that you can cope with whatever happens and are ready for anything. The opinions and viewpoints you express might be a little too forceful for the other people in your life, so try to be assertive but not aggressive in your approach. Although there should be a strong wave of feeling between couples, a tendency to be overly possessive or compulsive could cause a problem in your romantic partnership unless you apply restraint. Virgo singles engaged in pursuing a lover might need to find a different approach. Let the object of your desire know there is an attraction without giving the appearance of coming on too strong.

23. TUESDAY. Vibrant. Virgo energy remains high. Because of your efforts, everything that needs action will progress smoothly and in an orderly manner. If you are finishing purchasing gifts, resist sales talk and don't be pressured into buying things that may not suit the recipient. Consider leaving the car at home and taking public transportation. Finding available parking could cause lots of frustration even for the usually coolest Virgo. This is a good day to visit friends or an elderly relative you may not be able to see for the rest of the year. You will enjoy getting together with someone you are fond of.

24. WEDNESDAY. Comforting. On this Christmas Eve you are bound to be busy but might also feel the urge to do something out of the ordinary. If you decide to do something daring, make this a safe and fun activity for all of your companions. Intellectual pursuits or a game that stimulates the mind can be a pleasant way to occupy your leisure time. Bring out the chess or checkers set, board or computer games. This can be a great way to keep children and guests happily amused. If you are entertaining over the next few days, ensure that you have all the supplies you need before your favorite stores close for the holiday.

25. THURSDAY. Merry Christmas! You should be all ready for a happy day, whether hosting a gathering or not. Being surrounded by your immediate and extended family is a memorable way to spend this day. Caroling can give your singing voice a good workout while putting you and the entire audience in a festive spirit. A compassionate frame of mind may find you extending hospitality to someone who is currently away from loved ones. Or you might decide to volunteer your services for a few hours catering to the less fortunate. Prepare for a surprise development later. Enjoy a rousing conversation about what was and what might be.

26. FRIDAY. Joyful. Another happy day is on tap for Virgo. If you entertained yesterday, it is your turn to socialize and be catered to today. Get dressed in your finest and enjoy the social atmosphere. If adult children or guests stayed overnight, make sure that everyone does their bit to help clear up yesterday's festivities. Even the health-conscious and diet-conscious Virgo could be in the mood for some serious overindulging. If you are going to abandon your usual eating regime, do so for this one day only, and plan to resume your healthy habits tomorrow.

27. SATURDAY. Energetic. Motivating Mars steps into Capricorn, joining Pluto, Sun, Moon, Mercury, and Jupiter there. This increases your fire and enthusiasm as well as providing a burst of vigor to your love life. As much as this can be fun, it also comes with a warning to take some precautions so you do not become exhausted. Guard against burning yourself out with too much partying and romancing. Problems with a youngster could arise. Virgos with children may not enjoy the blessings of parenthood as much as usual. Spend time on a pastime that teaches as well as gives pleasure. Investigate a creative pursuit that you wish to develop further.

28. SUNDAY. Powerful. Intense and energetic influences are in force as active Mars merges with powerful Pluto in Capricorn, your house of leisure, treasure, and pleasure. The festive spirit has not yet passed you by. Virgo individuals will have plenty of good cheer and conversation to share with other people. You are the one who will most likely set the pace for others to follow, if they can keep up. This is not the time to allow anyone to add additional responsibilities to your workload. Be extremely careful when participating in any type of hobby or recreational pursuit that carries some type of risk. Avoid dangerous exploits altogether.

29. MONDAY. Rewarding. Even though Virgo emotions remain intense, those of you back on the job should be able to remain reasonably focused and on top of employment duties. Discipline and desire to work hard in your chosen field can find you making good progress. You are likely to receive recognition for past and current efforts. You might need to confront an unusual problem concerning a coworker or service provider. Your sensible approach should soon have the issue resolved to everyone's satisfaction. Amorous feelings are significantly on the rise, so prepare for a romantic encounter that fulfills your deepest longings for passionate union.

30. TUESDAY. Helpful. If you can channel your energy wisely, this should be a productive day. Trivial issues are likely to cause the most frustration, but only if you allow them to get the better of you. Aim to let situations unfold in their own good time. Be as creative and inventive as possible. Working solo on an employment project can be stimulating. You will like the feeling of no one watching your every move. If you are entertaining tomorrow evening, spend time finalizing arrangements to ensure that you have everything in hand. Resting and relaxing at home might be your preferred option tonight.

31. WEDNESDAY. Festive. Both happy and lucky energy prevails throughout the day, bringing 2008 to a successful close and beginning 2009 on a high note. This positive influence is a cue to become involved in a creative or artistic venture that will showcase your skills and talents. Many choices of venues and activities for celebrating the New Year is a happy possibility, making this a night that you are likely to remember for years to come. Wherever you decide to socialize, energy will remain high, allowing for plenty of high-spirited fun and games. One person in particular hopes you'll pay extra attention.

VIRGO
NOVEMBER–DECEMBER 2007

November 2007

1. THURSDAY. Promising. Delays can be a good thing, so do not let them cause frustration. Your ruler Mercury is ready to go direct again after a retrograde period. Today, it would be wise to revisit previous territory, with past decisions still up for review. You can make suitable changes now and formulate a sound strategy for going forward. Thorough knowledge will be a key factor in gaining success. Get all the bugs out of the works. Virgo students and apprentices who have been cramming and honing skills may be ready for final exams. Stepping forward on a new path gives you a great feeling.

2. FRIDAY. Mixed. It's no good trying to stand on stubborn ground right now. Sacrifice of some nature seems unavoidable. Possibly it's required on behalf of a customer or coworker. Willingly stepping away, with grace and compassion, gives another someone the necessary inches, but they could take the proverbial mile. Still, letting a person go out on a limb is fine if they want to. Act on your conscience and avoid getting trapped in the situation. A compulsion to rescue a person who's done something stupid might overwhelm you. Beware of creating a codependent relationship.

3. SATURDAY. Productive. As the stereotype predicts, Virgo can be uplifted by launching into a cleaning frenzy or a filing and ordering frenzy. So make good use of the Moon rising in your sign today. Right now is ideal for working bees and a massive tidying up of home or office. If this sounds way too huge a task, at least start small. Organize a room, a closet, or simply a handbag. Pursuing practical everyday intentions with the determination to see a job out will give you a sober focus that may isolate you from loved ones. Never mind, at the end of the day they will be happy that you have transformed some part of the shared environment and made it nicer.

4. SUNDAY. Exciting. With the Moon still in your sign, today is excellent for gratifying yourself. Treat yourself with a pleasurable reward for an ambition you have achieved. This gift to yourself will maintain your self-esteem and a positive outlook. You might be bursting with energy. Put it toward socializing and seeking stimulation. Being bored and alone won't suit you now. There's delightful distraction to be found in going out and about rather than staying in. Admiration for a companion's daring will amuse you for a while. Virgo athletes and spectators alike can revel in a win for the team. Connect with a group of people who enjoy the same buzz as you.

5. MONDAY. Encouraging. Some kind of personal metamorphosis seems to be in process for Virgo. You might be tired of where you have been living, and are now ready to move to something different. However, a housemate can get very resentful about such an event. This kind of reaction will only reinforce why you thought about moving in the first place. A partner's emotional scenes may cut a relationship off for good. When it's over, both of you will know it and will declare it with finality. Hanging on and fighting what is inevitable would be self-destructive. Endings will happen best if permitted to take their natural course.

6. TUESDAY. Successful. Your Virgo passion for perfection needs a positive outlet for you to be truly satisfied. Experiment with your own personal style in all things. However, it is always useful to consult various authoritative sources on what is currently fashionable. Be careful, though, not to get so caught up in a trend or fad that your capacity for originality is lost. You have plenty of leeway to do your own thing with your living quarters and your wardrobe. Whatever you purchase or invest in, make sure it has long-lasting intrinsic value. This advice applies to people, too. What's on the inside counts way more than the façade.

7. WEDNESDAY. Observant. Much is sure to be learned now from such close contacts as relatives, neighbors, teammates, even casual acquaintances. Someone may have scored a notable win, which somehow contributes to changing their style. They may decide to do a radical makeover, even resorting to cosmetic surgery. When a familiar person doesn't seem that familiar anymore, this can prove perturbing. Changes in another could have the consequence of urging you to be different. Crucial information regarding financial assistance is signified to arrive. So check your messages frequently and promptly return calls.

8. THURSDAY. Satisfying. Correspondence of all kinds puts you in touch with people, keeping you in the loop and on the same page. Expect calls, e-mails, letters, and cards to contribute a better awareness of where others are at. There's great satisfaction to be had in pulling things together, creating or recreating a sense of order. But do not limit your focus to workplace order and its details. Reach out to other human beings and get clear about what is expected and where things are going. Use your intuition and communication skill for people, not things. Neighbors and relatives can be especially helpful, either to you or your partner.

9. FRIDAY. Motivating. A New Moon in Scorpio may seem forbidding if you prefer everything out in the open and in the light of day. However, don't let preconceptions lead you astray. This is a genuinely happening day of positive potential. A deep sense of togetherness can fuse members of a team even more closely together. By illuminating and strengthening a common objective and direction, everyone can pull together and achieve much in the coming month. Just don't expect the same sense of urgency or speed to maintain itself. Contingency plans would be wise. Hard and fast schedules may be broken if they're too inflexible and unresponsive to events.

10. SATURDAY. Relaxing. Yesterday might have done you in, and the wind is out of your sails for most of today. Perhaps it was a big night out on the town that has left you a bit flat this morning. In any event, it's not normal and sustainable to maintain peak levels of excitement and anticipation for extended periods. Otherwise, you would physically burn out. So easy days like these are meant for taking it easy. Just cruising the neighborhood, window-shopping, and catching up with casual acquaintances over coffee could be enough for you to do now. Chatty visits can occupy you until you're ready to go home for a quiet evening.

11. SUNDAY. Positive. Your ruler Mercury breaks into new territory today, entering watery Scorpio. Your thoughts will be deep and serious, which aids greater awareness and enables better understanding. Family needs may run counter to your own agenda, so choices must be made about what will and won't be done. Sacrificing something personally urgent on behalf of others at home will be worthwhile. As a Virgo you seldom shirk your duties and you usually keep your promise. Revealing conversation with those closest, possibly neighbors and relatives, is preferable over social events and active pastimes. By listening carefully, you'll learn something significant.

12. MONDAY. Good. If the option exists to spend the day at home, take it. You may be of a mind to enhance the living environment. Perhaps warmer colors are needed indoors, with accompanying decor to keep wintry feelings at bay. If you think the house needs a total makeover, you may decide to embark on a major renovation. Even moving things around makes a big difference. The concept of feng shui, which teaches the art of placement, might be applied. Plan a dinner for the whole household. Spare no effort in creating a lavish spread. It will raise everyone's spirits and maintain enthusiasm for a mutual project.

13. TUESDAY. Steadying. Before settling in to serious endeavors, go out early for your regular round of exercise. Recreational sports and games can be enjoyed with companions before the working day gathers momentum. The motivation of a coach or trainer could push you beyond comfort zones and toward the achievement of a personal best. Friendly competition with peers can achieve the same ends of stretching your capacity and realizing greater potentials. Study of complex subjects is favored now. You can make strides in grasping difficult concepts and deepening your knowledge. Commitment and discipline will be rewarded.

14. WEDNESDAY. Interesting. If a confrontation looms, sidestep it. A flexible approach will work better than a head-on clash. When someone dumps frustration and discontent at your door, refuse to react to their misplaced aggression. By presenting them with an entirely unexpected response, you may help them to see around and beyond whatever is bothering them so much. Competition is likely a feature of activities now, but it should be in the right spirit of challenge and fun rather than being too deadly or serious. A fast-talking, quick-thinking third party might help you and a buddy to see eye-to-eye over a matter in dispute.

15. THURSDAY. Troubling. Progress could come to a standstill. The work of a team may grind to a halt as finances dry up. Career-based income may reach a turning point and temporarily turn down for the next few months. With Mars now retrograde until February next year, forget any plans for borrowing. The implementation of new technology within an organization is going to take longer than originally scheduled. New partnerships need time to build understanding and establish equilibrium over the months ahead. Your membership application to a club might have stalled, but persistence should result in an eventual favorable decision.

16. FRIDAY. Tricky. Changed circumstances can lead to a revision of work schedules and methods. Working smarter, not harder, could be the solution. Good works and good service are fated to be rewarded today. Helping out will pay off for a change. Keep an eye on the bottom line and what people want to buy. Your questioning curiosity might be turned on fellow workers, as you watch them in action and wonder what makes them tick. There is a possibility of your becoming attracted to someone or something that isn't good for you. No matter what you tell yourself, you'll probably follow your heart, which may not turn out to be the wisest choice.

17. SATURDAY. Misleading. At best, misunderstandings abound. At worst, deception is afoot. So that means take special care under all circumstances today. Guard your safety while traveling anywhere. Someone's mistake can be costly for you. Getting directions confused is highly probable. Take maps and double-check verbal instructions to prevent getting lost. The lure of escapism and of intoxication is strong, especially if you feel under stress. But don't mix work with pleasure. Saying too much to the wrong person can be embarrassing, even undermining. Before you speak, think twice about what others are going to hear.

18. SUNDAY. Variable. To be alone or with others may be today's dilemma. Even if you are in company, you may not be sociable or emotionally accessible. But perhaps you don't get to make the choice one way or another. Your partner may need to go out for good reason, leaving you on your own for the day. Or your partner could persuade you to accompany them to some social gathering in which you have little or no interest. Either way, you may feel very much separate from others or excluded from a group experience. Virgo visitors and volunteers at a hospital or nursing home will brighten the lives of those residents who need compassionate contact.

19. MONDAY. Enticing. Bright ideas and motivating insights can propel you into the day, straight into intriguing encounters with individuals of interest. A spontaneous meeting with a friend could have a sexual charge you hadn't detected before, making you wonder. Slow-burning fuses can be lit in this period, but they may smolder for a long time before finally catching fire. The seeds of a deep bond could be planted now. Unlikely bedfellows might suddenly team up to eventual mutual advantage. Company today is lively, upbeat, clever, and stimulating. Loosen up and enjoy the show. Colorful characters lead to places you'd never imagine or dare to go.

20. TUESDAY. Distracting. A person who trusts your fine Virgo judgment can confide their problems and unload their mental burdens on you. Perhaps you've got the strength to hear them out and to provide a shoulder to lean on. The essential difference between friends and intimates starts to make itself felt now. A closeness with a certain associate can become romantic, setting tongues wagging and the rumor mill working overtime. But the real issue is whether it's the right thing for both of you, especially if one of you is attached elsewhere. It's not too late to back out of a relationship that is inappropriate or potentially divisive.

21. WEDNESDAY. Diverse. There can be cost overruns and delays in delivering a project or service. A direct communication with the waiting customer will settle impatience or pressure, and they'll be pleased about being kept in the loop. A sticking point may be reached with a loved one concerning an intended purchase. This is the right time to discuss the budget and come to a sensible agreement. With give-and-take and goodwill, both of you should be pleased with the outcome. A deepening intimacy with a fellow worker could be developing romantic potential. Fitting them in to your social circle, however, may not be easy.

22. THURSDAY. Purposeful. Journeys for reward and profit should proceed as planned, even if they're on the slow side. Perhaps it's best to go alone, keeping arrangements as simple as possible. Attempts to transport a whole group of people, even to take a small support team along for the ride, could be thwarted. And on this Thanksgiving holiday the logistics of travel could become maddening. Any time you spend away from home should be kept short, sweet, and to the point. With today's movement of the Sun into the sign of Sagittarius, your solar sector of home and family, home base is looking better than ever. You won't want to be on the road for an extended period.

23. FRIDAY. Disquieting. The usual Virgo clarity and presence of mind could temporarily desert you today, leaving you feeling stranded. Don't make the mistake of scheduling mission-critical tasks now, as results might leave a lot to be desired. Presentations, performances, teaching, and communication events might disappoint. Connecting with an audience can be an elusive goal. It's possible that someone will be caught out, not really having the information or knowledge they claim to possess. Or they could be lying outright. Your trust in politicians and officials can take a nosedive when their hypocrisy is revealed for all to see.

24. SATURDAY. Challenging. Today's Full Moon calls for tough measures to right what is wrong or to steady a shaky situation. The consequences of recent mistakes or errors of judgment can have fallout in certain relationships and alliances. Your natural critical faculties kick in when things go awry or fail to live up to expectations. Before taking aim at targets of blame, honestly accept your responsibility in whatever has unfolded. While it's hard to admit fault or inadequacy, others will respect that sort of honesty and integrity from you. If the buck stops with you, own it. But whatever role others have played in creating a problem must be made clear to them as well.

25. SUNDAY. Pleasant. This is a day to put troubles aside. Gaze upon the positive and hopeful in your life. Some Virgos could need positive reprogramming to counter any overly critical or negative tendencies. Dress in your finest, then get out into the world to be seen. Churchgoers can be uplifted by joining others in the act of public worship. A pious profile is likely to be good for your reputation, as well as for your business! Take a break from an inconsistent partner. Enjoy cultural experiences on your own. For those of you with refined tastes, galleries, museums, and theaters may be the places to go. Money buys quality, and you'll want to possess some now.

26. MONDAY. Helpful. Today a team or some kind of cooperative endeavor may need your guiding hand. You can steer a club meeting in the right direction. People are receptive to nurturing and motivation, making this a great time for you to get a process or project back on track. Create a forum where everyone can contribute to the mix of understanding about where things have gone and where they are headed. This helps all involved to gain a better appreciation of what must be done and what role they must play. Hanging out with special pals will be more comfortable for you if the gathering happens at your place.

27. TUESDAY. Reassuring. Whatever was initiated yesterday continues its momentum today. A general enthusiasm and upbeat anticipation within a group should be used to advantage. New members can be inducted and welcomed with open arms. However, a deeper experience and familiarity with them can only come over time. Pushing too hard and too fast for rapid integration might make people anxious and self-conscious. Becoming suddenly swept up in a social happening is sure to be a stimulating change from humdrum routines. But before you know it, there may be immediate expenses that dampen your mood on the way home tonight.

28. WEDNESDAY. Renewing. Many Virgos will have earned a day of rest. Remember, you don't need to be sick or totally exhausted to take a break. If you have saved up leave, this is a good time to cash it in and opt out of the rat race. Realize that you are not as indispensable as you think, and the world will get by without you at least for a moment. Personal affairs on the home front hold more appeal now. Tending to the garden of domestic and familial relationships is a wise move if you want them to flourish. With the Moon rising in your sign, there may also be a need to get in touch with yourself through relaxation and quiet reflection in an undisturbed environment.

29. THURSDAY. Exceptional. This is a dreamy day, great for imaginative processes and scoping the future. Try not to clutter or block a flowing inner vision and creativity by focusing on routine chores. A heightened quality of experience can be spiritually renewing. The sheer beauty of existence in all its glory can be eye-opening, reminding you of bigger perspectives and mysteries. Compassion and understanding come more easily today, giving you a sensitive touch for all activities. Virgos in the caring professions are favored with magical support in healing endeavors. Miracles can happen, but not by expecting them or relying on them. Simply letting things be can work wonders.

30. FRIDAY. Comforting. There's a limit to conscious intellectual understanding, and you may have reached that point. It's sometimes hard for Virgos to admit and accept where knowing stops and faith begins. But without hope and trust in existence, life can become a very tough slog. Let's face it, even if you had all the parts, you still couldn't build the world. So stop all that analysis and deconstruction already! Life is a mystery and that's that, no matter how far you drill down into the detail and the mechanisms. Embrace the pleasures of a loving family and a secure nest. Renew courage for life's adventure. You don't have to understand everything and everybody, just accept it!

December 2007

1. SATURDAY. Difficult. It could definitely feel like heavy going today, mostly because other people are just not cooperating. Maybe you need to look at your own inflexibility and stubbornness rather than turning the tables of blame onto others. While it may seem preferable to stick to a plan of action come hell or high water, life is just not like that. Virgos who have recently settled into a new routine could be in for a rude awakening when the wheels bog down or start falling off. Take the example of easygoing pals and accommodating relatives. Don't be so hard-line in dealings. Bend rather than break. Then your agenda has a chance of being met.

2. SUNDAY. Erratic. With your ruling planet Mercury now in Sagittarius, many Virgos won't be happy campers. Your style may not suit the people who are a strong presence in your life. Domestic scenarios need a liberal dose of give and take, live and let live. If you insist on control at all costs, you might suffer. But it doesn't have to be that way. The power may not rest in your hands, so let go and see what comes. Digging at old family wounds by name-calling and judgmental criticism is destructive. If you can't be a force for good, then don't do anything. You are responsible for what you say regardless of any provocation by others.

3. MONDAY. Improving. Even if earnings, profits, and cash flow are cooking along, that doesn't mean you should spend it all. With hefty seasonal expenses approaching fast, now is the time to look carefully at the household budget. Keep enough money in reserve for close family, especially if you've got kids or will entertain over the holiday period. Be tough about sticking to the plan, otherwise there will be regrets. Keeping up with the wild antics of partying friends can drain your coffers. And the cost of membership in curious groups may be soaring. Covering all the bases may not be possible. Something needs to go.

4. TUESDAY. Promising. Why not beat the last-minute rush to buy everyone presents? Start holiday shopping today. Gifts that have already been decided on are the ones to go for first. Relax while perusing the sales. Enjoy the pleasant experience of choosing ideal purchases for each person who means something special. You'll be surprised how easily just the right thing magically appears in front of you, even when you're not trying. What can't be afforded this week should be put on hold for later. Business Virgos begin to feel the benefit of the season, as shoppers start spending big.

5. WEDNESDAY. Happy. A family enterprise might be paying dividends now, contributing substantially to the bottom line and rewarding everyone involved. The security of a cozy home keeps you cheerful and productive, with the wheels of industry and commerce turning profitably. Bringing home the bacon means a warm welcome from those who live with you or depend on you. Routine errands and trips are better left until later in the day, as transit will flow better then. Calls, visits, and messages to loved ones should come naturally after business is taken care of. Meet your date or lover later for a fun night out on the town.

6. THURSDAY. Frenzied. The party season appears set to kick in with a bang. Celebrations abound in multiple scenarios, involving club members and customers as well as neighbors and relatives. Things could get messy on behalf of a good time, but there's no omelet without first cracking eggs. Rather than taking offense at whatever chaos ensues, see the fun, join in, and take the ride. Intriguing information can be exchanged in your social circle. If you want to be in the loop, circulate in person and via all communication devices. In the midst of merriment, some sudden and shocking interruption seems imminent. Whatever that is, it will be a surprise!

7. FRIDAY. Social. Hanging out with friends might be hard to avoid. There may be so many invitations that you've got to accept at least one, if not some of them. Don't use the excuse of a disorganized household to skip an outing. It will be more fun than you think, with strange, weird, and wonderful characters spicing the mix. The compulsory round of obligatory corporate parties is likely to be in full swing. Make the best of whatever largesse is offered, and you might even be pleasantly surprised by making a promising contact or two. Virgos who started partying early in the day may want to call it quits before dark. The later it gets, the more inviting your own home becomes.

8. SATURDAY. Cloistered. There's still a heightened buzz in the air despite the fact that it's a dark Moon period. Bunkering down in the warmth and comfort of your own home seems the safest thing to do. But restless friends may attempt to spirit you out on risky ventures with uncertain outcomes. Perhaps a good compromise would be to invite guests to your place instead. Some Virgos may have a sense of being left out of a shared experience. Alienation from the people you live with is a real possibility, especially if you've kept yourself to yourself. To be part of things, you have to open up more and also show a genuine interest in the lives of others.

9. SUNDAY. Disquieting. Today's New Moon in Sagittarius could promote wild and wacky vibes. People close to you may begin behaving unpredictably, even out of character. Perhaps it's the silly season taking a grip. But there may be a need for thorough and permanent change, which is just beginning to assert itself. The likely candidates to raise issues are your partner, immediate family members, and permanent members of the household. It would be foolish to brush aside whatever comes up, no matter how unexpected or inconsistent it appears at first. Wise Virgos will assess restlessness and upset as early warning signals, then make necessary changes before it's too late.

10. MONDAY. Challenging. Mark today as a power day! Controlling behaviors will be expressed openly by parents or relatives who think they know it all. It's likely they truly believe they're implementing master plans for your own good. Competitors in business and rivals in career could raise the bar on their challenges to your status. There's no room for complacency, and you'll probably need all the help you can get to deal with threats to security. Home and family are the highest priority now, and should be given quality time and deserved attention. Your own kin are likely the best allies, offering the greatest resources in support.

11. TUESDAY. Reassuring. Many Virgos may feel you've returned to greater order and self-control. The first step in accomplishing such a feat would be a realistic assessment of situations. Forget about fudge factors or unsustainable rose-tinted lenses. Then marshal all your available reserves of strength to take practical, effective action that will bolster your position. Defensive tactics may be a wise strategy, especially if you feel up against the wall. Maybe you're taking it all too seriously, putting unnecessary pressure on yourself. Ease up on self-recriminations, take small steps to achieve limited objectives. Being around kids or playful characters will lighten the load.

12. WEDNESDAY. Steady. Common sense prevails, much to the relief of the rational and dutiful Virgo. Stick to routine plans and responsibilities, and this day can proceed smoothly and relatively uneventfully. People around you may have their heads full of crazy ideas, but you can stay calm and centered. Hopefully your example and influence will be grounding for others too. You can appreciate small joys and pleasures in a relaxed fashion. Friends and neighbors can be relied on for affectionate company and entertaining conversation. See the fun and humor of life. There's even romance for the daring.

13. THURSDAY. Productive. Work takes precedence over play. Dedicate yourself to accomplishing the routine tasks of an ordinary day. Proceed through the to-do list in an orderly fashion, from most important to least important. By ignoring any temptation to waste time in feel-good conversation, and resisting the lure of sexual innuendo in workaday encounters, much can be accomplished. You'll be glad, because there's more where that came from. It's not only self-discipline that is essential today. You may need to direct the activities of teammates who wander off topic. Rewards will come from a decent day's work, and nothing less.

14. FRIDAY. Stirring. Even Virgo workaholics need a break now and then. The real spirit of the holidays is likely to touch you deeply today. There's no need to feel foolish or embarrassed if sentiment, gratitude, and compassion begin to gently assert themselves in your actions and encounters. You may feel moved to do good works for charitable and community causes, or at least to promote them. Empty lip service doesn't count, though. You're advised to sidestep the cant and nonsense that certain religious and moral hypocrites spout at this time of year. Genuine care, sensitivity, and social conscience are easy to spot, and deserving of respect and support.

15. SATURDAY. Harmonious. The concerns, needs, and interests of significant others are front and center now. It can simply be a matter of following wherever a partner or companions lead. There's no need to resist, as a fun time is guaranteed. Parties and gatherings may be scheduled early, which makes it easy for Virgos who haven't been to bed yet! In the course of mixing socially, valuable new contacts can feature, making attendance all the more worthwhile. Singles may meet someone of note, while couples get to share a good time in fine company. Home before midnight will suit you best. Conserve energy for tomorrow.

16. SUNDAY. Delightful. It's another of those wild days when anything goes and probably will. Attempts at getting things done are probably futile and fruitless. This is a rare time to share socially and emotionally, which really comes only once a year. New relationships and associations should be full of anticipation. The act of getting to know someone can be a thrilling adventure. Lovers will be sweet to each other, and there may be a round of early gift giving. Friendly spontaneous encounters abound for Virgos prepared to get out on the street and around the neighborhood. Surprise phone calls and unexpected e-mail from afar will be heartwarming.

17. MONDAY. Stormy. Avoid buying into arguments or disputes, as they may run deeper and be more bitter than you're prepared to handle. Acting as a go-between is likely to be a thankless role that achieves little, if anything. Putting up with complaints and emotional manipulation, especially from those closest, may seem unavoidable. However, you can insulate yourself from such behavior by refusing to take on the negativity of others. An unfavorable response from family members to your current partner of choice surely is unfair, unwarranted, and unwanted. Pause to see things through their eyes before flying off the handle.

18. TUESDAY. Energetic. The company of motivated individuals will fire you up today. Stubborn Virgos who feel the compulsion to lead people and control events could be frustrated in such attempts. A much better strategy is to follow up on what the dynamic characters around you are able to initiate. Getting the ball rolling may not be your greatest strength, but you certainly have the ability to see things through until they're up and running. Intimate relationships are a hot topic, although sexual styles don't necessarily fit easily now. Your inclination to subtle and erotic mindplay and delicious flirting may not dovetail with a lover's lusty physicality.

19. WEDNESDAY. Opportune. A welcome astro event occurring last night is a boon for Virgos. Jupiter entered Capricorn, your solar sector of romance, recreation, children, and creativity. This planet of good fortune is now in a compatible earth sign, and you're sure to benefit in the year ahead. Things can change for the good as you play more, express more, and generally have more fun. Jupiter transit is good news for artists, athletes, and lovers. Some Virgos may begin to feel the urge to start a family or to add another child to the brood. However you respond to this fresh emphasis on the pleasures of life, you want your partner's wholehearted participation.

20. THURSDAY. Expectant. A playful holiday atmosphere reigns over workaday humbug. Try not to feel guilty if you really don't want to work today. You've likely already done your fair share anyway. Planning a vacation overseas would be a pleasure. Stick to the big picture with an overall objective rather than getting overloaded with the fine details of schedules and bookings. First, determine an ultimate destination according to whatever purpose you have in mind. Attending events, concerts, and parties may be on the cards this evening. The later it gets, the more intoxicating the social scene becomes. Don't lose your way or indulge beyond safe limits.

21. FRIDAY. Hectic. There may be teammates missing in action today. But you may not be at work to notice! Employers and managers should anticipate staff shortages, and prepare to run the ship with a skeleton crew. Virgos trying to get things done will be frustrated by an inability to have calls answered or by waiting in long lines for service. Transport arrangements can test your ingenuity, as everyone else wanting to travel is clamoring for a seat. Keeping customers happy is going to be a challenge if you're understaffed or if communication lines become overloaded. It's not an average day, and creative solutions are required.

22. SATURDAY. Gratifying. Today marks the solstice, a seasonal change, and the first day of the Sun in Capricorn. Your ruler Mercury just entered Capricorn on Thursday, and benefic planet Jupiter started its transit of Capricorn on Wednesday. These three planets are emphasizing the sector of your solar horoscope that deals with your creative potential and personal pleasures. So Virgo lifestyles should be on the up and up! Things will get progressively better, albeit at a gradual pace. You will begin to feel luckier. Fortune can smile on you in various ways. Perhaps you will win money or the heart of an admirer. Doing what pleases you is the key.

23. SUNDAY. Taxing. With both a Full Moon and a retrograde Mars in Cancer, this is no time to polarize in argument or competition. If it happens anyway, try to understand who is fighting for what, and why. Defusing tension will only be possible by employing a stern hand of authority. Point out what is right and fair from a high moral ground. Public debate on politics and religion seems tactless and heavy-handed at this time of year, whatever beliefs are held. Kids could become a handful, as the countdown to the holidays stretches their patience. Be firm in reminding them of appropriate behavior. A dispute with a feisty acquaintance might sour the day.

24. MONDAY. Fair. Recent antagonisms can be openly faced in the safety of a supportive group environment. It may be a domestic roundtable, a forum with extended family, a team meeting in the workplace, or an informal gathering of club members. Whatever the social context, open-minded solutions that suit all parties are a possible outcome. Nevertheless, if someone is stubbornly defiant with an ax to grind, there might be little that can be done to change that. Later, leave problems behind and celebrate Christmas Eve. Spontaneous enjoyment with loving friends is on tap this evening. You are moved by the spirit of the season.

25. TUESDAY. Merry Christmas! The Moon is transiting the familial and home-loving sign of Cancer for most of the day. This lunar influence promises a cozy, loving time amid relatives and friends. You might celebrate away from home, whether you've traveled a distance for the holidays or have just gone out to visit for a few hours. Unbelievably, certain people will still want to talk shop with you, so steer clear and give them a wide berth. An incongruent mix of people makes for a low-key experience, or at least it seems that way when the Moon enters Leo and your twelfth solar sector toward evening. Keep things short and sweet. Then you can have an early night and get the rest you'll crave.

26. WEDNESDAY. Quiet. Too much of the good life lately could put you in need of a period of recovery. Today is for downtime. Indulging and overindulging in rich food and drink may have left your digestive system gasping for breath. However tempting it may be to go on with fun and games, try to take it easy. Nothing is pleasurable without the good health to enjoy it. So take care of your physical well-being, and your mental outlook will rise in response. A new year is about to dawn, and you'll want to live to fight another day and welcome 2008 in good shape. High-powered performances may have left exhausted athletes in need of some pampering.

27. THURSDAY. Leisurely. It would be a mistake to venture too far out of your comfort zones today. The best place to be is in a warm, cozy home with pastimes and hobbies or other people to entertain you. Ensconcing yourself with your lover can be memorable and satisfying. Virgo parents will enjoy an uninterrupted opportunity to play with kids, sharing in their joy of new toys without the stress of busy schedules. You may contend with the competitive and strategic challenges of video games and Internet gambling. Some Virgos, of course, prefer the traditional board games. Inveterate couch potatoes will probably watch a movie on the home theater.

28. FRIDAY. Lively. With the Moon rising in your sign, a sense of duty takes a grip today. Hardworking Virgos will be at it again, hopefully with a cheery demeanor and a dash of creative verve. Sport and recreation will hold great appeal. Energetic vacationers will want to play as hard as you usually work. Exercise is a must, even just to walk off a few extra pounds. The care of children features, and they may need your help and adult expertise to figure out how to set up or play with gifts they've received. Restrain yourself from spoiling their fun by being too stern or serious. Remember, you were young once!

29. SATURDAY. Indulgent. Early risers will be stimulated by remarkable encounters when pursuing a favorite weekend hobby or sport. Other enthusiasts might introduce you to an innovative or novel feature of a shared interest. Or they could demonstrate better methods from their bag of tricks. Kids are likely to be up first thing looking for action, and are probably expecting or demanding parents to provide it. Creative thinkers, artists, and craftspeople can make productive use of provocative collaboration and intelligent feedback. Single Virgos playing the field, seeking a potential lover or date, should find one person genuinely fascinating and worth pursuing.

30. SUNDAY. Edgy. This could turn out to be a testy and expensive day. Tension may build over preparations for celebrations. Whether you're throwing a New Year's party or attending one, there will be pressure and frustration in finalizing what is needed. Materials for costumes, decorations, or food may not be available or meet your standards. Work around it with creative fixes. If what you intend to purchase costs too much, buy anyway on behalf of a good time. Expect your mood and that of others to be feisty and reactive. It may be appropriate to express regrets that this year is ending, then determine to do better in the year ahead.

31. MONDAY. Diverse. If you're hosting an event or catering for others, trust that everything will fall into place. While it may not meet the highest Virgo standards, the experience is sure to be appreciated and enjoyed by all. For many of you it could be business as usual today. It should be a profitable day, giving reason to celebrate tonight. As a retrograde Mars moves into Gemini again, the atmosphere returns to light sociability instead of brooding moodiness. A lively, chatty vibe means you'll hear a lot of stories and meet a wide variety of people in rapid succession. Don't become so distracted that the essential significance of the night is missed.

WHAT DOES YOUR FUTURE HOLD?

DISCOVER IT IN *ASTROANALYSIS*—

COMPLETELY REVISED THROUGH THE YEAR 2015, THESE GUIDES INCLUDE COLOR-CODED CHARTS FOR TOTAL ASTROLOGICAL EVALUATION, PLANET TABLES AND CUSP CHARTS, AND STREAMLINED INFORMATION.

ARIES	0-425-17558-8
TAURUS	0-425-17559-6
GEMINI	0-425-17560-X
CANCER	0-425-17561-8
LEO	0-425-17562-6
VIRGO	0-425-17563-4
LIBRA	0-425-17564-2
SCORPIO	0-425-17565-0
SAGITTARIUS	0-425-17566-9
CAPRICORN	0-425-17567-7
AQUARIUS	0-425-17568-5
PISCES	0-425-17569-3

Available wherever books are sold or at penguin.com

As seen on CBS's "Crossing Over"

John Edward
One Last Time

A Psychic Medium Speaks to Those We Have Loved and Lost

His television appearances have made millions of people believe in the afterlife—and in his ability to reach it.

Now Edward's many fans can read his remarkable true story and compelling accounts of his most important readings.

Edward empowers readers to tune in to their own psychic abilities, to read and understand signs of spiritual contact they may be experiencing every day without even knowing it.

"Compelling...poignant."
—Publishers Weekly

0-425-16692-9

Available wherever books are sold or at penguin.com

B095

NOW IN PAPERBACK FROM BERKLEY

Beyond These Four Walls
Diary of a Psychic Medium
by

MaryRose Occhino

The extraordinary memoir from the "remarkably gifted medium"* who has helped many with their struggles—and faced her own as well.

Born to a family of "intuitive" women, MaryRose Occhino has used her "celestial whispers" to open the minds and hearts of people seeking a connection with those who have passed on. Then, at the age of thirty-nine, she was diagnosed with multiple sclerosis and forced to face her own hard times.

Now she tells her fascinating story—of learning to see beyond the walls of this world, while making the most of life in the here and now.

"Sensitive, caring, humorous and accurate, she is among the very best mediums in the world."
—Gary E. Schwartz, Ph.D.,
author of *The Afterlife Experiments*

Available
wherever books are sold or at penguin.com

B099

Penguin Group (USA) Online

What will you be reading tomorrow?

Tom Clancy, Patricia Cornwell, W.E.B. Griffin, Nora Roberts, William Gibson, Robin Cook, Brian Jacques, Catherine Coulter, Stephen King, Dean Koontz, Ken Follett, Clive Cussler, Eric Jerome Dickey, John Sandford, Terry McMillan, Sue Monk Kidd, Amy Tan, John Berendt...

You'll find them all at
penguin.com

*Read excerpts and newsletters,
find tour schedules and reading group guides,
and enter contests.*

Subscribe to Penguin Group (USA) newsletters
and get an exclusive inside look
at exciting new titles and the authors you love
long before everyone else does.

PENGUIN GROUP (USA)
us.penguingroup.com